The central problem this study focuses on is the existence of the poetic subject/narrator of the psalms as a physical and spiritual being. Physicality is studied both from the perspective of the internal organs (heart, stomach, kidneys and liver) and from the perspective of the body and head. It is shown that the position of the limbs and the direction of the gaze are related to the religious experience and that it can be expressed not only with words but also by location in space and time, gestures and silence. A pious person may turn to God both as part of a collective (within a cult) and from solitude (for example, from bed), which is connected with the opposition of *numen locale* and *numen personale*. The person of the psalmist is outlined on the basis of Israel's religion and priestly activity, and is shown not only as a theological, narrative or poetic construct, but also as a biological being whose location in the world is crucial for understanding his address to the Lord. The author's fundamental thesis is well-argued from the perspective of cognitive linguistics and is illustrated with many appropriate quotations from the Bible.

Boris Beck, PhD
Associate Professor, Faculty of Political Science,
University of Zagreb, Croatia

David was a brave warlord with the gentle soul of a poet who expressed his intense feelings in many psalms. That is why the book of Psalms is a field of study for the poet's soul and feelings.

Judaism is a collective communal religion, but the individual has great weight in it. In the Bible, too, every biblical figure has a national dimension and a private, personal dimension. Hence, the great importance of Daniel Berković's research, whose work deals with the personal and emotional religious experience of King David, as expressed in a special way in the book of Psalms. This work, a doctoral thesis, is a valuable biblical-theological research text. The author discusses questions that are constantly being updated by biblical scholars and theologians. It is a work that makes an important contribution to the anthropological study of biblical figures and, in this case, of the psalmist King David. This study is primarily aimed at the wider scholarly community, particularly in the field of theology and biblical studies, but I believe it will be of great interest to a wider readership interested in the Bible.

Rabbi Professor Kotel Dadon
Chair of Judaic Studies, Faculty of Humanities and Social Sciences,
University of Zagreb, Croatia

Personal and Private Religious Experience in the Biblical Psalms

Daniel Berković

ACADEMIC

© 2025 Daniel Berković

Published 2025 by Langham Academic
An imprint of Langham Publishing
www.langhampublishing.org

Langham Publishing and its imprints are a ministry of Langham Partnership

Langham Partnership
PO Box 296, Carlisle, Cumbria, CA3 9WZ, UK
www.langham.org

ISBNs:
978-1-78641-003-0 Print
978-1-78641-168-6 ePub
978-1-78641-169-3 PDF
DOI: https://doi.org/10.69811/9781786410030

Daniel Berković has asserted his right under the Copyright, Designs and Patents Act, 1988 to be identified as the Author of this work.

All rights reserved. No part of this publication may be reproduced, stored in a retrieval system or transmitted, in any form or by any means, electronic, mechanical, photocopying, recording or otherwise, without the prior written permission of the publisher or the Copyright Licensing Agency.

Requests to reuse content from Langham Publishing are processed through PLSclear. Please visit www.plsclear.com to complete your request.

All Scripture quotations, unless otherwise indicated, are taken from the *New American Bible, revised edition*© 2010, 1991, 1986, 1970 Confraternity of Christian Doctrine, Washington, D.C. and are used by permission of the copyright owner. All Rights Reserved. No part of the New American Bible may be reproduced in any form without permission in writing from the copyright owner.

Scripture quotations marked (NRSV) are taken from the New Revised Standard Version Bible, copyright © 1989 National Council of the Churches of Christ in the United States of America. Used by permission. All rights reserved.

Scripture quotations marked (RSV) are taken from Revised Standard Version of the Bible, copyright © 1946, 1952, and 1971 National Council of the Churches of Christ in the United States of America. Used by permission. All rights reserved.

Scripture quotations marked (NAB) are taken from the New American Standard Bible®, Copyright © 1960, 1962, 1963,1968, 1971, 1972, 1973, 1975, 1977, 1995, 2020 by The Lockman Foundation. Used by permission.

British Library Cataloguing-in-Publication Data
A catalogue record for this book is available from the British Library

ISBN: 978-1-78641-003-0

Cover & Book Design: projectluz.com

Langham Partnership actively supports theological dialogue and an author's right to publish but does not necessarily endorse the views and opinions set forth here or in works referenced within this publication, nor can we guarantee technical and grammatical correctness. Langham Partnership does not accept any responsibility or liability to persons or property as a consequence of the reading, use or interpretation of its published content.

Contents

Chapter 1 1
Introduction
    1.1 Introductory Remarks 1
    1.2 False Synonymy 2
    1.3 Interpreting the Psalms 3
    1.4 Who Is the Psalmist? 7
        1.4.1 Producer 7
        1.4.2 Performer 7
    1.5 The Psalmist and the Torah 9

Chapter 2 13
Literature Review
    2.1 Robert Culley 13
    2.2 David Clines 14
    2.3 Benjamin Glass and Susanna Cahn 15
    2.4 Bernd Janowski 16
    2.5 Philip King 17
    2.6 Neil Messer 17
    2.7 Sue Gillingham 19

Chapter 3 23
Personal and Private Aspects of the Subject
    3.1 Person and Personality 24
    3.2 Subject and Subjectivity 25
        3.2.1 The Self: Given or Made? 26
        3.2.2 The Self and "Theoria" 27
        3.2.3 The Self and the Psalmist 28
    3.3 Appropriation and Interpretation 29
    3.4 Personal Piety and Privacy 30
        3.4.1 Personal Piety 30
        3.4.2 Privacy 30
    3.5 Concluding Remarks 31

Chapter 4 33
Religious Typology
    4.1 Israelite Religion 35
    4.2 *Numen Locale* and *Numen Personale* 36
    4.3 Centralization and Personalization 37

Chapter 5 41
The Religion of the Heart of Flesh
- 5.1 The "Heart of Flesh" 42
- 5.2 Anthropology and Psychobiology 45
- 5.3 Heart and Soul 45
- 5.4 Eyes, Face and Hands 48
- 5.5 All That Is within Me 50
- 5.6 Communal Anthropology 53
- 5.7 Individual Anthropology 57

Chapter 6 61
The Psalmist and His Prayer
- 6.1 The Process of Spiritualization 62
- 6.2 Personalization and Appropriation 63
- 6.3 The Lord Is My Portion 65
- 6.4 Priestly Intervention 68

Chapter 7 71
The Pious Man
- 7.1 The *Tsadiq* 72
- 7.2 *Anawim* 73
- 7.3 The Pious Man 76

Chapter 8 79
Cult-Free Psalms

Chapter 9 83
Silence and the Uttered Cry
- 9.1 The Psalmist: His Discontent and Strife 83
- 9.2 Silence and Personal Piety 85
- 9.3 Silence Is a Pressure Cooker 86

Chapter 10 89
The Silence of God
- 10.1 The Silence of God as Punishment 89
- 10.2 The Silence of Death and Suffering 91
- 10.3 Priestly Silence 92

Chapter 11 95
Silence Will be Broken
- 11.1 Moses or Elijah? 97
- 11.2 How Many Messiahs? 99

Chapter 12 101
  Realms of Piety and Privacy
    12.1 Solitude Vocabulary 101
    12.2 Solitude Narratives 102
    12.3 Solitude or Conventions 106

Chapter 13 109
  Realms of Privacy
    13.1 Anthropological Dimensions 109
    13.2 Location 113
    13.3 Privacy and Prayer 113
    13.4 Ritual Acts and Private Piety 115

Chapter 14 119
  The Temporal Aspect
    14.1 Always 120
      14.1.1 Always (תמיד) 120
      14.1.2 Always (עולם) 120
      14.1.3 Psalm 16 121
    14.2 Day and Night 123
      14.2.1 Psalm 42 125
      14.2.2 Psalm 77 125
      14.2.3 Psalm 88 126
    14.3 All the Days 127
      14.3.1 Psalm 23 127
      14.3.2 Psalm 27 127

Chapter 15 129
  Anthropology
    15.1 Four Domains of Anthropology 129
    15.2 Biblical Gastroenterology 130
      15.2.1 Intestines and Religion 131
      15.2.2 Stomach, Womb and Guts 132
      15.2.3 Kidneys, Liver and Bowels 136
    15.3 Limbs, Head and Soul 140
      15.3.1 Lifting Up or Falling Down 140
      15.3.2 Hands Up 141
      15.3.3 Eyes Lifted Up 141
      15.3.4 Face Lifted Up 144
      15.3.5 Soul Lifted Up 145

Chapter 16 149
    Location
        16.1 Private Places 150
        16.2 Bed..151
            16.2.1 Psalm 63...152
            16.2.2 Psalm 6...153
Chapter 17 155
    Conclusion
Bibliography... 157

CHAPTER 1

Introduction

1.1 Introductory Remarks

Reflections over the issues of the individuality of the psalmist and somewhat perpetual discussions over the collective "I" in the Psalter, even though this cannot be sidestepped, do not make us prisoners of a one sided discussion.[1] The historical legacy of the redaction-critical approach and the form-critical method, important as they are, in theological academic terms a common knowledge, ought to be cherished by all means as our heritage, yet not to become a ballast at the expense of other significant areas of research. In the terms of Old Testament study perhaps somewhat neglected is the area of the anthropological domain. Nevertheless, the past decades show a growing number of studies in that realm, as we will show in the literature review.

The primary task of this work is not so much the question of the psalmist as a collective "I" individual or a collective representative. The objective is to investigate the religious experience(s) of the psalmist as an individual in his personal and private emotive and emotional experiences, in the context of the anthropological and the poetic-narrative. Questions of the individuality of his personality or even if the collective representation revealed the psalmist's personality disclosed in his privacy, cannot be avoided. The issue and the importance of the collective experiences of the Israelites in their public

---

1. Here we shall be using the term "psalmist" rather than the "poet." We differentiate between the two notions and ideas. There are scholars such as Sigmund Mowinckel who insist on using the term "poet." Mowinckel, *Traditionalism and Personality*.

religious manifestations (temple liturgies, sacrificial practices) are beyond any doubt, yet we are also attentive of the psalmist as an individual, with all the marks of his individuality. The psalmist (or the poet) is not simply a puzzle piece in the big puzzle of the collective. It is individual anthropology and matters of psalmist's individuality, personality and privacy, emotional or emotive stamina, even of the poet himself, that concerns us.

Throughout the Psalter, and other Old Testament texts, it seems evident that Judaism of biblical times was not solely an elitist and entirely clergyman-centred religion. Notably, and beyond any doubt, the cult practically shaped its religiosity. However, there are clear indications throughout the Old Testament that the Israelite religion was designed to be a "religion of the heart" and not only of the cult. If that is so, then it inevitably elevates a believing person in their individuality, as well as their privacy. There seem to be many aspects of individual anthropology which we cannot bypass lightly. The psalmist as a pious individual exercises his piety not only in the public religious events, but even more profoundly as an individual in their privacy.

1.2 False Synonymy

Crucial and central to this undertaking are interests of the psalmist's privacy, personality, emotive and emotional issues. However, some clarifying and distinguishing undertaking on the conceptual and particularly definitional level will be neccessary. It is not unusual to encounter a deficit in the linguistic or lexical demarcation lines between concepts like *personal* and *private*, or *emotive* and *emotional*. On the semantic level, we ought to ensure clarity and accuracy in terminology and comprehension. It is not uncommon that in language and meaning, some terms may be regarded as synonymous even when that is not the case. This work's focal point is the relationship between the *personal* and *private*, and how the psalmist relates to his privacy. For personal persuasions may be evident in public, though in privacy it may be revealed in a different light. This will be noted below in the case of another false synonymy, that between emotive and emotional. If synonymy is to be understood simply as sameness, interpreting the notions of the personal and the private as synonymy would be a misnomer. The notions of private and personal may have similarities, but surely they are not synonymous in terms of sameness. Perhaps a creative example from daily life may be of some help, with a distinction between a personal vehicle and a private car. A personal vehicle is not inevitably a private car.[2]

Relevant to this work is a distinction between the notions of *emotional* and *emotive*. On many occasions, there will be a need to qualify the precise demarcation line between the emotional and the emotive. In many psalms, the psalmist displays swings in mood. In that, at times he may be moody, (*emotive*) at other times he may be reacting in agitation or emotional turmoil (*emotional*).[3] There are examples when the psalmist is in an emotional state and psychosomatic turmoil, such as in Psalm 38, where his heart throbs (סחר), pounds and shakes (38:8, 11). In Psalm 69, the insults have broken his heart (69:20); he gets emotive in his disorientation (69:10, 20b) or emotional in his anger (69:22–28).[4]

1.3 Interpreting the Psalms

The theme of the psalmist's personal and private piety is a subject which challenges and embarks on the issue of the nature of *Israelite religion and anthropology* and the concept of the Hebrew person, but most of all the identification of the *pious man* in the Psalter, as an individual experiencer of personal devotion.

First, the issue of identifying the psalmist as a *pious man* must be addressed. Who do we mean when referring to "the psalmist"? Do the existing superscriptions to individual psalms resolve the issue, as some may suggest? Can "the psalmist" just be a private worshipping individual? Let us assume that there are three stages in the process associated with every psalm: *production*,

---

2. In *Meaning in Language*, Alan Cruse devotes some attention to the topic of synonymy. He advocates for the distinction between *sameness* and semantic *similarity*. Cruse, *Meaning in Language*, 154.

3. Often in Scriptural texts, we will find an emotional concoction (between being emotive and emotional), such as of fear and anger. It can be found in many biblical characters (Cain, Moses, Elijah and Jonah). The anger of Cain towards his brother Abel (Gen 4) is already proverbial; Moses gets angry with God (Num 11:11–15); Elijah's emotional predicament is a blend of fear and anger (1 Kgs 19:3–4, 9); Jonah's condition is even more complicated (Jonah 4). Beyond his theological discomforts, in terms of modern thought we might say that Jonah was also a "clinical case" of depression and anger. Not only was he exceedingly angry (רעה גדולה) (4:1), and angry to death (חרה-לי עד-מות) (4:9) he was also bad-tempered, and God attempted to "deliver him from his evil" (JPS) (להציל לו מרעתו) (4:6).

4. On the question of the distinctions between the emotive and emotional, see Berkovic, "Grammar of Death," an unpublished doctoral work, ch.1.4.1.

performance and *experience* (see chapter 2). As we seek to identify "the psalmist," it will also reveal the need to identify the pious man of the Psalms. How does the individual Israelite relate to the Torah, and is it only in the context of public worship and the cultus?

Second, there is the question of the essential nature of the Hebrew religion in terms of *religious typology*. That is to say, what is the relationship between religion and emotion? And what is the nature of religious and emotional experience of an individual Israelite?[5] To be able to examine this relationship, all we have at our disposal is language as an attire of the devotees' experience. Psalmodic language has a powerful capacity to articulate and express the experience. A variety of religious experiences are markedly conveyed and articulated in poetic forms. The poetic forms and types are not ornamental literary embellishment, they are instruments of conveying a message and not an end in themselves. Such language is here to decode and understand the nature of the devotees' experience. It is that language which becomes our servant and not the lord. However, it would be a mistake not to utilize the tenets of form critical method, though one ought to be careful of the risk that *form* criticism becomes *formula* criticism.

It is only with the development of cognitive theories and processes, in the latter half of the twentieth century, that cognitive linguistics opened up this freedom for language and literature to treat emotions with respect, rather than just being a "nagging source of 'hot' noise."[6]

The psalmodic literature and versatile poetic compositions clearly reveal all the vigour of the psalmist's experiences, and particularly in distress. In fact, there seems to be consensus that in the lament Psalms, which become the core of personal piety, the psalmist reaches the point of being speechless, he was "dumb and silent," and decided to "refrain from any speech" (Ps 39:3). For him, it is a frightening experience, when God goes silent (Ps 30:8b), signifying the punishment of distancing himself from his people. This leads not only to national laments, but also to demonstrations of private and personal

---

5. An investigation into the background and history of development of religion, in particular Israel's faith (*Religionsgesichte*) will not be the focus of this work. Cf. Oesterley and Robinson, *Hebrew Religion*.

6. Eich, *Cognition and Emotion*, 3.

piety.⁷ Why the personal and private piety of the psalmist has not been given a more notable treatment deserves a brief note.

During the 1920s–50s, the primary interest of traditional psalmodic form critical scholarship was how the psalms *originated* as religious poetry. Even when deemed as "private religious poetry" or "private individual lyrics," the psalmist was still looked on as a professional poet composing ritual texts. The chief concern was the Psalms in Israel's worship, focusing on the Psalms as "cultic songs," finding their place in the liturgical life of Israel.⁸ It was of lesser concern to focus on the private "space" of the individual psalmist. The primary interest was in the "historicizing" and "particularizing" of Psalms as literature and ancient texts.⁹ Essentially it was *reconstructionist* in nature, attempting to reconstruct the history. Striving to discover the historical events, background and dates behind a particular psalm, and if possible even the historical person who wrote it, the scholarship of the day just didn't have "time" to deal with the individual. The identity of the Israelite individual only served its purpose to show that the individual's identity only exists in the manifestation of the collective.¹⁰ In his superb survey of the form-critical tenets of psalmodic studies, Mowinckel in *Psalm Criticism between 1900 and 1935* calls the historicizing a "mania" for fixing the date of every single Psalm.

The second reason why, in the days of the "fathers" of psalmodic critical scholarship, the individual was somewhat neglected, is in the language research of the day, which was then largely in the "pre-cognitive" stage of linguistic studies. It was the *form* and type(s) (Gunkel's *Gattungen*) that mattered more than the *meaning*, even when it also contributed to the whole picture of how a text was to be read and examined.¹¹

---

7. In relation to the pious, in a distant land far from the temple and the homeland, during the exile, the Lord God says, "I have been to them as a little sanctuary." מקדש מעט (Ezek 11:16b).

8. Mowinckel *The Psalms in Israel's Worship*, 1,4,207

9. Gillingham calls this: "historicizing" and "particularizing" the Psalms. Gillingham, *Poems and Psalms*, 186. By "particularizing," she refers to setting each Psalm in a very specific, individual, communal setting. However, she notes that there have also been attempts, radical proposals, to see the Psalms only as private, non-cultic prayers. Cf. Quell, *The Cultic Problem of the Psalms*, and Szoreny, *Psalmen und Kult im Alten Testament*

10. Cf. Mowinckel, *Psalms in Israel's Worship*, ch. 3, "The I and 'we' in the Psalms."

11. Cf. Berlin, "The role of the text in the reading process," 143–7.

Psalmodic scholarship has lately moved forward towards a "postcritical reading of the Psalms."[12] This however does not mean disregarding the past achievements of critical psalmodic scholarship.

Walter Brueggemann puts it this way:

> We shall try to take full account of the critical gains made by such scholars as Gunkel, Mowinckel, and Westermann, without betraying any of the precritical passion, naivete, and insight of believing exposition. Specifically, there is a close correspondence between the anatomy of the lament psalms (which Westermann as a critical scholar has shown to be structurally central for the entire collection) and the anatomy of the soul (which Calvin related to his discernment and presentation of biblical faith).[13]

As the transitions in understanding of the Psalms and linguistic developments took place, the reading of the Psalms was moving towards redefinition and opening up to the possibility that the Psalms may refer to and be read more personally and independent of liturgical activity.[14]

A key question here becomes a whole issue. That is, when an appellation the "psalmist" as it is commonly being used brings us to the question: who is really that "psalmist"? Presumably, the psalmist should be the one who composes a psalm. Thus, he is the one who compiles the psalmodic material (*producer*). Alternatively, he may be the one who, in public liturgical performance, enacts the psalmodic material (*performer*).[15] Finally, the psalmist may be the one who testifies to his very personal experiences (*experiencer*). Who do we then conceive that the psalmist may be?

---

12. Cf. Brueggemann, *Message of Psalms*, 18.
13. Brueggemann, 18–19.
14. Cf. Gillingham, *Poems and Psalms*, 184.
15. Similar psalmodic 'performers' were some of the worship group leaders, such as the sons of Korah. Korahaites, or the 'sons of Korah', were Levites and one of the leading worship groups. Korah's ancestors were Oholibah and Esau (Gen 36,5; 15–18). Korahites or the sons of Korah are mentioned in several Psalms headings, as in Ps 42 named as *'Maskil of the Sons of Korah '*. Most likely 'maskil' denoting a music genre. However, Korahites are also known as a rebellious group plotting against Moses during the desert years of the Israelites. They *'rose up against Moses. With them were 250 Israelite men, well-known community leaders'* (Num 16,2).

1.4 Who Is the Psalmist?

The inventory of the key issues in psalmodic studies endorses the identity of the individual in an important place. Within the range of key psalmodic issues there is a term frequently used, that of the "psalmist." Whether it is employed as a *generic* term or simply as *terminus technicus*, it is to be seen. It does seem that it is being used almost habitually. Who then is the psalmist? There are three proposed possibilities as to the identification of the psalmist in the scholarly usage. It is that of the (i) *producer*, (ii) the *performer*, or (iii) the *experiencer*.

1.4.1 Producer

Referring to the psalmist as the "producer" alludes to the way a psalm or a composition of the whole Psalter came about. A producer is a poet, professional or popular, an author or compiler of an individual psalm or the corpus of the whole Psalter. Croft suggests that what we have as the Psalter is a selection "deliberately chosen from a wider body of material."[16] He further suggests that this selection (the Psalter) follows well-defined criteria, with two principal aspects for choosing a psalm to be included in the body of the Psalter.

The first criterion is that which will include a psalm to be a piece of work used in public worship. As well, "many of the psalms which do mention an individual were delivered by public spokesman in the cult."[17] The second criterion is that of excellence. Croft maintains that "the efforts of the poets would be concentrated upon the psalms for public use."[18] However, one has to note here that according to the excellence criteria, for a psalm to be publicly presentable, some of the psalms may indeed not be appropriate.

1.4.2 Performer

The appellation "the psalmist" may allude to a "performer," either as the priest performing the cult liturgy or a public spokesman. This would be a professional liturgical poet attached to the temple. Perhaps it could also be

---

16. Croft, *Identity of Individual*, 133.
17. Croft, 133.
18. Croft, 133.

an itinerary priestly officer providing liturgical services for local sanctuaries; or even for more personal needs.[19]

Finally, and inevitably, there is a question of how is a psalm being internalized by the pious, in his personal faith or private piety, that is, the "experiencer." The *experiencer*, here designated as the *paslmist*, that is, the individual devotee, is the centre of our attention. An experiencer is a person engaged in mental or emotive acitivity. Here, the Psalter provides a striking portrait of the pious man in his personal and private devotion, faith and reliance on Yahweh (within or without existing cultic practices).

As for the identity of the individual, and the pious, some commentators conclude that the superscriptions to individual psalms point to authorship, thus also resolving the identity of the psalmist. For example, if the superscription reads *lišlomo* (a Psalm of Solomon) (Pss 72; 127), or the very frequent designation *lᵉdawid* (a Psalm of David), or *'lᵉmošeh'* (a Psalm of Moses) (Ps 90), the author's identity is designated, and consequently the identity of the psalmist.[20] The circumstances in which a psalm was written, or its stated purpose, also contribute to identification. In the cases of David and Solomon, this is supported by the understanding that both were poets. In his *Introduction to the Old Testament*, Georg Fohrer concludes:

> Among the names mentioned in the superscriptions, "Moses," "David" and "Solomon" are clearly intended to designate the authors of the Psalms, while the mention of guilds of temple singers like Asaph and Korah should probably be understood as denoting particular collections.[21]

In identifying the psalmist as a private individual, the earlier discussion in chapter 2 took into account the three stages that encompass the process; *composition* (of a psalm or psalter), public *performance*, and *participation* or

---

19. Cf. Gillingham, *Poems and Psalms*, 184.

20. The grammatical issue and ambiguity of meaning of the inseparable preposition *lᵉ* ("*lišlomo*," "*lᵉdawid*," "*lᵉmošeh*") should be accounted for. It is sometimes referred to as *lamed auctoris*, that is, a designation of authorship. Others consider it a lamed of "destination," that is, the object of reference. Cf. Kautzsch, *Gesenius' Hebrew Grammar*, 419, par. 129c; Jouon, *Grammar of Biblical Hebrew*, 474, par 130bN. Fohrer, on the subject, notes that in Ugaritic texts, this *lᵉ* does not specify the authorship but the protagonist or designation of a poem. Cf. Fohrer, *Introduction to OT*, 282.

21. Fohrer, 282.

the experiential aspect of any given psalm. These stages were described as *production, performance* and *experience*.

All three are important and demand the attention of any student of the Psalter. However, for obvious reasons related to the task and the interest of this work, the third phase concerns us the most. The traditional understanding of the psalmist has been of a professional poet attached to the Jerusalem cult, a "producer." The poet-producer may also have been entrusted indirectly to some extent in public performance. The psalmist, if this signifies the poet, and the worshippers all participated in the *group experience* of the worshipping community.[22] Such an almost exclusively liturgical understanding of the Psalms may be considered a rigid "cult-functional reading" of the Psalter.[23]

This traditional understanding and interpretation of the Psalter has been re-evaluated. The cult-function aspect, of course, cannot be neglected or ignored, but some revision and redefinition of the role of the cultus is necessary. Susan Gillingham, in her work *The Poems and Psalms of the Hebrew Bible*, in the section "The Psalmist as Liturgical Poets Serving a Private Cultus," discusses the shift in views and interpretations[24] in the redefinition of the psalmist. Though the Psalter is still understood as "composed poetry which served as prayers for individuals," it has now been redefined, first, along the lines of the relationship between the reader-listener, and second as a matter of personalisation and appropriation. What the worshipper hears and takes hold of for themselves then becomes an appropriation, through which the *hearer* also becomes the *experiencer*. In other words, they cease to be a mere listener but an individual who speaks for themselves.

1.5 The Psalmist and the Torah

Hans-Joachim Kraus, in his *Theology of the Psalms*, dedicates chapter 6 to the theme of the individual in the presence of God.[25] In his concluding remarks, in reference to Psalms 19 and 119, Kraus maintains that there has been a misconception in the understanding of the term "law" (Torah).

---

22. Broyles, *Conflict of Faith*:16; Croft, *Identity of Individual*, 133.
23. Gillingham, *Poems and Psalms*, 184.
24. Gillingham, 184–85.
25. Kraus, *Theology of Psalms*, 137–62.

The misunderstandings, however, begin, as has been said, with the translation of the term. תורה is not "the law," but "instruction," the gracious expression of the will of Yahweh as experienced by the individual.[26]

Several things which will reappear later should be noted here. First, how is the Law to be understood and described under new circumstances, and second, how does it relate to the personal experience of the psalmist?

As Kraus argued, the term (*torah*) is not a legalistic set of cult-orientated regulations, but a far more dynamic concept, an "active word." If God can be "heard to speak through the 'instruction' then one's life is 'revived.'"[27]

The Torah then ceases to be "law" in the sense of a mere collection of legal material that is static and legalistic. It becomes a dynamic body of personal instructions. It moves from ritual and cultic performance to the personal appropriation of God's Law. The Torah moves beyond a sacred written scroll; if it is to be written anywhere, it is on the worshipper's heart. The prophet announces a divine "novelty," a new covenant written on a different writing material than tablets of stone (Exod 34:1). The most suitable writing material for this new covenant (ברית חדשה) (Jer 31:31, 33a) is the human heart: "I will put my law within them, and I will write it upon their hearts; and I will be their God, and they shall be my people" (Jer 31:33b). The knowledge of God will now be founded on personal experience rather than the mere repetition of legal codes. The experience, initially and primarily, will be rooted in and grow out from knowledge of the forgiveness of sins (31:34b). Moreover, this new appropriation of Torah goes as far as to declare that, "No longer will they have need to teach their friends and kinsmen how to know the LORD" (31:34, NAB).

The psalmist concludes that the law of the Lord is perfect, "reviving the soul" and "rejoicing the heart" (Ps 19:8).[28] The law then becomes the word (דבר), which shows the way (Ps 119:105). Clearly, a person's relationship to the

---

26. Kraus, 161. Particularly see Kraus's discussion on page 162 in relation to understanding the Torah, and in relation to some of Gunkel's comments, such as the "dominance of the law" in the Psalter, but also the observation that the spirit of the prophets was living in the "pious circles among the laity."

27. Kraus, 161. Kraus then discusses the matter of life and death as viewed in the life and faith of the Israelite individual in the context of the Psalms. Kraus, 162–68.

28. שוב נפש and שמח לב.

Torah goes beyond rigid religiosity; it is marked by joy and refreshment. This is repeatedly confirmed in the so-called Torah psalms (sometimes categorized as didactic or wisdom psalms). In them, over and again, the emphasis is on personal devotion and the experiences of the individual, that is, torah piety.[29]

---

29. Cf. Brown, *Seeing the Psalms*, 16. One also wonders how some of the understandings and interpretations of the law in the times of the New Testament will fit such pictures of Torah as a dynamic concept. It seems that aspects of personal and private piety have lost its edge in the New Testament times.

CHAPTER 2

Literature Review

A brief survey of literature and bibliography provided in this work will show that literature covering the focal interest of this work may be scarce. This is particularly true in reference to the relationship between the nature of what is *personal* and that which belongs to a person's *privacy*. Unfortunately, it is not so uncommon that the ideas be treated as synonymous. This may indeed be an obstacle of *false synonymy*.

The bibliography covers three areas of interest, one is relating to general *psalmodic studies* (Mowinckel, Gunkel, Gillingham) and general characteristics of the Israelite religion. Another allotment of the enclosed bibliography concerns *biblical commentaries* in relation to specific psalmodic texts. Last but not the least, the short list of bibliography will contain the entries which focus on and cover topical areas of the psalmist's *personality and privacy*. Considering that the bibliography contains close to 400 entries, we can only provide a modest sample and an overview of the entries and authors which are immediately vital to the central argument of this work – the distinction between the *personal and the private*. For the efficiency and keeping the focus, we selected only several key titles and authors on the subject matter such as Clines (2008), Culley (1986), Gillingham (1987), Glas/Cahn (2017), Messer (2021), Mowinckel (1950), Prosser (1960) and Waren/Brandeis (1890).

2.1 Robert Culley

Culley and his study *Oral Tradition and Biblical Studies* (1986) is a well-researched and detailed overview of biblical studies. A large part of his work concentrates on the work of Hermann Gunkel and the historical development

13

of biblical studies (pp. 32–41). He gives important attention to an aspect of biblical studies, that of "oral tradion."

For our work here, the most valuable aspect in Culley's work is its contribution to biblical Hebrew poetry (pp. 42–45) and biblical Hebrew prose (pp. 47–51), plus the way author bridges or links poetry and prose in Hebrew texts. In this, he bases his work on William Whallon's *Formulaic Poetry in the Old Testament*. Whallon argues that Hebrew poetic parallelisms were actually a "prosodic requirement."

2.2 David Clines

Certainly very valuable to our work is David Clines's *The Book of Psalms, Where Men Are Men . . . On the Gender of Hebrew Piety*, which is also directly related to our study. Therefore, the work will receive more attention. Hebrew piety, manhood and masculinity is not a common topic in biblical scholarship.

Men do many manly things, but piety is probably not one of them. Manhood and masculinity does not relate much to piety. Yet, here we have the psalmist in his piety and his masculinity. Indeed David, or/and the psalmist in his maleness, according to many psalms, exercises "doing very many male things"[1] of which some are very consistent, such as "warfare and enemies," "honour and shame" and certainly the metaphors of "strength." How does Clines embrace and perceive masculinity and piety? Here is how he perceives and spans between masculinity and the piety of Hebrew psalms:

> I find that I can identify the maleness of the piety in the Hebrew psalms in these categories: the rhetoric of war, the ideology of honour and shame, the construction of enemies, the role of women, the concept of solitariness, the importance of strength and height in its metaphorical system, and the practice of binary thinking.[2]

The rhetoric of warfare is clearly manifest from the very beginning of the Psalter. In Psalm 2:9, it will be the nations that will be "ruled" and "crashed." In Psalm 3, Yahweh is the psalmist's "shield," in Psalm 18 the whole vocabulary

---

1. Clines, "Book of Psalms," 1.
2. Clines, 1.

is particularly in military disposition, with such words as: "fortress," "shield," "bow," "stronghold," "refuge," "deliverance."

Clines notices well another important concept that bridges masculinity and piety – that of "honour and shame." Apart from the wider Mediterranean basin, some would call the ancient Israel as an "honour-shame" culture. Honour and shame is indeed intrinsic to the Mediterranean and also to Middle Eastern cultures. It is peculiar to patriarchal societies and male ideology. Distinguishing marks of male ideology, are identified as: "strength, courage, daring, valour, generosity, and wisdom. Weakness, cowardice, and lack of generosity indicate lack of honour, and hence, are despised."[3]

2.3 Benjamin Glass and Susanna Cahn

In *Privacy Ethics in Biblical Literature* (2017), Glass and Cahn define and identify privacy as "the right to be let alone."[4] The right to be alone is also linked to personal dignity and private affairs. William Posser makes four domains of human privacy: (i) intrusion into private affairs, (ii) public disclosure of embarrassing private facts, (iii) publicity creating a false light in the public eye, and (iv) appropriation of name or likeness.[5]

Some would disagree that "undue publicity" is an intrusion on human dignity.[6] On the other hand, some biblical situations may shed a different light on this, such as in the case of Hannah, Samuel's mother. In her privacy of imploring Yahweh for begetting a son, she was declared a drunkard (1 Sam 1:12–16). Such "undue publicity," within the shrines, seem to be a breach of human dignity. On the other hand, Bloustein clearly states that "without privacy a person loses individual dignity, integrity and freedom."[7]

On the other hand, there is the whole question of the idea of human dignity wthin the text and context of the Old Testament times. Mowinckel addresses the subject in his words:

---

3. Clines, 4.
4. Glass and Cahn, "Privacy Ethics," 1.
5. Posser, William, "Privacy," 383–423.
6. Bloustein Edward, "Privacy as an Aspect of Human Dignity," 962–1007.
7. Bloustein, 979.

To be original, someone apart, a personality, whose right of existence depended on being different, would not to the ancient Israelites have appeared as an ideal or an end to attain, but on the contrary, as a *madness*, an *arrogance*, something *abnormal*, or, in their own words, an unrighteousness and a folly.[8]

The work of Glass and Cahn is another valuable contribution to our research, particularly their sections: "Privacy in Biblical Literature" and "Privacy in the Hebrew Bible."

2.4 Bernd Janowski

Arguing with God: A Theological Anthropology of the Psalms (2003, 2009) by Bernd Janowski is one of the rare studies of Old Testament anthropology that focuses on biblical psalmody. The introductory section entitled "What Is a Human Being?" covers fundamental areas of anthropology (Historical anthropology, Theological anthropology and the Language of human beings). The remaining ten chapters are divided into two parts: Part 1 (*From Life to Death*), and Part 2 (*From Death to Life*). Each chapter covers a psalmodic text with an appendix at the end of each chapter entitled: "Anthropological Keyword." For example, chapter 4, as a case study of Psalm 59 ("Swords Are on Their Lips"), is on "Anthropological Keyword 2: Revenge." All this makes the whole matter of research more relevant and applicable.

Janowski's first case study is Psalm 13 entitled, "How Long Will You Hide Your Face" (pp. 57–96)?, which is perhaps the most productive section in the work, after the catchphrase of the psalm "how long," pointing to the hiddenness of God. As for the keywords in the appendix, Janowski focuses here on two keywords: "seeing" and "hearing" (provided with some attractive ancient graphic illustrations).

In his anthropological objectives, Janowski inevitably tackles the psalmist's moods, emotive states as well as his emotional reactions. The psalmist's swings in mood (thus *Arguing with God*) frequently emerge in the psalmodic texts, particularly in the lamental psalms. Laments, though, are not to be regarded as an "illicit" aspect of faith. On the contrary, Janowski insists that

---

8. Mowinckel, *Psalms in Israel's Worship*, 43.

it is to be regarded as "an indispensible element of faith."[9] In this, Janowski promotes boldness in speech, the *parrhesia* (an open speech; speaking freely). His study is not a classical word-study, which was at one time methodologically a traditional approach to Hebrew texts. His lexical study is profound and with acumen, but in some sense minimalistic, only to serve the holistic anthropological aims of his work.

2.5 Philip King

In "Surrounded by Bitterness: Image Schemas and Metaphors for Conceptualizing Distress in Classical Hebrew" (2012), Philip King focuses on the distress schema language.

In the introductory section (chapters 1–2), King provides a survey and retrospectives over the distress language. Chapter 1 is assigned and structured as: "Historical Criticism and Idiosyncratic Language," "Form Criticism and Liturgical Language," "Literary Criticism and Intertextual Language," "Psychological Interpretation and the Language of Humanity and Cultural linguistic Interpretation," and the "Language of Conceptual Metaphor." Chapter 2 deals with "Culture, Language and Thought (Tradition of Linguistic Relativity; Linguistic and Biblical Studies to Cognitive Linguistics)."

The core of King's work is the "distress language scheme," centrally located over the aspects of conceptual metaphors.[10]

2.6 Neil Messer

Messer's focus on neuroscience and theology is challenging and important to our work over the aspects of the personal and the private in the Psalter. One of Messer's works is "Judging the Secret Thoughts of All: Functional Neuroimaging, Brain Reading and Theology Ethics of Privacy" (2021). This is a very specific study, in some ways futuristic in its scientific realm of neuroscience, in relation to biblical texts. In the opening section, Messer states that:

---

9. Janowski, *Arguing with God*, 39.

10. In some ways, King's chapters 6–9 correspond to this author's unpublished doctoral thesis on conceptual metaphors and the grammar of death. Berković, "Grammar of Death." In terms of conceptual metaphors, the author of "Grammar of Death" focuses on specific Hebrew vocabulary of PeYod and PeWaw verb groups.

> Of the many futuristic prospects offered by neuroscience, one of the more controversial is "brain reading": the use of functional neuroimaging to gain information about subjects' mental states or thoughts . . . if God knows and judges all our secret thoughts, do Christians have any stake in defending a right to mental privacy?[11]

The whole approach, bizarre as it may seem, is certainly applicable to our area of interest, the issue of privacy of the psalmist and his personality. Messer's sections entitled, "The Scanner and the Eye of God" and "Psalm 139 and the Panopticon," seem to aim at the very core of our study, focusing on the *personal* and the *private* of the biblical psalmist.[12] David Lyon (quoted by Messer) alludes to Psalm 139 as a "model prison":

> in the design for his model prison, the Panopticon: "Thou art about my path, and about my bed; and spiest out all my ways."[13]

Messer then summarises:

> it does not take much imagination to hear, in descriptions of neuroscience-based brain reading, echoes of biblical texts depicting God's complete knowledge of human creatures. In the words of Psalm 139, the technology seems to allow its users to "discern [our] thoughts from afar." (v. 2, NRSV)[14]

It may be going too far to claim that "before a word is on my tongue," (Ps 139:4) a neuroscientist can "know it completely" (Ps 139:4). Yet, the forensic uses of brain-reading described earlier might suggest that human agents are now able to imitate God in not only knowing, but also "judge[ing] the secret thoughts of all" (Rom 2:16).[15]

---

11. Messer, "Judging Secret Thoughts," 17.

12. *Panopticon* for "all seeing" – from the Greek *panoptes* and πανοψιος (the one who is observable to anyone).

13. Messer, "Judging Secret Thoughts," 25; Psalm 139:3.

14. Messer, 24.

15. Messer, 24.

2.7 Sue Gillingham

Gillingham's "Personal Piety in the Study of the Psalms" (1987), is theme-based and thematically immediately relevant to our study, thus we shall carry out a more extensive survey of her present work. The study is Gillingham's unpublished doctoral work:[16]

> [a] life centred interpretation of the Psalter, by assessing the personal insights and experiences which the composers brought to their psalms, whether or not they originally intended to be compositions for cultic use.

The thesis is in two parts. Part one consists of two chapters (chs.1–2; pp. 9–92).

Chapter 1 outlines the general development of Old Testament critical studies and psalmodic cult functioning contexts. With form-critical and literary-critical methods, in relation to psalmodic studies, Gillingham concludes that "it should be apparent that there is simply no one fixed method of interpretation in a study of the psalms."[17] She then concludes at the end of chapter 1 citing Walter Brueggemann: "It would appear that Psalm scholarship is now tending to move forward toward a recovery of personal piety in the Psalms."[18]

Chapter 2 is entitled "The Confessions of Jeremiah as Personal Prayers." In this chapter a theme of personal piety opens up, examining several chapters in Jeremiah as representation of the "intimate dialogue with God in psalmic form . . . and is directly relevant for understanding the nature of personal piety in the psalms" (Jer 11; 12; 15; 17; 18; 20).[19] Even though Gillingham, through chapter 2 analyses the issues of literary-critical and form-critical interpretations – in many ways this chapter with Jeremiah's personal prayers, seems to be a foundation for the whole thesis.[20]

---

16. Sue Gillingham defended her thesis in Oxford at Keble College (1987) under the supervision of Revd. Professor Ernest Nicholson. The structure of the thesis in its beginnings is somewhat unusual as the selected bibliography preceeds the Introduction to the thesis.

17. Gillingham, "Personal Piety," 29.

18. Gillingham, 29.

19. Gillingham, 42.

20. Gillingham calls her title of chapter 2, "The Confessions of Jeremiah," a "misnomer." This is to say that these are not so much: "confessions of sin," they are rather "protestations of innocence," or even "questions of doubt at the justice of God."

The *second* part of the thesis consists of chapters 3–8. Each of these chapters impart some focal themes that pervade the psalms. This is followed by a study of the words that describe and feature a given thematic unit.

The following is a pattern of Gillingham's forthcoming chapters:

Chapter 3: "Trust in God." Word study: יחל, אמץ, חסה, בטה.

Gillingham opens up this chapter with a statement saying that "trust in God prevades the psalms."[21] Yet, one has to bear in mind that a great number of psalms are actual lamentations, even questioning God's justice (Ps 73), and a problem of the suffering of the righteous (theodicy). Here and in the forthcoming chapters, Gillingham's word studies would have been strengthened by more notable input on the situational and the contextual view of theological and contextual elements in and through the Psalter.

Chapter 4: "Penitence before God." Word study: כסה, נשא, סלח, כפר, עבר, מחה.

The focal point of the previous chapter is the psalmist's craving to trust God. This seems to be prevalent, and comparatively there seem to be fewer urges to request the forgiveness. Penitential psalms are then much fewer in number. Yet, Gillingham points out: "the concept of penitence was familiar to many psalmists . . . many of the psalmists reveal an attitude of penitence even though the language offers no explicit vocabulary."[22]

This is well pointed out. In such psalms, there are the psalmist's requests for healing and/or restoration, which substantially, even though indirectly, is a penitence behind it all.

Chapter 5: "Death, Life and God." Word study: עפר, שחת, קבר, בור, מות, חיים, שאול.

Gillingham, here alludes to Barth, who suggests that the references to death in the Psalter may also be taken figurativelly, as a loss of strength. It is a well known reality in Jewish anthropology and vitality that weakness, illness or fragility is to some extent a way to death. On this, Aubrey Johnson's *The Vitality of the Individual in the Thought of Ancient Israel* (1949) is a vital work. It is beyond any reasonable doubt that both physical existence and bodily fragility are expectations of human life and death.

Chapter 6: "Communion with God." Word study: ידע, חסד, חפץ, רחם, אהב.

---

21. Gillingham, "Personal Piety," 94
22. Gillingham, 123.

Communion with God is not an exclusive privilege to the biblical psalmist. Gillingham frequently, and appropriately, alludes to the prophets, particularly prophet Jeremiah, and the psalmists as having similar experiences of the communion with God. She also points to the similarity of the life-settings of the two groups (prophets and psalmists). The words for Gillingham's word study are skilfully chosen.

Chapter 7: "Suffering before God." Word study: פעלי און, רשים, איבים.

Gillingham asserts: "most psalmists accept little responsibility for their suffering," and so it must have been due to other parties. Sometimes, whether in psalmodic or prophetic texts it may have been God himself, who does not "see" or "hear" the psalmist's distress or tribulations. This raises the questions of theodicy, the suffering of the righteous. But, one of the harshest sufferings for the psalmist, which is not physical or tribulation, is the silence and the hiddenness of God (*deus absconditus*) as in Isaiah 45:15 "you are a God who hides himself" or Job 2:13. In her word studies, Gillingham analyses the word "enemies" (*pa'al awon*), which "occurs in over twenty psalms and is supposedly implicit in over thirty more."[23] The question is posed, are they "living within the community"?[24] There are various theories, and she expectedly refers to Mowinckel and his theory about the sorcerers being the enemies.

Chapter 8: "Pleasing God." Word study: ישרים, אביונים, קדושים, חסידים, . . .

This chapter is somewhat an extension of chapter 6 (communion with God), in Gillingham's words the purpose of this chapter is to: "examine the extent to which the psalmists' particular experiences of God guided their understanding."[25] That is to say, what are the moral responses to God?

One of the words for the word study Gillingham puts across is the "saints" (*hasidim*). The question here was/is whether we have here a saintly individual psalmist who pleases God, or do we have here a particular party (bearing in mind we have here a plural noun). This would not be attractive within the cult-functions; others (Mowinckel) bring an "alternative proposal [of] [that] hasidim as referring to the whole nation of Israel."[26] Here, Psalm 85 is relevant where the saints clearly refer to God's people (Ps 85:9), his people

---

23. Gillingham, 254.
24. Gillingham, 254.
25. Gillingham, 311.
26. Gillingham, 315.

being in the midst of a crisis, the psalmodic text says that God will: "speak peace to his people, to his saints" (85:9), thus Gillingham concludes that "saints is used in synonymous terms with God's people" (p. 316). Curiously, the same terminology is familiar in the New Testament, particularly in the Pauline epistles (Phil 4:22; Col 3:12 or 1 Pet 2:9). Further in her word studies, Gillingham touches a similar challenge in reference to the *anawim* and *aniyim*, both "'pertain to the state of being physically poor' terms referring to the poor."[27] Similar discussion was/is going on whether we have here a religious party of the pious.

In conclusion, Gillingham's work is a great contribution to the idea of personal piety of the psalmist. She concludes that "the underlying assumptions were that the individual piety of the psalmists was the product of the individual self-consciousness" (p. 12). But also, after Kraus, it is regarded that "the emphasis is more on God's activity as perceived by the psalmists, than on man's personal experience of God."[28] Gillingham then appropriately refers to Prothero's study where he reflects on the "appropriation of psalms by individuals."[29]

On the other hand, Gillingham's work fundamentally belongs to a word-study domain. Such mode of study, analysis and techniques can readily be found in many excellent Old Testament Hebrew lexicons or theological workbooks. Gillingham's study lacks contextual and situational leanings in the area of the psalmist's personal piety as well as many aspects of the psalmist's piety in his privacy as we find it in the Psalter.

Our study aims towards the situational and contextual aspects (day, night, bed, morning, evening) (chs. 14, 16). Particular attention is given to the realm of privacy of the psalmist, making a clear distinction between the notions of the personal and the private (chs. 3, 12, 13), which are sometimes, and misleadingly, regarded as synonymous. Finally, the psalmodic anthropological aspect is of great importance and needs careful investigation (ch. 5).

---

27. Gillingham, 330.
28. Gillingham, 37.
29. Gillingham, 12.

CHAPTER 3

Personal and Private Aspects of the Subject

The demarcation between the very ideas and concepts of *personal* and *private* is significant, particularly in examinig the Psalmist's individual piety. The two notions may easily be, and erroneously, overlooked and regarded as synonymous. Distinction between the ideas and notions, private and personal are evident – this is particularly evident in the life of the biblical psalmist.[1]

To this distinction psalmodic critical scholarship has not paid adequate attention, resulting in lack of insights into the psalmist's personal and private piety. The issue has been neglected at the expense of more scientifically founded criteria, even though "prayers cannot simply be classified as literature or sentences to be examined using only linguistic scientific criteria."[2] In truth, "scientific criteria" and "religiosity" are almost oxymoronic. That is why manifestations or expressions of the personal are deemed *subjective*, while the impersonal is considered *objective*.[3] In the dichotomy between

---

1. In the language we use, we may have "private property" but we do not speak of "private injury," but rather of "personal injury." The injury is referred to be personal, but not private. Privacy considers a higher degree of confidentiality. Privacy is an antonym for the official. The psalmist's personal piety may be publicly ("officially") manifest, but in the most intimate experiences and his emotional or emotive states he withdraws into the privacy of his bedroom. See Ps 6:7.

2. Berkovic, "Grammar of Death," 127.

3. For more on this see: James, V*arieties of Religious Experience*. William James, in his final, 20th lecture, presented certain conclusions relative to religiosity and personality. Religiosity belongs to personal and personal destiny, while the scientific approach by and large excludes the personal factor. While religion revolves around the "interest of the individual in his private personal destiny," science, on the other hand, "catalogues her elements and records

the subjective and the objective, the subjective seem to be at a losing end. It is often followed by such reasoning, which is plain syllogism, that what is subjective is not objective. This anteriory puts the subjective in the inferior position. However in the words of William James, "the pivot round which the religious life, as we have traced it, revolves, is the interest of the individual in his private personal destiny."[4]

The issues of personal and private will make us at least to tackle the subject matter of the subject and subjectivity. Although this subject of the subject has been one of the central ideas throughout the history of literature, literary theories, philosophy, psychoanalysis and hermenutics.

3.1 Person and Personality

The word *person* is not known in Biblical Hebrew vocabulary. The closest to our understanding and the concept of "person"/"personality" is the Hebrew noun נפש ("nefeš") (soul). But even the "nefeš" as the individual is hardly ever seen as an isolated unit. It always seems to be in interaction with the community rather than the individual per se. It seems to be only an "indefinite extension" of the corporate personality.[5]

Even closer to our idea of person is the Hebrew idea of the "face" פנה ("pana"). The face seems to be a common denominator for the person-personality idea between the semitic but also the Indo-European mindset.

The bond between the *face* and the *person*, etymologically is a fascinating one.[6] When speaking of the face and personality, Aubrey Johnson points out that the face "was found to be extraordinarily revealing in respect of man's various emotions, moods, and dispositions."[7]. Yet, it is not only the expressiv-

---

her laws indifferent as to what purpose may be shown forth by them, and constructs her theories quite careless of their bearing on human anxieties and fates." James, *Varieties of Religious Experience*, 370.

    4. James, 370.

    5. Cf. Johnson, *One and Many*, 7–8.

    6. The word "person" comes from the original Latin noun "persona" (*f.*) and/or Greek πρόσωπον (*n.*) meaning "face." Originally the Greek "prosopon" was a mask covering the face. In the ancient Hellenistic and Roman theatrical performances, there were masks for covering the dead; "death-masks," just as there were a great number of masks to represent every possible character, emotion, age and sex.

    7. Johnson, *One and Many*, 40.

ness of the face that is so revealing of the person. It is also its various "fixing" or "turning" in a particular direction that serves for indications of purpose or intentions of the whole person. For example, God will in punishment and retribution "set his face against" his people (Lev 26:17).[8]

The face ceases to be a mere metaphor and metonymy; the "prosopon" becomes "an external aspect of an object, whether personal or impersonal."[9] In the Aaronic blessing (Num 6:24–26) the prosopon, the person and personality is in the face (פנה) of the Lord that shines upon his people. The face of God, that is, God himself in person turns towards man, providing his support and life. On the other hand, God can hide his face (himself) from the psalmist, which makes him panic stricken (Ps 13:1; Ps 30:7). God or God's face hiding from the psalmist has the effect of mortal threat: "Do not hide your face from me, lest I become like those descending to the pit" (Ps 143:7).

3.2 Subject and Subjectivity

One of the major concerns of literature, particularly narrative literature, relates to identity and function of the subject. Hence, the *dramatis personae* (literally, "the masks of the drama") or the main character in a drama. As a literary genre, drama primarily and commonly refers to a theater. However, in a wider sense drama and *dramatis personae* may also apply to general situations where an individual subject, or a member of a group, plays a crucial role in an episode. In this, the psalmist in the Psalter is also a *dramatis personae*. And, though the term the "psalmist" is widely being used as *terminus technicus*, it also ought to be identified in individual terms as the subject (see here: "Who Is the Psalmist").

The interest in the subject and the individual, apart from literary theories, persists in psychoanalysis, hermeneutics, literary criticism, feminist criticism, Marxist criticism, etc. May we be allowed to take as an example from contemporary history how the subject and the individual are determined in

---

8. Representative is how the linguistic, and then the theological *face-person* pair provoked a major division in the history of the Western world. It is indicative that in the Christian patristic times the Trinitarian controversies started with the conception of God's face and Christ as the "prosopon" of God. The face was an obvious "medium of self-expression, or presenting character." Prestige, *God in Patristic Thought*, 55.

9. Prestige, 55.

the Marxist theory. Jonathan Culler puts it this way, "Marxist theory sees the subject as determined by class position: it either profits from others' labour or labours for others' profit."[10] In somewhat comparable fashion, biblical subject can be determined by class position, but it is by far more determined by religion. This is where the psalmist as an individual, in his personal and private aspects, needs to be defined and determined. Throughout the psalmodic studies, the subject and the individuality of the individual (psalmist) was one of the key issues. This search for the psalmist as a private individual, against the bias that an individual in the Scriptural context is only an anonymous part of a corporate personality in biblical scholarship has been around for quite a while.

3.2.1 The Self: Given or Made?

Before we say some more about the issue of the psalmist as an individual, his personality and privacy, we ought to give at least some attention to the general discussion over various approaches and theories of the subject, not as a grammatical part of a sentence, but rather as an idea of the *individuality of the individual*. It is a question, whether the subject is "the self something given or something made ... and should it be conceived in individual or in social terms."[11] Culler continues and proposes four threads or issues in comprehending the individual as a subject. Let us briefly outline his scheme.

First, the individual can be viewed as the self as something "inner and unique." Second, Culler portrays the subject as that which is "made," meaning that the self is "determined by its origins and social attributes." Third, it is a combination of the previous two points. It combines the individual as "unique" ("inner and unique") and the individual which is "made" ("determined by its origins"). This then emphasizes the changing nature of a self. The fourth and final point emphasizes that the subject becomes the individual through "various subject positions" which one occupies.[12] Observing Culler's scheme, it strongly directs us to the etymology of the term "subject." This may impart some oxymoronic shades. Namely, the term "subject" comes from the Latin *subjectio* and *subjacceo*. Both terms convey the same idea: *subjectio*

---

10. Culler, *Literary Theory*, 109.
11. Culler, 108.
12. Culler, 108.

(submit, come under) and *subjaceo* (lie underneath, at the foot). As we had it so far, the subject comes across as that which is "inner and unique" of the individual. But then the etymology of the term "subject" gives us a completely different picture, as that which is in submission and not of uniqueness.[13]

3.2.2 The Self and "Theoria"

As we aim to portray the psalmist in his personal and private life, discerning between the subject and the object is very much needed.[14] For the differentiation between the subject and the object, a notion of *theory* (Greek, θεωρια) from the ancient Greek metaphysics becomes crucial.[15]

The primary meaning of *theoria* is "to observe" or "to look at." In ancient Greece, *theoros* or *theoroi* were official delegates or observers of cities' festivals and *theoria* was their duty. They were ambassadors from other cities, in diplomatic mission for truce between the cities. *Theoroi* were *spectators* and *witnesses*, which made *theoria* not only a duty and the event, but also a stage which was not merely an oversight and observation point, but also an observation point wherefrom the observer acquires knowledge. The subject (*theoros*) as an observer, cannot subject an object to himself, if he is in any way subordinate to the object of his observation; thus the *theoros* had to distance himself from the object of his observation.[16]

However, there is another somewhat different understanding of the *theoria* as an observation and the affiliation between the subject and the object. Namely, the Latin translation of Greek *theoria* is *speculatio* (from Latin *specto*, to observe, to re-search). Here, the one who is observing, the observer, is called the *spectans*, just like the *theoros* in *theoria*. But the *spectans* is also the *speculator*, that is, the one who lies in wait, as a researcher. But now comes a significant difference between the observer (*theoros*) and the Latin observer (*spectans*). Here comes an etymological play on words, from Latin verbal root *specto* also comes *speculum*, mirror. That is to say that while the *spectans* is

---

13. Culler provides some theories and models regarding the position and the role of the self and the subject. Culler particularly lists: Michel Foucault's portrayal in psychoanalysis; Marxist theory; the Queer theory. Culler, 109.

14. In his *Summa Theologiae*, Thomas Aquinas differentiates between *subiectum* and *obiectum* and the relationship between the subject and the object. Whereas, the object has this capacity (*ratio*) to evaluate the subject.

15. *Theoria* is a compound word consisting of: *thea* (a view) and *horan* (to see).

16. Biti, *Pojmovnik suvremene knjizevne teorije*, 385.

the observer, he is also performing an act of *intro-spection*. Indeed, as Biti sums it up, "*speculatio* as Latin translation of the Greek term *theoria* involves also the final abolishing in the separation between the subject and the object, while and instead they mirror each other."[17]

In this understanding of the ancient Greek *theoria* we now have both aspects included, that of the observation (*theoros*), where the subject is distanced from the object, and a dimension of the introspection and self-reflection, a mirroring between the subject and the object. Both of these understandings and interpretations of *theoria* are fully congruent with the psalmist's experiences, where he played a role as an observer as well as the experiencer. We then may conclude that the so-called "theoretical truth" may not be so "theoretical" but rather, on the basis of observation and self-reflection, a phenomenon of life and living.[18] This is well witnessed in the psalmist's personal and private living as we have it in the Psalter.

3.2.3 The Self and the Psalmist

For quite a while in biblical scholarship, particularly in the psalmodic studies, the individual as the subject was predominantly treated merely as a piece in a puzzle, rather than recognizing the individuality of the individual. Some eminent psalmodic researchers would claim that individual personality in biblical culture would be equal to arrogance, thus one of the fathers of the psalmodic studies will conclude,

> To be original, someone apart, a personality, whose right of existence depended on being different, would not to the ancient Israelites have appeared as an ideal or an end to attain, but on the contrary, as a *madness*, an *arrogance*, something *abnormal*, or, in their own words, an unrighteousness and a folly (italics mine).[19]

As one goes through the biblical texts, there seem to be quite a number of "abnormal" biblical individuals – to name but two "arrogant" biblical characters, Hannah and Job. Hannah, Samuel's mother, was proclaimed a drunkard; while in her bitterness (מרת נפש) she poured out her grief before

---

17. Biti, 385.
18. Cf. Hans Jonas, *Phenomenon of Life*.
19. Mowinckel, *Psalms in Israel's Worship*, ch. 3, 43.

God, which resulted in the priest imploring her to sober up (1 Sam 1:10, 14). On the expression (מרה נפש), "bitterness of the soul," see the discussion by Dermot Cox (1978) in *The Triumph of Impotence*. Perhaps such "abnormal" individuals are to be viewed simply as a record of general traditions or perhaps a thematic prototype. Even then, there is a case in point of *personal anthropology* vs. *collective anthropology*. In the matters of personal anthropology, particularly in the case of the abdominal idiom, it may prove difficult to put it in the framework of the collective anthropology. Surely, one cannot speak of *kidneys*, *liver*, *innards* or *wombs* in the context of a collective anthropology.

3.3 Appropriation and Interpretation

An attentive reader of the Psalter will note that comprehension or interpretation of the Psalms may not be his ultimate goal. For the attentive reader of the Psalms, the ultimate goal is *appropriation* of the psalmodic texts. It is a step further and beyond the neccessary intelligent comprehension and interpretation. In this case, the reader is not only to adopt the text in comprehension, competent interpretation or appraisal of its authoritative value. Appropriation is the reader's adoption of the text as if it is one's own, it is a matter of self-identification.[20]

Perhaps the best example of appropriation is Jesus's self-identification with the psalmist. It is a powerful display of the last weeks of his life, in the Gethsemane experience (Ps 22) and finally in his death on the cross (Ps 31). For better and more adequate perception of the Psalter and the psalmist, we propose that appropriation of the psalms is a better way of mastering and understanding of the Psalter.[21] We acknowledge that the Psalter is an editorial collection, composed and compiled for liturgical purposes, but we also recognize that it aims to be an appropriation material. This brings us to tackle the issue of the the psalmist as a private individual and the subject matter of appropriation.

---

20. Cf. Schokel, *Manual of Hebrew Poetics*, 90.

21. We agree and concur with Alonso Schokel saying that biblical psalms are "an extreme, and almost inevitable case of appropriation." Schokel, 90.

3.4 Personal Piety and Privacy

3.4.1 Personal Piety

Personal refers to everything that is immanent to a particular person, whether material (*property*) or immaterial (*emotion*). The personal is a combination of each individual's emotional and behavioral patterns. The consciousness and self-consciousness of all that is personal, includes forms of public expression. The psalmist often yearns to exercise his personal devotion and piety in public worship. One such example is Psalm 27 (see also 61:4) where in his heartfelt yearning for the nearness of God, the psalmist seeks to affirm his faith and exercise his deep-seated personal piety in public worship: "One thing I ask of the LORD; this I seek: To dwell in the LORD's house all the days of my life, To gaze on the LORD's beauty, to visit his temple" (Ps 27:4 NAB).

Some commentators call this kind of psalmodic poem a "spiritual song." Gunkel categorizes the Psalm as the "spiritual cult-free psalm" and assembles a collection of 12 such Psalms.[22] However, it is not quite clear why he concludes, oddly, that the collection has "no relationship to the worship service."[23] Others insist that the psalm should be interpreted in the context of liturgy.[24]

Gunkel concludes that this collection of "spiritual songs" or "spiritual cult-free psalm" is "suitable for private use because they consist of genres for the individual"[25] Others, however, do not recognize the earthly exercise of personal piety, but rather consider it as "eternal bliss with YHWH in heaven," where the "Lord's house" designates a divine heavenly habitation.[26] Whichever of these interpretations we accept, the psalmist clearly and powerfully demonstrates his personal piety, which he wishes to show publicly (27:6b).

3.4.2 Privacy

On the other hand that which is "private" is confined to the person concerned, and not publicly expressed. It requires private space, "taken away" (Latin *privatus*) from public eyes. In Biblical Hebrew there are two concepts of the awareness and perception of what is strictly private. One is to do with the

---

22. Pss 7, 16, 17, 25, 26, 27, 28, 32, 33, 34, 35, 37.
23. Gunkel, *Introduction to Psalms*, 346.
24. Craigie, *Psalms 1–50*, 231.
25. Craigie, 231.
26. Dahood, *Psalms I*, 167.

verb בוש (to be ashamed) which designates something to be kept strictly to oneself, that what is intimate. Sometimes it refers to the "private parts" of the human body (Deut 25:11).

The other is the verb לוט (or לאט) (to cover, hide, to be secret or keep in private).[27] Privacy is a matter of seclusion and secrecy (בלט).[28] Jesus of Nazareth, the Jewish rabbi, urged his pious compatriots and followers to exercise genuine personal piety in private.[29] Such as we find in the Gospel of Matthew: "when you pray, go to your inner room (ταμεῖόν), close the door, and pray to your Father in secret (κρυπτῷ). And your Father who sees in secret will repay you" (Matt 6:6). The New Testament Hebrew rendering of Matthew 6:6 (κρυπτῷ) is סבב (to surround) and סתר (hide).[30] Using a compound expression of the two verbs (סתר סביבו) conveys this privacy even in the more intense way than the original Mathean Greek.[31]

The psalmist's personal piety is often exercised in such privacy. For him this can be designated *spatially* and *temporally* – spatially, on his *bed* or a *couch*, his *room* (Pss 6, 63); temporally, it can be at *all times* or *day and night* (Pss 6, 16, 17, 42, 63, 77, 88).

3.5 Concluding Remarks

Although it may seem as being a contradiction, while the collective is being recognized as a ruling social organization, at the same time and that point the individual is being recognized as a subject to be concerned with. In the words of Andre Lacocque this can be summed up in his commentary to the book of Daniel,

> man became a citizen of the world, of the oikoumene. And in a paradoxical, yet comprehensible way, this enlarging of men's

---

27. 2 Sam 19:5. The לאט is hapax legomena.

28. For example: "Saul commanded his servants, 'Speak to David in private.'" (דברו אל־דוד בלט) (1 Sam 18:22 NRSV).

29. Such "private meeting" with their God involves seclusion – *entering* into private space and *closing* the door behind.

30. Cf. HNT Salkinson-Ginsburg Hebrew NT. Greek κρυπτῷ = secret, hidden, private. Cf. Rom 2:29: "He is a Jew who is one inwardly (ἐν τῷ κρυπτῷ), and real circumcision is a matter of the heart, spiritual and not literal." (RSV)

31. This also echoes the enclosures of monastic foundations (Latin, *claustrum*, English, *cloister*) which separate and seclude the pious from the outside world.

horizons to universal dimensions had the consequence of atomizing society into individuals. In the process of the disintegrating of social structures which had been second nature to him, man found himself alone, hence unique, with particular problems which could no longer be resolved by collective solutions.[32]

Following Lacocque's summary of how the collective and the individual interact, we conclude that the collective "I" and the collective personality of biblical Israel, is in coexistence with that which is personal and private. We cannot accept that the Israelite individual in his/her individuality is to be viewed as arrogance, madness and something abnormal.[33] We shall demonstrate in this work that the the two, the collective and the individual in his/her individuality are not mutually exclusive but rather complementary.[34]

Let us look into some characteristics of the Israelite religion to observe what is its basic nature. Is it more of a transcendental or a literalist type of religion? Is the community a ruling factor or more of individualistic religious experience?

---

32. Lacocque, *Book of Daniel*, 235.
33. Mowinckel, *Psalms in Israel's Worship*, ch. 3, 43.
34. Lacocque, *Book of Daniel*, 235.

CHAPTER 4

Religious Typology

If ancient Judaism was an elitist, clergy-centred religion, with the cult and liturgy thoroughly shaping its religiosity, has it ruled out any form of personal and private piety? Was Judaism also a religion of the heart; whereas the heart of the pious may also be serving as a metaphor for the temple (Ezek 11:16b)? Although this is not the occasion to tackle the subject of the origins, history and development of religion, some knowledge of early Semitic religion is in order to place an individual in the wider perspective of personal and public piety.[1] Of course, this question of the nature of Hebrew religion can be, and should also be viewed from the perspective of the general history of religion (*Religionsgeschichte*). But our task here is to deal with religious experience as encountered in the canonical book of Psalms – particularly expressions of "personal religion" and its private expressions. In the Psalter, quite an advanced stage in the development of the history of religion is evident in the intense synergy between faith (religion) and emotion. The relationship between religion and emotion, which has been traditionally well attested to, is markedly present in the Psalter. This also implies typical features in terms of the religious typology found in the Psalter.

---

1. In rudimentary form, we can at least sketch the basics of the earliest stages of religious beliefs as found in the history of religion, some of which are evidenced in the Hebrew Old Testament religious context, from the earliest animistic stages and objects of worship, to later polytheism, or ancestor worship, and finally to monotheism. Here are some of the religious history elements found in the Old Testament: *trees* (dendolatry; cf. Gen 21:33; Isa 1:29; Hos 4:13); *holy hills* or *high places* ("bamot," elements of polytheistic tendencies, cf. Lev 26:30); *stones* (erected at the spots of theophanic events, cf. Gen 35:14; Deut 4:28); *ancestor worship* (as an expression of the human need for continuity, cf. Sir 44:8–15; 2 Sam 18:18, cf. Sheriffs, 2004:1–16); *necromancy* (cult of the dead, a desire to know the future, cf. 1 Sam 28). Oesterley and Robinson, *Hebrew Religion*, 3–107.

In his study, *Religion and Emotion*, Hans Schilderman investigates the subject of how emotion and religion relate, by asking why and how distinctions of religious types cohere with emotional states. He begins his investigation with the hypothesis that,

> *transcendent* religion tends to be associated with positive moods and emotions, whereas a *literal* approach to religion is more often associated with negative moods and emotions.[2] (italics mine)

In the case of the psalmist's religiosity and piety, this conclusion presents certain dilemma, as the psalmist's emotional display spans a range of emotional states; and this seems to be one of the major issues in psalmodic studies in general (see chapter 2).

A detailed analysis of Schilderman's investigation is not appropriate here and more detailed discussion will be furnished while considering the psalmist emotions. However, two alternate views should be taken into account now. One is the so-called "emotional interpretation of religion" (EIR), in other words, blind faith steered by emotion.[3] The other is the so-called "religious interpretation of emotion" (RIE), which fundamentally sees religion in terms of specific emotions, not based on knowledge, metaphysics or morality. This view is upheld and particularly well explained by Rudolf Otto in his opus, *Das Heilige: Uber das Irrationale in der Idee des Gottlichen und sein Verhaltnis zum Rationalen*. Otto's understanding of religion is rooted in human ability to sense the "numinous" ("mysterious"), which is purported by the *mysterium tremendum*, sometimes translated as "ominous fear," or fear of God. There is also *tremendum majestatis*, or that which is awesome and inaccessible.[4] This awesome experience of God and his holiness is certainly one of the key experiences of the psalmist. The experience of the *tremendum* even in the lamental psalms is evident. Many aspects of the RIE understanding of religion are applicable to the psalmist's experiences.

---

2. Schilderman, "Religion and Emotion," 85.

3. "Emotion – as the dark unexplainable motive of action – competes with reason," whereby religion becomes the shelter and master of emotion. See: Schilderman, 87.

4. See: Otto, *Das Heilige*, chapter 4.

4.1 Israelite Religion

Moving on to the examination of the religious typology of the Israelite religion, some general remarks are necessary. The issues of Old Testament theology methodologies are not at stake here. The "history-of-religion" (*Religionsgeschichte*) and the historical development of any religion, including that of Israel, cannot be ignored. Religion and the study of the history of religion (more specifically, the Israelite religion) need not only be viewed as or significantly reduced to a purely historic discipline, which "records impartially the beliefs of the religious community."[5] However important, useful or influential a particular approach may be, it should not be taken in isolation.

For quite some time, the Psalms were considered almost exclusively through the study of the forms (*Formsgeschichte*). Accordingly, the key in understanding of the biblical literature was not so much in dividing it and grouping of the *sources* of different traditions (documents), but rather a study of the (literary) *forms*, which had their origin in the prewritten and preliterary stages. Both the documentary and the form critical approach are *reconstructionist* in nature. They are concerned with the attempt to reconstruct either the sources or the literary types in the literary development of the Old Testament. The literary types were meant to be a solution in the interpretation strategies, following the similarities and analogous forms of the religious forms of the surrounding peoples around Israel.

If the methodologies which study forms have had such a sweeping influence, potentially even reductionist in understanding the Psalms, the actual religiosity and individual piety of the psalmist easily become of lesser or only incidental importance. To repeat Martin Noth's warning, the danger is that form criticism and its apparatus simply become *formula criticism*.[6]

---

5. Kaiser, *Toward an Old Testament Theology*, 10. See also the wider discussion in Kaiser, 4–11.

6. Walter Kaiser presents types and methodologies in approaches to studying the Old Testament. These are the following four types or methods: (i) the *structural* type, which approaches Old Testament in terms of structures borrowed from systematic theology, (ii) the *diachronic* type, which is basically representative of the Religionsgeschichte method, that is, looking through successive time periods and religious development, (iii) the *lexicographic* type, often called the word studies, focusing on vocabulary and use of words, and (iv) the *biblical themes* type, which searches a key term in the Old Testament which may cover or create a cluster of theological focus for the whole of the Old Testament. Kaiser, 9–10.

There are fundamental sets of rudiments regarding Israelite type of beliefs and religion, which ideally strive to remain unchanged, and encourage either the collective manifestation of religion or individual private piety, as in the case of the psalmist.

So the Israelite religion should be discussed in terms of religious typology, not only the history-of-religion tradition. What kind of predominant traces of religious experience (piety) can be observed in religious practice, whether collective or individual? The answer will naturally also touch on the psychology of religion, experience and emotion, rather than just the cultus and religious institutional organisation. For, piety is exactly that – a step beyond formally organised religion.[7]

4.2 *Numen Locale* and *Numen Personale*

Religious experience and experience of God are often perceived in conceptual terms as *numen* and the numinous, experience of the divine or supernatural which invokes fear and trembling (*mysterium tremendum*).[8] This is not a type of panic fear (dread or fright), though to *tremble* and *tremor* is initially associated with that type of fear. It is the most intimate experience of awe. In biblical Hebrew, for such experience of the *tremendum* we have (אימה) or (פחד) both terms refer to the "terror of JHWH" (Exod 23:27; Job 9:34).[9] Such awesome experience of the transcendence blends with another, that of the *majestas* (majesty), that which is of a superior other-worldly power.

---

7. In his study of religion and emotion, Hans Schilderman classifies religions as *transcendent* and *literal*. The former participate more in divine realities (personal experience), while the latter are more limited to the realm of the immanent (the cultus and the collective). Schilderman relates emotive states and emotional experiences to these two classificatioins. The conclusion seems to be that transcendent religion is more associated with positive moods and emotions, while literal religion is more associated with negative moods and emotional states. Schilderman, "Religion and Emotion," 85.

8. The idea and the meaning of *numen* (Latin *numen, -inis, n.*) essentially refer to divine, efficacious and sovereign ordinances; it also can mean "a wink from gods" or a personal divine commandment, for example, *inimica Trojae numen magna deum* or *numine Italiam petere*.

9. The English language for such experiences has few terms which well describe the feeling. Certainly first, it is the *awe* and *awesome*, then there is the adjective *aghast* (stunned, dismayed). German Grauen is close to the English verb *terrify*. The experience may also be described as *uncanny* (unearthly, other-worldly, ghostly, strange). Cf. Otto, *Das Heilige*, chapter 4.

Finally, the experience of the *numinous* is not only *tremendum* (Latin *tremere*, to shiver; *tremendus*, awesome), and *majestas*. The *numen* is also experienced as that of the fascination, the *fascinans*, that is, as being fascinated and amazed. It is a wonder that befalls the experiencer or the observer (Ps 48:6).

There are two valuable works on the subject. One introductory and the other more exhaustive. In his *Einfuhrung in das Christentum* (*Introduction to Christianity*), Joseph Ratzinger articulates *numen* by drawing a basic distinction between *numen locale* and *numen personale*. The former refers to localising a deity following personal religious experience, simply equating the location with the deity. The latter relates to a very personal, non-localised experience of God. So, *numen locale* is a very localised god; while *numen personale* is a very individual, personal experience of God. Another work, which is more detailed and extensive, a great classic on the subject, is Rudolf Otto's *Das Heilige: Uber das Irrationale in der Idee des Gottlichen und sein Verhaltnis zum Rationalen.*[10]

4.3 Centralization and Personalization

According to the above discussion, can the Israelite religion, without going into a general discussion of the history of religion, be classified as a *numen personale* type? The witness of the biblical texts provides sufficient evidence for assessing the Israelite religion, in its more primitive religious developmental stage, and during the later stage. There seems to be a common denominator shared by, possibly, contrasting developmental stages.

Two rival strategies can be identified. One is the tradition of the centralisation of worship (Deut 12:5), which might seem to be an exemplary model of localising a deity, though this was clearly not its primary aim. Other texts positively wrestle with centralisation/localisation endeavours, pleading for the personalisation of faith and piety (eg. 2 Sam 7:5–16). Brueggemann is right when he says that the call for Yahweh's presence among the Israelites was in itself "endlessly problematic."[11] The rationale for such a statement

---

10. See Ratzinger, *Einfuhrung*, chapter 2, "Biblical Faith in God, and Otto, *Das Heilige*, particularly chapter 2 on the definitional level of the numinous; then chapter 4 on the experience of the numinous termed the *mysterium tremendum*, and then chapter 5 on expressions of the experience of the numinous in the numinous hymns, essentially biblical psalmody.

11. Cf. Brueggemann, *Theology of Old Testament*, 675.

rests on the programmatic tensions between the two schemes or theologies found in the Old Testament. One side was held by the priestly tradition, with its agenda for centralizing the cultus, while the other was represented by Deuteronomic theology and Deuteronomistic circles. They supported the sovereign freedom of Yahweh, while encouraging and even demanding individual piety, as advocated strongly by the prophets. The prophets were themselves disciples of the Deuteronomistic tradition, acknowledging that, "particular communal practice (immersion in and influence of a tradition and perspective) and inexplicable, originary personal experience."[12]

The centralization manifesto instructed the Israelites not to worship or seek the Lord anywhere and everywhere they thought fitting, but only in "the place which the LORD your God will choose." (Deut 12:5 NRSV). They were to put his name and there seek his dwelling (שכן) only there. Though this may seem like a blatant localization of the deity, its rationale was not to make Yahwism the *numen locale* type of religion. It was more to do with preventing the people from adopting the religious customs of the surrounding nations (12:4).[13] The intention was to prohibit Israelites' worship at sites where pagan shrines were already being used. The Yahwistic place of worship was to be determined by Yahweh. In fact, it could be argued that no single place was to be chosen, but places which "Yahweh shall choose in any of your tribes."[14] Thus, the Israelites were confronted with the same question as other religions, that is, can the deity only be revealed in a particular place or places?[15] The difference between public worship and personal piety does not seem to have been an issue in the early days after the Exodus.

On the other hand, while the plans for building a dwelling for Yahweh, the House of the Lord (בית יהוה), were under way, the *vox dei* replies in the form

---

12. Brueggemann, 624. In reference to the prophets of the Old Testament, Brueggemann concludes that "the emergence of individual persons who speak with an authority beyond their own is indeed an odd, inexplicable, originary happening in Israel." Brueggemann, 622. It ought to be said that the Deuteronomistic tradition did not foster "spiritual lone rangers," for no other reason than that such individuals did not and could not live in a social or religious vacuum.

13. The centralisation theme was already proffered in Exod 20:24 within the Book of the Covenant where the people were commanded to worship "in every place where I cause my name to be remembered I will come to you and bless you" (Exod 20:24 NRSV).

14. Nicholson, *Deuteronomy and Tradition*, 53–54.

15. The Israelites went through this experience during the desert wanderings, when apart from the Ark and the Tent, there was only inaccessible Mt. Sinai as a sacred site of the divine presence.

of a rhetorical question: "Are you the one to build me a house to dwell in?" (2 Sam 7:5 NRSV). It is a question which implies a negative reply. Moreover, Yahweh overturns the plan and affirms his freedom and sovereignty, by introducing his own plan and design and establishing a royal house. King David was then informed, "The LORD will make you a house." (7:11 NRSV). There is a parallel narrative regarding King David's designs to build the temple to Yahweh in 1 Chronicles 17. In that account, there was no rhetorical question, but a clear statement: "You shall not build me a house to dwell in" (17:4 RSV). Only after Yahweh establishes the royal house will he decide and choose the person to build him a dwelling (1 Chr 17:2).

Consequently, there was a constant dilemma, exhibited in the tension between Israel's expectations of having Yahweh's presence with them at all times in his divine, but earthly dwelling (clearly localized in the temple in Jerusalem), and Yahweh' nature as the sovereign, free God of the wilderness, who "moved about in the tent" (מתהלך באהל) (2 Sam 7:6), and "walked with all the children of Israel" (7:7). In one sense, they did not need to go to Yahweh's place of residence, since he was always with and among them, providing immediate and lasting access to his presence. On the other hand, the priestly tradition's strategy was to localise Yahweh's presence and integrate it into cultic, sacramental practices. Walter Eichrodt observes well the dangers of tensions between institutional religion and personal piety:

> The more emphatically a religion becomes tied to the sacred sites, the more dangerous are their inevitable effects on the idea of God and on his worship. The holy place, especially when it is also thought of as the dwelling-place of the divinity, leads to the localisation of the Godhead and the limitation of his sphere of influence.[16]

According to the biblical text, this tension indicates possible incompatibility between where Yahweh dwells and where Yahweh manifests himself.[17] In other words, the sacred localities where Yahweh dwells are not necessarily where Yahweh manifests himself.

---

16. Eichrodt, *Theology of the Old Testament*, 103.
17. Eichrodt, 103.

The tension between a localised God (*numen locale*) and a free God of the people (*numen personale*) is clearly exhibited throughout the Psalms. At times, the psalmist is eager to experience Yahweh in his dwelling in Zion, while at others he longs to have Yahweh with him day and night. Yahweh dwells in Zion (ישב ציון) (Ps 9:12). His title may be even rendered as: "Yahweh of Zion" (יהוה מציון), or according to the parallel expression of Psalm 135:21 as the "resident of Jerusalem" (שכן ירושלם) (Ps 76:3).[18] From his sanctuary on Zion, Yahweh sends help and support (Ps 20:3). Therefore, Zion becomes a metonymic association for Yahweh. The captives of Psalm 137:1, who "sat mourning and weeping when we remembered Zion," were not just experiencing homesickness because of their physical and geographical separation from Jerusalem, but felt deeply the separation from their God, his presence and his help. The Israelite religion clearly included certain fundamentals relating to religious experience in terms of *numen personale*, and hence strongly developed personal and private piety, while the cultus and theophanic experiences, though highly personal, led to the institution of organized religion which knew the divine as *numen locale*. The features of Israelite religion were thus neither predominately *numen locale* nor *numen personale*. In any case, the two are not mutually exclusive. But how can a balance be found between tradition and personal experience?

---

18. Dahood translates this, "Blessed be Yahweh of Zion, the Resident of Jerusalem" (Ps 135:21). Dahood, *Psalms*, III, 262–63.

CHAPTER 5

The Religion of the Heart of Flesh

Israelite religiosity has close association to its anthropology. Biblical and psalmodic piety are closely related to the Hebrew view of the man's constitution and his constitutional parts.[1] There are a number of psycho-physiological terms, such as: "heart," "soul," "spirit," "body," "bones," "feet," "hands," "face," which are not only anthropological constituent parts but also frequently play an important part in conveying emotional/religious experience, as a means of non-verbal communication.[2] Thus, the *anthropological dimension* must be given serious consideration in relation to the psalmist's piety (or for that matter, even when discussing human religiosity in general).

In religious practices, different parts of the body need referring to, which shall be assessed in the forthcoming chapters, but for now our base is set with the very core of (Israelite) religiosity, that of the *heart*. In the Israelite view of humans, the heart is not only the seat of emotions or decision-making (though religion is almost without exception easily coupled with emotion).

---

1. Biblical anthropology of the Hebrew person is a complex subject covered in many in-depth studies, essays and scholarly works. Some outstanding referential studies include: Hans W. Wolff, *Anthropology of the Old Testament*; major sections of Johannes Pedersen's *Israel: Its life and culture*; and Aubrey Johnson, *The Vitality of the Individual in the Thought of Ancient Israel*. On various aspects of anthropology as it relates to Hebrew psychology and expressions of emotion, a number of studies published in periodicals are available. There is the issue of "corporate personality"; cf. J. R. Porter, *The Legal Aspects of the Concept of Corporate Personality in Old Testament* (in *Vetus Testamentum*, 15 (1965)) or H. W. Robinson, *The Hebrew Conception of Corporate Personality* (in Beihefte zur Zeitschrift für die alttestamentliche Wissenschaf (BZAW), 66 (1936)). See also Mowinckel's *Psalms in Israel's Worship*, ch. 3.

2. Gruber, "Many Faces of Hebrew," and *Aspects of Nonverbal Communication*; Barre, "Wandering About"; Labarre, "Cultural Basis of Emotions."

It is also the real location and the source of genuine religiosity and piety. But there are certain qualifying requirements for that to be so.

5.1 The "Heart of Flesh"

The expression "heart of flesh" (לב בשר) clearly echoes the words of Ezekiel. The idiom is unique to that prophet, and as such it will not be found in the Psalter.[3] So, why do we find it necessary to use this idiom and build on something which is textually absent from the Psalter? How relevant and congruous is this to the matter of the psalmist's personal piety? It would be a mistake of literalist reading if the idiom as we use it here is being read only as Ezekiel's phrase, without connecting it to the psalmist's piety. Indeed, the nature of the psalmist's religion (and equally so, for Ezekiel) is the "fleshy" and "pure" (Ps 24:4; Ps 51:10), also the "new" heart, as basic premises to genuine Israelite religiosity.[4] The phrase(s) we opt for here we take as conceptual in nature, referring to the very foundations of genuine Israelite religion.

Actually, the concept of the *fleshy* heart is not inherent and unique to Ezekiel. The idea of the *fleshy* heart as opposed to the *stony* heart (or the heart which is hardened) is typical for the Psalms. The admonition of the worship leader in Psalm 95 calls upon the gathered pilgrims: "Do not harden your hearts as at Meribah" (Ps 95:8). The hearts need to be "fleshed" (Ezek 37:6) and the stone broken. The "broken hearted" (לב נשבר) (Ps 51:19) are not only the ones who are emotionally disturbed and desperate, they are the ones whose hearts are fleshy and ready to be responsive and sensitive to God. There is also this idea of a *new heart*. Furthermore, it has been instructed that they, the people, should "get yourselves a new heart" (ועשו לכם לב חדש) (Ezek 18:31).[5] Or, as the psalmist would have it, the *new spirit* (Ps 51:31) denotes spiritual renewal and personal devotion widespread throughout the Old Testament,

---

3. Compare: Ezek 11:19; 36:26; so is the phrase "new heart" (לב חדש). See: Ezek 18:31.
4. See also: בר-לבב and לב טהור.
5. Eichrodt, 246: "the imperative of the exhortation is a response to the indicative of God's saving action; God's gift of salvation does not leave a man alone, but calls upon him for a response to God's offer, to enter upon the new potentiality of life."

and so it is in the psalter.⁶ The psalmist's soul longs for and his heart and flesh yearn for God (Ps 84:2).

In terms of psychobiology, the heart is made of flesh, that is, being sensitive, rather than as irresponsive as stone, which becomes a constant reminder for a genuine piety for the Israelites.

At this point, Hans W. Wolff provides some useful pointers and cautions. First, regarding methodology, he cautions the use of the "anthropologisation of theology." That is to say, anthropological problems should not be resolved simply by "screening off" theology.⁷ Anthropological conclusions should not be brought about on the basis of theologically preconceived ideas. While we agree on the dangers of theologizing biblical anthropology, it is hard to agree with von Rad's passing remark that there is "absolutely no unity in the ideas of the Old Testament about the nature of man."⁸ It is even more difficult to agree with him since he draws on A. R. Johnson and J. Pedersen, who actually both insist on the unity and totality of the Hebrew person.⁹ Following A. R. Johnson and Levy-Bruhl, it would be more correct to argue for a variety of "extensions of the personality."¹⁰ On the other hand, von Rad acknowledges that there is an underlying conceptual idea and unity in the Hebrew anthropology of the concept of *nepheš* (the soul).¹¹ In addition to that, Wolff also recommends caution regarding dichotomous or trichotomous anthropology, in which body, soul and spirit are set in opposition to each other.¹² Hans J. Kraus, who is an advocate of the form criticism approach, is right apropos Israelite biblical anthropology when he infers that it: "must have a theological orientation, that is to say, it must investigate how man in Israel is seen in the presence of God."¹³

---

6. Speaking of the Messianic salvation hope as the religious core of the Israelite religion, Eichrodt speaks of the "transforming power of the Yahweh religion" which seizes and spreads not only through the people as a whole but also "catches on" to an individual devotee. Eichrodt, 499–500.

7. Wolff, *Anthropology of Old Testament*, 3.

8. Von Rad, *Old Testament Theology*, 152.

9. Pedersen, *Israel*, 100; Johnson, *The Vitality*, 3.

10. Johnson, 3; Pedersen, 100.

11. Von Rad, *Old Testament Theology*, 153.

12. Wolff, *Anthropology of Old Testament*, 3, 7.

13. Kraus, *Theology of Psalms*, 143.

Kraus's assertion does not contradict Wolff's remarks on the "anthropologisation of theology." It clearly alludes to the specific relational and situational points of departure of Hebrew anthropology. Kraus's observation is along the lines of the argument here that the Israelite concept of the person (individual or corporate) is closely associated with God, thus an inherent part of both corporate and individual piety. While the subject, as an individual, undisputably assumes both apects, personal and private.

Hebrew anthropology does not rest only on this *relational* element between the subject and the collective, its other anthropological prop is the undivided *totality* and *unity* of the Hebrew person. According to the biblical myth of creation, the Creator shapes and forms the first human being from the earthly dust like a potter (Gen 2:7). Although the description has counterparts in accounts and myths of cosmogonies of the time, the Israelite version "preserves the stamp of the Israelitic manner of thinking."[14]

> Yahweh, as a potter, moulded man of clay or earth, and into the moulded image he breathed his breath, in which manner man became a living soul . . . It is not said that man was supplied with a nephesh, a soul, and so the relation between body and soul is quite different from what it is to us. Such as he is, man, in his *total* essence, is a soul.[15]

Although the anthropological terminology varies, the totality and unity of the Hebrew person is often described by the somewhat elusive term "soul," along with the "heart" as a centrepiece of the Hebrew person.[16]

---

14. Pedersen, *Israel*, 99. In the Sumerian myth, the creation of man is described in the Hymn to Eridu (that is, the "mighty place"); Eridu was an ancient Sumerian city and still is regarded as the oldest city in the world. Eridu was where god Enki descended from heaven and settled. "When kingship from heaven was lowered, the kingship was in Eridu." In the same hymn, the emergence of man is described as "the men had broken through the earth like grass" (Sumerian hymn to Eridu). Beyerlin, *Near Eastern Religious Texts*, 76; Leick, *Mesopotamia*, 4–9.

15. Pederson, 99. Aubrey Johnson, in his *Vitality of the Individual*, following Pedersen, further expounds this awareness of totality or "grasping of a totality" in ancient Israel's anthropology.

16. For a discussion of anthropology in the Psalms, see chapter 2. Various aspects of anthropology and piety in the Psalms are tackled in Kraus, *Theology of Psalms*, 143–50.

5.2 Anthropology and Psychobiology

An examination of the psalmist's personal experiences and individual piety ought to pay attention to two crucial, referential points of interest. One is biblical Hebrew *anthropology*, and the other is *psychobiology*.[17] The former looks at the human psyche, the non-material self and its composition (soul, spirit and psyche). The latter is a kind of blend of physiology (the functioning of organ systems) and psychology (feelings, emotions and moods). Psychobiology interprets how the constituent parts of the human body, whether anatomical (internal organs, heart, liver, bones) or physiological processes, relate to human emotional states and feelings. Of particular importance is the psalmist's psycho-physiology, relating to both internal organs, and visible, external parts of the anatomy.

5.3 Heart and Soul

The heart demonstrates various emotional states. It can beat wildly, "My heart pounds (חול) within me; death's terrors fall (נפל) upon me" (Ps 55:5 NAB). What is more, it becomes heated and hot in the psalmist's emotional condition: "I was dumb and silent, I held my peace to no avail; my distress grew worse, my heart became hot within me (חם לבי בקרבי), . . . then I spoke with my tongue" (Ps 39:2–3, RSV).[18] Both descriptions cover physical and mental conditions.[19]

The focal and referential points of Hebrew anthropology are the *heart* (לב) and *soul* (נפש).[20] Both terms, elusive as they may be, particularly the *nepheš*, imply an awareness of the totality or completeness of human beings. The heart is not merely a physical organ, and there is more to it than the contraction

---

17. Kraus rightly cautions against possible assumptions that "an abstract world of concepts lies behind the texts," that is, that we attempt to concentrate on man himself as "the eternally unchanging human." Kraus, 143. That is to say that as far as anthropology is concerned, humans cannot be viewed as non-relational and non-contextual.

18. Rashi has here, "and in our thought it was aflame within us like fire and that is what was causing us to speak." Gruber, *Rashi's Commentary*, 323. Rashi takes here, as in Ps 38:11, the utterance as that of personified Israel.

19. For more on medical and psychosomatic conditions of the psalmist, one ought to look up the outstanding discussions by G. R. Driver in "Some Hebrew," and M. L. Barre, "Wandering About."

20. See Kraus, *Theology of Psalms*, 145; Wolff, *Anthropology of Old Testament*, 10;40; Pedersen, *Israel*, 99.

of its muscle. The writer long ago, anyway, most probably did not make a connection between the beating of the pulse and the heart.[21] Two biblical stories illustrate the connection between the physical organ and personal emotional experience.

The first story refers to the story of a rich man called Nabal, the "Fool," as Hebrew etymology will have it, reported in 1 Samuel 25:36–38. After a very merry night, "he was very drunk" (25:36), which shows the unpleasant character of Nabal. The next morning, he was told some distressing news by his wife whereupon "his heart died within him, and he became as a stone" (1 Sam 25:37 RSV).[22] In the religious language of the biblical texts the heart of stone is that which refers to what is numb and insensitive. Nabal was all that, but in this story, it also alludes to Nabal's physiological condition which clearly refers to a heart attack, since about ten days later after his heart failed and he became like a stone, he died (1 Sam 25:38).

The second story (Jer 4:5–31) is that of the prophet Jeremiah's experience of what sounds like a heart attack upon receiving news of a forthcoming national catastrophe: "My breast! My breast! How I suffer! The walls of my heart! My heart beats wildly, I cannot be still; for I have heard the sound of the trumpet, the alarm of war" (Jer 4:19).[23] We may not be able to learn much about the physiology of the heart from the ancients, but the heart and soul are the seats of the psychosomatic experiences and personal religious encounters as encountered in the Psalter. The anthropological vocabulary of Hebrew personhood includes other words that cover the personality; particularly "flesh" (בשר) and "spirit" (רוח). However, the heart and soul constitute the centre of Jewish personhood and personality in its totality.[24] Consequently, the piety of the individual and the piety of the community revolve around anthropologically conceptual ideas of personality, expressed through body parts, which also and particularly demonstrate personal and highly intimate

---

21. See Wolff, *Anthropology of Old Testament*, 41. Similarly, in modern discourse the heart is not merely a physical organ, but expresses the fullness or totality of experience, such as "Hearty thanks" or "from the bottom of my heart," etc.

22. (וימת לבו בקרבן והוא היה לאבן).

23. Compare Jer 23:9 – "My heart within me is broken, all my bones shake; I am like a drunken man, and like a man whom wine hath overcome; because of the LORD, and because of His holy words."

24. Wolff, *Anthropology of Old Testament*, 1973.

experiences.[25] Delineating between the individual and the collective usage should enable the individual's piety to be portrayed.

As already indicated, there are certain assumptions regarding "certified" piety. The essential prerequisite of acceptable, true piety is a "clean heart," that is, a "heart of flesh" (as opposed to a "heart of stone"). Finally, God is to be sought with the "whole heart." These prerequisites refer to either individual or communal godliness. The expression "whole heart" evidently means eliminating calculated motives or interests (for example, avoiding danger), rather than the devotion of the whole being.

Westermann comments on the Deuteronomist's instruction on how to seek the Lord, "Seek the LORD, your God; and you shall indeed find him when you search after him with your whole heart and your whole soul" (Deut 4:29; and see Deut 30:2).[26] He concludes, "Evidently it is a matter of a very spiritual process, and not of a return to correct cultic forms."[27] This conclusion is very similar to von Rad's idea of the process of spiritualization.

---

25. See the work of Aubrey Johnson and Johannes Pedersen. In the late thirties and early forties, Aubrey Johnson wrote a couple of volumes in reference to religiosity and the religious anthropology of ancient Israel (A. Johnson, *The One and the Many in the Israelite Conception of God* (1942) and *The Vitality of the Individual in the Thought of Ancient Israel* (1949). These relatively short volumes are extremely well focused and documented, and may serve as important referential works in the area of Old Testament anthropology and religious typology. Johnson published his work in the era of the fathers of Form Criticism (Mowinckel, Gunkel) and at a time when Form Criticism scholarship introduced completely new approaches and methodology to OT studies, so biblical anthropology did not gain that much attention. However, at about the same time (1926–1940) Johannes Pedersen published his voluminous and influential *magnum opus* in two volumes (approx. 1,200 pages): *Israel. Its life and Culture* (Oxford University Press). The work is of a much wider scope, but also addresses the anthropological and religious topos of Israel. See especially Pedersen, *Israel*, chapter: "The Soul, Its Power and Capacity," 99–181. Although Pedersen gives significant place to the Jewish *soul*, it is not quite clear why he omitted the *heart* which holds such an important place in Israel's psychology and anthropology.

26. In relation to an almost equivalent saying by the prophet Jeremiah (Jer 29:13), Westermann says that Deut 4:29 resembles Jer 29:13 so much that a connection must exist. On the other hand, he asks, "Is it so certain that the well-known letter of Jeremiah is quoted here? Is not the hypothesis just as likely that Jeremiah adopted a contemporary phrase used in sermons? The saying too in Jer 29:13, 'with all your heart' also sounds very Deuteronomic. A quite similar admonition (Isa 55:6) occurs also in the preaching of Deutero-Isaiah." Westermann, *Isaiah 40–66*, 51.

27. Westermann, 50.

5.4 Eyes, Face and Hands

Other body parts, which we can group as facial, limbs or innards, are the bearers of very important anthropological motifs in emotional and religious expressions.[28] Among other biblical examples, a verse in Lamentations (2:11) is intriguing for containing a number of body parts (eyes, soul, heart, internal organs), all used to express a very vivid emotional state: "Mine eyes do fail with tears, mine inwards burn, my liver (מעה) is poured upon the earth, for the breach of the daughter of my people" (Lam 2:11 JPS).[29] This is a powerful description of how the internal body organs produce external manifestations. It is a two-way street. The external manifestations (eyes and tears) relate to the internal organs (liver) whose distressed condition results in the physical state of weeping.

The "face" and facial expressions are often used with idioms which designate mood, feelings or attitude. The face "lifted up" denotes benevolent inclination or happiness (Num 6:26), or acceptance (Job 42:8; 9b), while a "fallen face" denotes anger or resentment. Here is how Zophar from Naama instructs Job on how to re-establish his integrity and regain genuine piety. The text is one of many examples where the parts of the body are used as indicators of moods and attitudes.

> If you set your heart aright, you will stretch out your hands toward him. If iniquity is in your hand, put it far away, and let not wickedness dwell in your tents. Surely then you will lift up thy face without blemish; you will be secure, and will not fear. (Job 11:13–15 RSV)

---

28. For example, the facial body parts: "face" (פנים), "eyes" (עין), "ears" (אזן); or the limbs: "hands" (יד), "feet" (רגל) and the internal body parts: "kidneys" (כליה), "belly" (בטן), "inward parts" (מעה).

Angela Thomas, in her PhD thesis, and many other scholars, have examined the role and place of Hebrew anatomical idioms in expressing emotional states. Angela Thomas's thesis ("Anatomical Idiom and Emotional Expression in the Hebrew Bible and the Septuagint: A Comparative Study (Roehampton University, 2008) is available at the Roehampton University Research Repository, http://roehampton.openrepository.com. See also, Gruber, "Many Faces of Hebrew"; Collins, "Physiology of Tears"; Smith, "Heart and Innards"; Driver, "Some Hebrew"; Boyle, "Law of Heart"; Kruger "The Face and Emotions," 651–63.

29. The expression "my liver is poured upon the earth" (JPS) (מעי נשפך לארץ), occurs nowhere else in the Old Testament. The liver here should not be equated with heart or soul, on the basis of some texts and translations of Ps 42:5; 40:9; Isa 16:1 where מעי from מעה is rendered heart. KD, vol. 8, KD, Lamentations, 392. On this, consult Smith, "Heart and Innards," 427–28, and footnote @@ with Sasson's explanations.

The Lord's face "lifted" denotes divine favour: "The LORD lift up his countenance (face) upon you (ישא יהוה פניו אליך) and give you peace" (Num 6:26 RSV). A "fallen face" (נפל פנים) denotes anger and resentment. God asks Cain: "Why are you angry, and why has your countenance (face) fallen?" (ויפלו פניו) (Gen 4:5 RSV).[30]

Also, the hands that are clean ought to be stretched towards God. Just like the heart that is clean, designates innocence. In his disappointment, the discouraged psalmist concludes, "All in vain have I kept my heart clean (זכה) and washed my hands in innocence (נקה)" (Ps 73:13 RSV). The pious psalmist asserts his innocence by washing his hands: "I wash my hands in innocence (בנקיון)" (Ps 26:6 RSV). Craigie suggests that the words themselves may have been recited while the actual symbolic washing of hands took place.[31] The gesture of hand-washing in innocence is attested as a liturgical precept in the ritual of cleansing blood-guilt (See Deut 21:6–9). It also suggests that the outward manifestation of clean hands symbolizes the innocence of the inner being, the heart. Only the "innocent" or "clean" of hands can approach God (Ps 24:4 נקי כפים). In the New Testament, we witness a similar course of action during Jesus's trial, when Pilate washes his hands (Matt 27:24), while the Jews accept the responsibility and thus assent to blood-guilt (Matt 27:5). The washing of hands apart from its hygienic aspect till this day has its moral and ethical bearing in distancing oneself.[32] Having clean hands (and hearts) for the pious and righteous man, also connotes growing stronger (See Job 17:9).[33] When Job is discouraged by mockers and appalled by the unrighteous, in his disillusioned piety he concludes,

> Upright men are appalled at this, and the innocent (נקה) stirs himself up against the godless. Yet the righteous holds to his way, and he that has clean (טהור) hands grows stronger and stronger. (Job 17:8–9 RSV)

---

30. See also: Gruber, "Many Faces of Hebrew," 252; Smith, "Heart and Innards."
31. See Craigie, *Psalms 1–50*, 226.
32. See 2 Sam 3:28.
33. Note a variety in the lexicon of purity, innocence and cleanliness of heart or hands: נקה (innocence, Ps 26:6; 73:13), (ברר) (זכה) (טהור).

Job himself was not growing stronger and stronger here. On the contrary, his vitality was fading away (17:1–2), yet though disappointed, his personal piety impelled him to hold to his way and preserve his integrity (17:9).[34]

5.5 All That Is within Me

Another designation of an anthropological dimension close to emotional and religious experience is the term קרב. The noun refers to the innermost part of the human being. In his soliloquy, the psalmist reaches deep into the most central, innermost part of his being to give praise to God: "Bless the LORD, O my soul; and all that is within me" (כל כרבי) (103:1 NRSV).[35] The centre may also be an actual point, as in the "the midst of the land" (בקרב הארץ) or it can designate all the land in its entirety (See Isa 5:8; 10:23). In a temporal sense with the prepositional ב (בקרב), it designates the middle of the year. The prophet Habakkuk pleads for the Lord to renew and revive his works and the glory for his people "in the midst of the years" (בקרב שנים). In this context, the expression probably means "at the appropriate time," the "kairos," rather than a very specific, precise time (Hab 2:3).[36]

The verbal form קרב carries the meaning "coming close" or "approach," whether in the sense of spatial proximity to the object or the intimacy with the subject. As they sojourned in Gerar, in the story of Abraham and Sarah, Abraham presented his wife as his sister. Abimelech, the king of Gerar wished to incorporate Sarah in his harem, but he had not "approached her" (לא קרב אליה), that is, he had not had intimate relations with her (Gen 20:4). The verb is used also to designate approaching the divine presence. When Moses approached the theophanic burning bush, the voice from heaven commanded him to "come no nearer" (אל תקרב הלם) (Exod 3:5). Eventually, it becomes a technical term in the cultic world of worship and relates to approaching

---

34. Clines, *Job 1–20*, 396–97.

35. Similarly in Pss 5:10 and 55:16, the קרב designates the innermost part, the innards of the human being. The evildoers are corrupt from the very depth of their being (Ps 5:10): "evil is in their dwelling, and within them" (Ps 55:16).

36. Keil, *KD*, vol. 10:95, "Habakkuk," 49–116. According to Keil, the prophet here also prays that the Lord's saving intervention will not be delayed too long.

the divine presence while presenting the burnt sin offering (Lev 22:18; Num 17:3).³⁷

For us it is more important to observe the anthropological dimensions of the phrase "all that is within me." Particularly, when it designates the innermost part of a human being during a personal intimate religious experience. In that sense, קרב can be paralleled to the "heart" or "soul." It experiences similar personal, emotional (Ps 39:3; 55:5) and/or religious (Ps 103:1) episodes. The prophet affirms, "My soul yearns for you in the night, yes, my spirit within me (אף רוחי בקני) keeps vigil for you" (Isa 26:9).

In Psalm 39, the heart "became hot within me" (חם לבי בקרבי) (Ps 39:4).³⁸ The term *bqr* (nominal or verbal form) describes and refers to the entire human being, giving it a very personal tone. The "hot heart" in Deuteronomy 19:6 describes the almost uncontrollable anger of a vengeful person.³⁹ The psalmist displays a similar emotional condition and reaction (Ps 39), bottling up his emotions for a while, then bursting into speech. In contrast to this "hot heart," Psalm 103 describes a different intimate and personal experience. The psalmist addresses himself in a soliloquy of praise: "Bless the Lord, O my soul"; and "all that is within me" (כל קרני) (Ps 103:1).

In the words of Artur Weiser, this psalm is

> one of the finest blossoms on the tree of biblical faith. Its roots reach deep down to where the most powerful springs of biblical

---

37. The nominal form: *qorban* (κορβαν) refers to the cultic offerings which consist of (personal) sacrificial dedication not only in the cultic context but also in relation to God. It occurs about 80 times in the Old Testament, almost exclusively in Leviticus and Numbers, with the exception of one appearance in Ezekiel (20:28). In the New Testament, κορβᾶν is a transliteration of the Hebrew קרב. In Mark 7:11 it describes how a gift (κορβᾶν) of support for the needy can be revoked by the process of sanctifying such gift, which then becomes holy and dedicated to God, that is, "that which is offered to God as a korban becomes 'holy' and so is no longer available for ordinary use." Cranfield, 237. In such or similar circumstances a *korban formula* was used, either as a dedication formula so that a person could benefit from a gift, or as means of preventing the gift from being used for a particular purpose. In the latter case, the formula would sound something like "May such-and-such be korban to you." Cranfield points out that the formula was often used "hastily in anger." Cranfield, 237.

38. On the similar note, see Ps 38:11: "My heart shudders, my strength forsakes me." There the סחרחר (from סחר, to go around) is a *hapax legomenon*. Dahood, *Psalms*, I, 236.

39. פן-ירדף גאל הדם אחרי הרצח כי-יחם לבבו: "lest the avenger of blood pursue the manslayer, while his heart is hot" (Deut 19:6).

piety flow. The man who speaks in this psalm is able to talk from personal experience.⁴⁰

Weiser appropriately notes and warns against assuming that such personal experience and expression are "a compilation of quotations taken from other sources."⁴¹ Another of the psalmist's yearnings for God's nearness is portrayed in Psalm 73, which is traditionally categorized as a wisdom Psalm, though it clearly includes a complaint character. At the conclusion of the Psalm, the psalmist says, "But for me, it is good to be near God" (קרבת אלהים) (Ps 73:28 NRSV). The phrase "nearness of God" appears only once more, in Isaiah 58:2, though here in a more cynical context.⁴² As for the expressions "I am always with you" (תמיד עמך) (73:23) and "It is good for me to be near God" (73:28), Dahood reckons these actually denote the future life and afterlife of the psalmist.⁴³

> If the first colon of verse 28 conceptually contrasts the lot of the Psalmist with that of the apostates who shall perish (*yo'bedu*, vs.27), we must conclude that the poet is referring to his future happiness in heaven.⁴⁴

Though Dahood's reasoning has a certain inner logic, it does not account adequately for the remainder of the text (Ps 73:17–28) in order to justify such conclusion. The psalmist is still being guided by God's counsel (73:24) and only after that (אחר) will he be taken (לקח) into God's glory.⁴⁵ God is also near the psalmist even during trials of faith, doubts or sufferings; and throughout his earthly life. The psalmist, upon coming into God's presence (73:17), realizes that even here and now it is better to be in the nearness of God and put his trust in him (73:28b). He is impelled to tell others of God's works (73:28c), for only then will the ultimate, final encounter with glory

---

40. Weiser, *Psalms*, 657.

41. Regarding this psalm, Weiser says that in this jubilant song of praise of fatherly love, the "poet is to be included in the great line of witnesses to God's Kingdom of grace that leads from Moses and the prophets to Christ." Weiser, 657.

42. Delitzsch translates here, "They desire the drawing near of Elohim." Delitzsch in *KD*, vol. VII: Part III 384–85.

43. Dahood, *Psalms*, II, 196.

44. Dahood, 196.

45. It is not necessary to translate this as JPS ("receive me with glory") and NAB ("receive me with honour").

be accomplished. This is in fact an example of the psalmist regaining and refreshing his personal piety. After almost slipping and falling into a "spiritual abyss" (73:2), his "zest for living" has been renewed.[46]

5.6 Communal Anthropology

Israel as a collective noun employs the same anthropological references as the individual person. Body metaphors and parts play an important role in the Israelite experience of God, whether personal or corporate, though it is true to say that most references to internal body parts appear almost exclusively in personal emotional expressions.[47] The heart as a physical organ is traditionally also used with its metaphoric meaning beyond its fundamental anthropological designation. Essentially it relates and designates the core and the essence of things. For example, the phrase: "the heart of" may refer to natural elements like the "sea." The "heart of the sea" (לב ים) will refer to the mighty waters or the sea depths (Exod 15:8, Ps 46:2; Ezek 27:4). Prophet Jonah was thrown into the "heart of the sea" (Jonah 2:3). A particular group of people may have heart: nations (Isa 19:1), prophets (Jer 23:26), warriors (Jer 48:41); or a distinct individual characteristic: humble (דכא) (Isa 57:15), brokenhearted (שבר) (Isa 61:1), wise (חכם) (Eccl 7:4).

With biblical authors, the phrase "the heart of the people" (לב העם) (Num 32:7–9; Josh 14:8; Isa 6:10) in nearly all usages alludes to the popular sentiment or attitudes.[48] It can be said to be "sluggish," "rebellious," "stubborn" or "hardened." Isaiah is told by Yahweh to make "the people's heart sluggish" (fat) (Isa 6:10).[49] Their hearts will be "covered over with the grease of insensibility."[50] In the powerful lament psalm of Isaiah 63, the people complain that their hearts have been hardened.

> Why do you make us wander, O LORD, from your ways, and harden our hearts so that we do not fear you? . . . Why have the

---

46. Weiser, *Psalms*, 514–16; and Terrien, *Psalms*, 529.
47. Smith, "Heart and Innards"; Collins, "Physiology of Tears."
48. See also: Josh 14:8; 1 Kgs 12:27; Isa 6:10; Ezek 21:20, etc. There are equivalents in New Testament expressions of communal anthropology: "the heart of people" (καρδία τοῦ λαοῦ). Cf. Matt 13:15; Acts 28:27.
49. "Make the heart of this people fat (שמן)" (השמן לב-העם הזה) (Isa 6:10).
50. Delitzsch, *KD* vol.7, 200.

wicked invaded your holy place, why have our enemies trampled your sanctuary?" (Isa 63:17–18)

These "whys" represent the charges brought against God, who has permitted their hearts to grow hard, or even worse, has tolerated his sanctuary being trampled by pagans (Isa 63:18). The psalm in Isaiah 63 (63:7–19) is considered "probably the most powerful psalm of communal lamentation in the Bible."[51] The place of lament in Old Testament theology, or indeed in religion in general, stimulates and cultivates personal piety, as a basic attempt to establish a personal relationship with God. Throughout the Old Testament and Psalter, "from beginning to end, the 'call of distress,' the 'cry out of the depths,' that is, the lament, is an inevitable part of what happens between God and man."[52]

This is probably why in Isaiah 63–64, the people call upon God as their father. They request and yet question divine compassion: "Where are . . . your surge of pity and your mercy? O Lord, hold not back, for you are our father" (63:15). Again, in their distress they call upon the fatherhood of God, "Yet, LORD, you are our father; we are the clay and you the potter: we are all the work of your hands" (64:7). Likening God to a father is very rare in the Old Testament (Isa 9:6; 43:6; Hos 11:1–5). These are the only two Old Testament instances of calling upon God as a father. It should be remembered that the Israelites were surrounded by a pagan and polytheistic religious environment of myths, in which the physical fatherhood of gods was a common religious motif.[53]

In Isaiah, the people were "sentenced" to a sluggish heart, but in Jeremiah, the prophet is told that the heart of the people is stubborn (סרר) and rebellious (מרה): "But this people has a stubborn and rebellious heart" (Jer 5:23). The heart of the people tremble in fear, as in Isaiah 7:2 (נוע). According to another report, the "fainthearted," or rather "the soft hearted" (רכך לבב) (see Deut 20:8) were not required to go to war as they would have a demoralising effect on the rest of the community and army, thus posing a potential danger. Von Rad notes that the soft hearted actually showed a lack of faith,

---

51. Westermann, *Isaiah 40–66*, 392.

52. Westermann, "Role of Lament," 22.

53. Some commentators argue that in the post-exilic period, the danger of pagan religious influence diminished considerably. Westermann, *Isaiah 40–66*, 393.

endangering the whole nation. Commenting on Deuteronomy 20:8, he states that this text is a

> specifically Deuteronomic concern that fear would be lack of faith. Discouragement, regarded as lack of faith, is not only a personal affair for the man who has been assailed by it; it threatens the whole army.[54]

During the conquest of the Promised Land, the Reubenites and Gadites, due to their particular interests, "discouraged (נוא) the hearts of the Israelites" from crossing the River Jordan and entering the land (Num 32:7).

Along with the heart, it is the face that displays moods and feelings even more visibly as a matter of psycho-physiology; Like the perspiration of the face which may signify a hard labour. On the day of judgement in Genesis 3:19, the first human couple were sentenced thus: "By the sweat of your face (בזעת אפיך) you shall get bread to eat." Some translate this as "in sorrow shalt thou eat it."[55] It was meant not only to apply to the particular human couple, but as a permanent disadvantage for the whole of humankind.

Collective or social anthropology is in many cases evident in the Old Testament and the Psalms. It concerns not only the individual's identity but also his/her belonging to a group. For the ancient Israelites, it was important to have a sociocultural and religious construct which gave them a collective sense of communal identity.[56] For the Israelite, it is not so much the individual that matters but the community. It is, in Mowinckel's words, a matter of the species and the specimen. But he does not annul the importance of the "specimen."

> The species was the original entity, which manifest itself in the single specimen. Likewise with human beings: the tribe – Israel, Moab, etc. – was not looked upon as a sum of individuals who

---

54. Von Rad, *Deuteronomy*, 132.

55. After אף; = nostril, face, anger; Keil, *KD*, 1:103–4.

56. Identity should be regarded as an anthropological category, and this "collective self" is an underlining mark of the *autonomy* and *unity* of an ethnic group. Smith, *National Identity*, 74–75. Since historically the Israelites had more than one problem with their homeland (autonomy) their collective anthropology focused on religion. Smith, 33. It was only at a later stage that there was a rise in Jewish nationalism.

had joined together . . . it was the real entity which manifested itself in each separate member.⁵⁷

It is this "real entity" of individuality that we are interested in the psalmodic piety. Although Mowinckel gives some concession to the Israelite individual and individuality, he also argues that the personhood in its individuality in the biblical Israelitic world would be considered more as a folly and foolishness. In other words, being different within the communal world would be reckoned as peculiarity or even as arrogance. Mowinckel concludes that, "the basic reality in human life is, for the Israelite, not the individual, but the community,"⁵⁸ and such an individual in their individuality and personality is only to serve the higher causes; to be an ideal expression of their common good. Mowinckel observes that:

> To be original, someone apart, a personality, whose right of existence depended on being different, would not to the ancient Israelites have appeared as an ideal or an end to attain, but on the contrary, as a madness, an arrogance, something abnormal, or, in their own words, an "unrighteousness" and a "folly."⁵⁹

It is true to say that such demonstration of originality, individuality, or simply being different, was not an ideal in the ancient Israelitic culture. On the other hand, it is difficult to agree entirely with Mowinckel's observation. The Old Testament witnesses a number of examples of individuals who are "different" and "abnormal" in their originality. To name but a few:

The "arrogance" of *Joseph* the dreamer of dreams (בעל החלמות), Gen 37:19); where even his loving father had to rebuke his "originality" (Gen 37:10). *Hannah*, Samuel's mother, was proclaimed to be a drunkard (1 Sam 1:14). *David* acted abnormally for a king and his wife declared him a fool and a primitive man (ריק) (2 Sam 6:20).

---

57. Mowinckel, *Psalms in Israel's Worship*, vol. 1, ch. 3.
58. Mowinckel, 42.
59. Mowinckel, 3.

5.7 Individual Anthropology

When Kraus states that the *Hebrew individual, rather than the individual in Israel* ought to be investigated he is only partially correct.[60] If we endorse such a point of departure to Hebrew anthropology, it would seriously narrow and limit most of the religious and emotional experiences to corporate events.[61] Israelite anthropology should be set in the context of the man-God relationship – and that should not exclusively be in the context of public worship. The private individual in his piety is clearly portrayed in the role of both "experiencer" and "patient."[62] The biblical texts include more than several accounts which draw a rather accurate picture of the individual in personal, mental, emotional, religious, and pietistic experiences.

For example, in their discontent and despair, many individual biblical characters relate to God with great fervour.[63] Their complaints are addressed to God, and are rarely the grumbling expressions of unbelief accredited to the rebellious people at large. Rather, they send out pleas for help, sometimes using embittered, desperate language. Moses presents a serious ultimatum in his address to God: "If you are going to deal with me in this way, please kill me now" (Num 11:15 NASB). Elijah is weary of life and utterly depressed; he voices his desperation to God, wanting to die: "It is enough now, O Lord, (רב עתה יהוה) take away my life" (1 Kgs 19:4 NRSV).[64] Samuel's mother, Hannah, when expressing her troubles, is said to have been "pouring out her soul" (שפך נפש). In her bitterness (מרת נפש), she wept painfully (ובכ תבכה) (1 Sam 1:10, 15). These are just a few very personal experiences unconnected with any group or collective events. Indeed, most of these are taking place away from a public event or sanctuary worship setting.

---

60. Kraus, *Theology of Psalms*, 138.

61. See here: Chapter 2.

62. "A person engaged in mental activity instantiates the 'experiencer' role . . . We can recognize different types of experiencer, based on the kind of mental experience involved (intellectual, perceptual, emotive)." Langacker, *Concept, Image, and Symbol*, 210.

63. The distress and complaints of the psalmist have long been the focus of scholarly interest in psalmodic studies, yet his personal piety has been somewhat neglected, probably due to the history of the prevalent methodology of Form Criticism. Recently there have been more studies that significantly incorporate the issue of the psalmist as a private individual. See also: King, *Surrounded by Bitterness*; Broyles, *Conflict of Faith*; Brueggemann, *The Message of Psalms*.

64. The same phrase – ישאל את-נפשו למות ("it is better for me to die"), as a request to die is found only once more in the similar state of mind of the prophet Jonah (Jon 4:8).

Let us consider some psalmodic texts with positively personal and individual anthropological vocabulary.

The psalmist prays for a "clean heart" (לב טהור) (Ps 51:12), or in his distress his heart is full of "sorrows" (יגון בלבבי) (Ps 13:3). The prerequisite for finding the path to God is approaching him with a "whole heart" and a "pure heart" (Jer 29:13; Matt 5:8). The prophet witnesses that this was not always the case; even when the people declared, "Let us press on to know the LORD" (Hos 6:3), they did not do so with their whole hearts. But, in the dire straits of persecution of suffering, the psalmist decides to *seek* the Lord with "all his heart" (Ps 119:2) and glorify him likewise (Pss 9:2; 86:12; 111:1; 138:1). While, in his distress, his heart pounds madly in his chest (לבי יחיל בקרבי) (Ps 55:5).[65]

There are other, more visible anthropological and psychosomatic manifestations of his mental state. These have to do with the psalmist's eyes (weeping), feet (wandering) or knees (trembling). When he is exhausted from crying, his bed is drenched with tears, "I am weary with sobbing; each night I soak my bed, with tears my couch I drench" (Ps 6:7) (transl. Dahood). Some commentators think this too extravagant a metaphor and seek to tone it down.[66] Dahood is right when he comments that "exegesis must be governed by other criteria, as appears from similar extravagant language," and provides similar examples.[67] Agitated and disoriented, the psalmist wanders around in a gloomy mood, while he asks God: "Why must I go about mourning (למה קדר אלך)?" (Ps 42:10). He then prays to God to lighten his darkness (Ps 43:3).[68] His *knees* tremble and as he awaits the outcome of his trials, he is exhausted by fasting (Ps 109:24). He is agitated and afraid, yet not inclined to curse his enemies, for "though they curse, may you bless" (Ps 109:28). The psalmist's psychosomatic state is the result of all these factors.[69]

---

65. See Driver, "Some Hebrew," 257.

66. The psalmist's couch flooded with tears, Briggs comments on the intensity of grief: "tears burst from the eyes in a flood, wet the couch, and cause it to dissolve, as in stream of rushing water. The figure seems extravagant to Western taste, but not to the Oriental . . . it is still more extravagant in MT and Vrss . . . make my bed swim" (See Ps 6:7; Briggs, *Critical and Exegetical*, 1, 48).

67. Dahood, *Psalms*, I, 38.

68. Cf. Barre, "Wandering About," 182–83. Pss 42–43; also in Ps 35:14 and Ps 38:7, as in Job 30:28, where there is a collocation of הלך+קדר /gloomy + walk, referring to a gloomy mood.

69. See ברך + כשל. The verb כשל usually relates to stumbling and physically falling or being brought down (Ps 64:9). Here, it seems that the Psalmist was completely weakened

From the previous discussions, it is clear that Yahweh's desire is to give all his people a "new heart" (לב חדש) which will be a "heart of flesh" (לב בשר) to replace their "heart of stone" (לב האבן) (Ezek 11:19; 36:26). Only with a sensitive, feeling heart will they be able to walk with God and truly be his people. Such an experience of God penetrates right to the innermost being (*bᵊqirbi*) of all the people and the pious individual.

The subject of collective anthropology permeates with that of the individual. While some of the features described could be "collectivized," it would require great ingenuity to completely "collectivize" the Psalms, transforming every individual "I" into a collective "I." In fact, it would be a serious mistake to reduce Israelite anthropology to communal for the sake, or in the interest of a particular methodology. In their insistence on collective personality, form criticism scholars easily bypass or ignore the tenets of individual anthropology, particularly in the area of private piety. Mowinckel's statement that the traditional Jewish and Christian interpretation "took for granted that the psalms were originally private, individual poetry"[70] can be acceptable in part, as *some* of the mentioned traditions held a fairly low estimate of cult and liturgy.[71]

We have at this point reached closer to finding the characteristics of the righteous and pious man who, though he is part of the community and corporate devotion, demonstrates aspects and modes of private, personal piety.

---

by the charges raised against him and the uncertainty of the outcome, in addition to fasting and praying.

70. Mowinckel, *Psalms in Israel's Worship*, vol. 1, ch. 1, par. 4.

71. Further, detailed and valuable discussion on the "I" and the "we" in the Psalms can be found in Mowinckel, vol. 1, ch. 3, par. 1.

CHAPTER 6

The Psalmist and His Prayer

Gunkel discusses communal complaints[1] before moving on to individual complaint psalms,[2] and in connection with the psalmist's use of "you" when addressing God, says:

> The nature of the prayer as such, the God is addressed as "you" (singular). This "you" appears regularly throughout the entire complaint, no matter whether the complaint is communal or individual. This happens because the prayer is not defined (as one tends today) as a conversation (or dialogue) with God. Rather, the prayer is a speech to God. Even this venture of the heart in child-like trust, when one speaks to God and pours out one's heart before him, is peculiar for the prayer of antiquity (Fr. Heiler, Gebet, pp.147f.). Here, the basic presupposition is that one can say something to God that can influence him.[3]

Further to this, John Wevers notes that the psalmist's prayer is intended "to sway the deity to hear and answer the suppliant".[4] In terms of literary structure, Wevers observes that the prayer itself is always in the "imperative mood, though its final recapitulation is often in the third person jussive."[5] For example: "Hear my voice, LORD, when I call" (Ps 27:7), or "Hear the sound of my pleading" (Ps 28:2).

---

1. Gunkel, *Introduction to Psalms*, 82–98.
2. Gunkel, 121–98.
3. Gunkel, 86.
4. Wevers, "Study in Form Criticism," 81.
5. Wevers, 81.

In his form critical study of individual complaint in the Psalms, Wevers is mainly concerned with cultic prayers, particularly the effects of invoking God's name. He also notes and remarks on the sudden changes in the tone of the prayers, from complaint to the joyous certainty of being heard:

> The feeling of uncertainty suddenly disappears to be replaced by the joyous consciousness of being protected and hidden by the hand of a higher power. The suddenness of the change is apparently the result of the psychic impact of repeated petition and expressed longing for an answer. Such a psychological phenomenon is certainly not impossible; it, however, applies only to private prayer.[6]

Expressions in the language of the psalmist's private prayer demonstrate his personal piety, as a consequence of his inability to "hide" in the sacred institution, thus he prays, "Hide me (סתר) in the shadow of your wings" (Ps 17:8), and declares, "I keep the LORD always before me; because he is at my right hand, I shall not be moved" (Ps 16:8 NRSV).[7]

6.1 The Process of Spiritualization

Personal invocation of the blessings of being hidden with Yahweh creates a "process of spiritualisation" in von Rad's words.[8] It advances the psalmist's personal spirituality, despite the lack of a place of cultic liturgy, sanctuary or sacred institution in which to practise his/her faith; therefore:

> If we listen to these Psalms with an ear directed to the question as to what these blessings of being hidden with Yahweh really consists in, we come upon expressions saying very much more about the bliss of spiritual communion with Yahweh.[9]

Naturally, a form critical psalmodic tradition which cultivates the temple and cult spirituality exclusively will not support such a view. The traditional tenets of this methodology may not embrace the prospective discovery of

---

6. Wevers, 81.
7. Compare to. Pss 27:5; 64:2.
8. Von Rad, *Old Testament Theology*, 1:402.
9. Von Rad, 1:402–3.

new spiritual realities, which may only indirectly be linked to the cultus and temple. The function of the sanctuary was to be a holy place and also a *sanctum*, a protected enclosure, inviolable in all circumstances.[10] Thus, when the psalmist is outside the sanctuary, the language of protection becomes symbolic, and the "epitome of all divine protection."[11] Kraus then concludes that there is no need to speak of spiritualizing the psalmist's relationship with God, as von Rad does. He concludes: "spiritualising is not a term that can be applied to this process. What is involved is a transposing into an analogous, but no longer institutional destiny of the individual."[12] This is a sweeping assertion and Kraus does not account for all the expressions of the psalmist who yearns for God, "always" or "day and night" (Ps 16:7-8). In these instances and interpretation, he opts for solutions which point to the priestly life and joining the ranks of Levitical priests, so as to be in the divine presence and protection "day and night."[13]

The very proclamation, "Your love (חסד) is better than life" (Ps 63:4) demonstrates the radical nature of the process of spiritualization. Life itself becomes transformed into a continuous prayer.[14] The continuous worship of the psalmist clearly goes beyond institutional religion. It reveals a profound, refreshing spirituality, such as in Psalm 36, "With you is the fountain of life, and in your light we see light" (Ps 36:10).[15]

6.2 Personalization and Appropriation

The processes of spiritualization and personalization/appropriation are two sides of the same coin. If a process of spiritualization is happening, as von Rad suggests, then it is accompanied by a growing sense of individuality and developing personal piety. It has been suggested on more than one occasion, that one of the major issues in psalmodic studies is the identity of the

---

10. See the above discussion on the *numen locale* and *numen personale*.
11. Kraus, *Theology of Psalms*, 159.
12. Kraus, 159.
13. Kraus, 160. Interestingly, Kraus "allows" for the individual's open relationship and personal piety which "does not display the traits of a rigid religiosity" when he speaks of (mis) understanding the term "torah." Kraus, 161.
14. In the New Testament, this is echoed in Paul's very personal meditation on life and death: "For to me to live is Christ, and to die is gain" (Phil 1:21).
15. באורך נראה-אור.

individual in Hebrew thought and the Hebrew Bible; no doubt it is also a major concern in this matter of personalization and appropriation.[16]

If there is an increase in personal piety outside organized religion, in which the worshipper communicates independently and spontaneously with heaven, why is his personal and private experience couched in such highly versified, skilful poetry, and the richness of imagery as we find it in the Psalms? Is the psalmist a professional poet, or perhaps a priestly group responsible for psalm production? There is no doubt that the Psalter is inspired poetry, central to public worship and *composed for* (?) this purpose. But, Bewer rightly notes that "many poets have contributed; some of them were geniuses of poetic power, others were common versifiers."[17]

As for the personal psalmist's piety, it is generally accepted that a process of appropriation is in operation. What do we mean by this? The individual takes an existing psalm and in the appropriation process epitomizes it for himself, making it his own experience.[18] On the other hand, the view that in this it imposes upon the worshipper a kind of magical power through the use of a psalm and unifies models which direct a worshipper to articulate their faith and experience is implausible.[19] Proponents of "generalized psalmodic language"[20] may easily become victims of what Martin Noth calls "formula criticism," as opposed to form criticism. They maintain that generalized psalmodic language can serve as a set of formulae to be imposed on

---

16. The problem of the identity of the psalmist and the individual in Hebrew thought and the Psalter has been a struggle since the modern beginnings of the psalmodic scholarship. Is Sigmund Mowinckel's contribution in ch. 3 of "'I' and 'We' in the Psalms" in *The Psalms in Israel's Worship* is particularly to the point. Mowinckel postulates that it is the species rather than the specimen that counts – "species was the original entity, which manifests itself in the single specimen" (p. 42), thus the tribe is a "living personality," so the individual's personality is only an ideal expression of what is common to all.
Johannes Pedersen (in *Israel: Its Life and Culture*) discusses extensively the notion of the individual in a lengthy chapter, "The Soul: Its Powers and Capacity" (pp. 99–181). "Every community forms a unity, but the unity is not mechanical; it does not consist in obliterating the individual, but in imbuing him with the common character and spirit of the community." Pedersen, *Israel*, 57.

17. Bewer, *Literature of Old Testament*, 360.

18. Modern hermeneutical understanding brings in another aspect, that of the reading process. See Berlin, "Role of Text."

19. See Chapter: "Priestly Intervention."

20. Broyles, *Conflict of Faith*, 17.

worshippers in order to direct their experience. Craig Broyles, in *The Conflict of Faith and Experience in the Psalms*, explains this interpretation:

> worshippers thus received these psalms as models through which they might properly articulate their faith and experiences. If a worshipper encountered distress and then took up an appropriate psalm, the psalm would have guided him in the interpretation of his distress . . . even if a worshipper came to a psalm with no immediate experience of distress, the psalm would have evoked in his imagination the sense of that distress. In worship the Psalms not only follow religious experience; they lead it.[21]

Such an approach may lead to religious "dictatorship," whereby experience is imposed and interpreted at the same time. Though this may represent one kind of worship, it does not take into account the genuine personal piety of the individual, but rather provides him with generic, dictated, readymade experiences. Some of the deepest episodes of the psalmist can hardly be superimposed. The Psalter is a treasure-house overflowing with new discoveries of spiritual reality, and so it is no exaggeration to agree with von Rad that, "this faith no longer had need of anything external, neither the saving history nor objective rites, for Yahweh's salvation appertained to it from within itself."[22]

6.3 The Lord Is My Portion

In the context of the psalmist's personal private piety, it is particularly appealing to observe the frequent expression, "the Lord is my portion" (Pss 16; 119; 142). It occurs, for example in Psalm 16: "The Lord is my portion (הלק) and my cup, you have made my destiny secure" (Ps 16:5).[23]

---

21. Broyles, 17.
22. Von Rad, *Old Testament Theology*, 403.
23. יהוה מנת-חלקי וכוסי אתה תומיך גורלי Here the NAB translates "destiny," for גורל with its primary meaning "lot." This is appropriate to the actual performance of throwing the "lot." In Arabic, the noun "garwal" means "pebble." It comes with different verbs, with: שלך (Mic 2:5), טול (Prov 16:33), נפל (Jonah 1:7), יצא (Num 33:54) (see Dommershausen, *Theological Wordbook of the Old Testament* (TWOT), 2:450). As for the etymology of the "portion," the verb חלק, means primarily "to divide," that is, acquire by law an apportioned inheritance or a "portion in life determined by God." In other words, the term is used both in social and religious contexts. In Deut 32:8, Yahweh has apportioned Israel to himself. Tsevat, "Chalaq," 447.

The "portion" here designates the nearness of Yahweh and it is parallel to a similar expression used in Psalm 73, "As for me, the nearness (קרבת) of God is my good" (Ps 73:28). The correspondence between "portion" (הלק), "nearness" (קרב) and קרבן (offering) are evident here in the spiritual content, though both expressions have come to be also religious technical terms.[24] The word "portion" echoes the legal and sacred apportionment to the tribe of Levi. God told the Aaronite priestly clan that, "You shall not have any heritage in the land of the Israelites nor hold any portion among them; I will be your portion and your heritage" (Num 18:20). For the Levites, Yahweh was their "portion" and "destiny" and their livelihood came from fulfilling their cultic functions; they were to live "from Yahweh's table."[25] The same phraseology appears in Deuteronomistic (e.g. Deut 10:9; 18:1) and priestly (Num 18:20) traditions. Although initially, it bore a purely material significance in apportioning of the land, the phrase evidently carries a potential spiritual content. Indicatively, the religious and spiritual significance of the term "portion" included the naming of a child. Here, von Rad comments on its theological significance, that is:

> in no way due to later attempts to find theological meanings, as can be gathered from the Levitical name Hilkiah ("Yahweh is my portion," 2 Kgs 18:37; 22:4), which is attested even in the pre-exilic period. How popular must the understanding have been even then when it could determine the name of a child.[26]

Kraus disagrees, as earlier noted, with von Rad on potential spiritual contents and the "process of spiritualisation." He is inclined to assign a symbolic or metaphoric character to such psalmodic language. In regard to the lack of a sacred institution and thus a cultic refuge, Kraus explains the psalmist's

---

24. The phrase קרבת אלהים ("nearness of God") uses the verb קרב (to draw near), the verb and its various cognate nominal forms, apart from its primary meaning "to come close, near." There are also more technical uses of the term, like *qorban* ("offering"), which among other things can denote self-sacrifice as an acceptable act of worship. See *Theological Wordbook of the Old Testament* 2:811–812.

25. Von Rad, *Deuteronomy*, 80. This phrase certainly also refers to the three basic (priestly) functions of the Levi tribe: (i) to *carry* the Ark of the covenant, Deut 31:9 (cf. Num 3:31; 4:15); (ii) to *stand* before Yahweh, Deut 18:5 (also may refer to the phrase "to wait upon the Lord," Driver, "Textual and Linguistic Problems," 174–75); and (iii) to *bless* the name of Yahweh, Deut 21:5 (and see Num 6:23).

26. Von Rad, *Old Testament Theology*, 404.

language of prayer as "transposing into the analogous, but no longer institutional, destiny of the individual," while the institutional sanctuary "becomes the epitome of all divine protection."[27] This may be true, but it certainly does not rule out the development of private piety. Kraus's additional explanation that the psalmist's passionate wish to "dwell in the house of the Lord" or "gaze on the Lord's beauty" (Ps 27:4) is simply an ambition to join the priestly ranks does not seem very convincing, particularly when set against von Rad's position on the process of spiritualization.

Not only that, but the Lord is the psalmist's "portion for ever" לעולם (Ps 73:26) and his dearest wish is the nearness of God (קרבת אלהים) (73:28).[28] This phrase appears again only in Isaiah 58, in relation to "they seek me day after day, and desire to know my ways" (Isa 58:2). The latter, however, seems to be "a variety of attempts to hold fast to God"[29] through the medium of a formal worship service (Isa 29:13), while in Psalm 73 the "nearness" (עמד) may refer to life after death, as some commentators would interpret.[30] However, there is no valid reason why, in the context of 73:23–24, the psalmist's earthly life should not be understood as his renewed dedication and a life of a devotee. Moreover, verses 23–28 display the psalmist's personal piety that reveal his plea and struggle between life and death, in the dispirited context of the whole of Psalm 73, though there are indeed clear indications of the life to come.[31]

---

27. Kraus, *Theology of Psalms*, 159–60.

28. "For me, the nearness of God is my good; I have made the Lord GOD my refuge" (ואני קרבת אלהים לי-טוב) (Ps 73:28). Dahood translates here: "Myself, the nearness of God will be my happiness." Dahood, *Psalms*, I,187.

29. Westermann, *Isaiah 40–66*, 334.

30. Cf. von Rad, *Old Testament Theology*, 405; Dahood, *Psalms*, II, 196. Referring to Ps 49:16 "But God will redeem my soul from the power of the nether-world; for He shall receive me," von Rad says: "This statement can hardly be referred to anything other than a life after death, for the thought of the whole psalm revolves, in the sense of the problem of theodicy, around the question of the grace of Yahweh in the life of the individual, and comes to the conclusion that the proud rich must remain in death. This then, death, is the last great separator." Von Rad, 406.

31. Von Rad, 405. Dahood translates v. 24, "Lead me into your council, and with glory take me to yourself." Dahood, *Psalms*, II, 187.

6.4 Priestly Intervention

As for the suddenness of change in mood of the praying psalmist, there are various interpretations. Gunkel, for instance, believes it is due to an external event.[32] In relation to this swing in mood, Gunkle argues that this is to do with priestly intervention: "In our opinion, they certainly lead to the conclusion that a priestly salvation oracle originally preceded the certainty of being heard."[33]

Gunkel then insists that there is a fixed association between the cultic priestly oracle and the petitioner's prayer. However, he then "fences himself off" by saying that although this fixed style continued to operate widely, "the priestly oracle does not constitute the entire explanation for the certainty of being heard."[34] Gunkel actually follows Begrich's explanation in reconstructing cultic priestly intervention as a matter of consolation to the one praying in distress.[35] After the prayer of lament, the priest utters an oracle of blessing, which had an illocutionary effect and became so efficacious that the psalmist radically changes his mood.[36] On the suddenness of mood change in the psalmist's prayer, Friedrich Heiler, on the other hand, in his masterly and now referential work on prayer (*Das Gebet*), suggests a psychological explanation for this phenomenon.[37]

There are several things which should be noted in reference to the psalmist in prayer. We can agree with Gunkel and others that prayer is speaking to God in an endeavour to influence the divine mind. However, many of the psalmist's prayers show a conversational nature and may not include any

---

32. "How does one explain the sudden change of mood which is so noticeable in this motif? Does it concern an internal process of the one praying? After all of the turmoil of the internal struggle, after the despondency or the doubt, does the heart of the one praying finally find stillness and confidence?" Gunkel, *Introduction to Psalms*, par. 6, 23: 182.

33. Gunkel, par. 6, 23: 183.

34. Gunkel, par. 6, 23: 183. This hesitant explanation is probably due to the historical approach to the Psalter, that is, that every psalm was written for a particular historical occasion. This would then help to date each psalm precisely.

35. Von Rad, *Old Testament Theology*, 401.

36. See, Wevers, "Study in Form Criticism," 81. Wevers also suggests a more "magical" solution, on the basis of the efficacy of the invocation and use of the divine name. Wevers, 82.

37. Heiler's work on prayer, "Das Gebet," was his doctoral dissertation endorsed and defended at the University in Munich, 1917. The full title of Heiler's work is: "Das Gebet: Eine religionsgeschichtliche und religionspsychologische Untersuchung" (Reinhardt, Munich, 1919).

external intervention.³⁸ The psalmist is heard and answered (ענה), the poor man cries and the Lord hears (שמע) him (e.g. Ps 34:4, 7).³⁹ In the light of the psalmist's prayer and priestly intervention as discussed above (Gunkel, Wevers), Yehezkel Kaufmann presents a somewhat different understanding and interpretation. He introduces an idea of *popular religion* and the concept of the *temple of silence*. He argues that, for the psalmist, the individual prays for himself, so prayer belongs almost exclusively to *popular religion*. Although the professional singers of psalmody became a part of the Levite class, according to Kaufmann, "psalmody is a creation of popular poets." He goes as far as to state that the Psalms were not part of the sacrificial cult, or for that matter, any other priestly rite.⁴⁰ Kaufmann states:

> The priestly temple is the kingdom of silence. In Egypt, Babylonia and in the pagan world in general, word and incantation were integral parts of the cult; act was accompanied by speech. The spell expressed the magical essence of cultic activity. In more developed form, pagan rituals might be accompanied by mythological allusions relating to events in the life of the gods. . . . Not only have spells and psalms no place in the priestly cult, even prayer is absent . . . Priestly speech is found only outside the Temple apart from the essential cultic act. . . . This silence is an intuitive expression of the priestly desire to fashion a non-pagan cult. . . . Therewith the Israelite cult became a domain of silence.⁴¹

This seems to indicate discrepancy with the traditional views presented above. Kaufmann makes the point that the cult isn the "temple of silence could not contain the abundance of popular religious sentiment" and thus the individual "prays for himself."⁴² He actually wishes to prove that silence in the cult is rooted in the wish "to make a clear break from paganism."⁴³

---

38. Albertz, *Personliche frommigkeit*, 24–37; Brueggemann, *Message of Psalms*, 54.

39. See also Pss 81:7; 118:5, 21.

40. Kaufmann, "The Religion of Israel," 110, cited in Knohl, "Between Voice and Silence," 18.

41. Kaufmann, 303–5 in Knohl, 17–18.

42. Kaufmann, 303–5, 309, 110 in Knohl, 17–18.

43. Knohl, 19–20. For Kaufmann and Nahum Sarna on the social gap between the elite priestly class and the circle of poets see: Knohl, 18.

CHAPTER 7

The Pious Man

How can we identify the pious individual in the Psalter? In Israel's thought, and more specifically in the Psalms, the pious man is essentially portrayed as the *tsadiq* (צדיק), the righteous man. Though it is true to say that the *tsadiq* is primarily identified as the one who keeps God's commandments, this is notably his relationship to Yahweh, rather than merely a legalistic observance of the Law or perfection. That is why this righteousness is so often found in parallel with compassion and grace. For God loves justice and righteousness (צדקה ומשפט), but he is also steadfast in his love (Ps 33:5), "In you, LORD, I take refuge; let me never be put to shame. In your justice, deliver me.... I will rejoice and be glad in your mercy" (Ps 31:2, 8). What lies behind this complementary affinity of righteousness and mercy or grace (love) is a constant realization of (covenantal) fellowship. So that "the relationship of legal obligation has become the relationship of grace,"[1] because "the steadfast love of the LORD is from everlasting to everlasting for those who fear him, and his righteousness to children's children" (Ps 103:17 NRSV). This is the point at which the Israelite individual and their piety ought to be addressed.

Some commentators maintain that the identity of the individual and individual piety was a later development in Israel's faith, in the course of the emancipation of the individual from the overpowering influences of the community. This was perhaps because the individual had a greater opportunity to speak for themselves. So, von Rad writes:

> In the older period the individual was bound up with the life of the community, but in the course of time he clearly achieved

---

1. Eichrodt, 247.

independence of it. He became more conscious of himself and of his relationship to God and consequently felt a more urgent need to justify himself in his personal existence before Yahweh.[2]

Although there may have been a novel consciousness of individual existence and worth, it is too strong to say there was a "severance from the community" or that the *tsadiq* was "standing completely isolated in relationship to Yahweh." The *tsadiq's* relationship with the community may have been repressed to some extent, but it can hardly experience a full severance.[3]

7.1 The *Tsadiq*

In his *Old Testament Theology* (vol. 1), G. von Rad dedicates a major section of his work to the individual and his/her standing before God.[4] He elaborates the Old Testament concept of "righteousness" (צדקה) on the one hand, and on the other, the position of the "righteous" individual (the *tsadiq* (צדיק) in the sight of God.[5] The term and concept *tsedeq* (צדק) is not only a notion of righteousness, nor merely an abstract or theoretical consideration. It always denotes a real relationship between two parties, rather than the "relationship of an object under consideration to an idea."[6] Israel lived and practised issues of righteousness and the righteous in every situation in life.

> It was only at a very late phase in her (i.e. Israel) existence that she made these ideas (i.e. of tsedaqah) the subject of theoretical consideration: for most of the time she lived with them uncritically and practised them in every situation of life. This life, in which Israel had to orientate herself with such basic presuppositions of faith, was a life of suffering and serious dangers for community and individual alike. What this means is that Israel took a supremely realistic view of life's sufferings and dangers, saw herself as exposed to them vulnerably and without defence,

---

2. Von Rad, *Old Testament Theology*, 1:380.
3. Von Rad, 1:380–81.
4. Von Rad, *Old Testament Theology*. The whole of chapter D (1:355–459) is dedicated to the subject.
5. Von Rad, 1:355–453.
6. Von Rad, 1:371.

and showed little talent for fleeing from them into ideologies of any kind.[7]

Both von Rad and Kraus present their debates on the *tsedaqah*, following Pedersen. Pedersen organizes the whole concept of the *tsadiq* around a few essential terms which presuppose the right action or a state of the person. Mostly, it revolves around the wholeness and purity of the soul and the heart. Also, it is to do with the firmness and the soul being straight, thus the psalmist speaks against those who are stubborn and wicked. They are the generation whose heart is not firm and upright (דור לא הכין לבו) (Ps 78:8).[8] Therefore, the whole concept of righteousness and the *tsadiq* is strictly a relational concept, not a legalistic and static one. In that sense, the *tsadiq's* righteousness is sustained and upheld through their personal relationship to his God.

7.2 *Anawim*

How does this term *anawim* (the oppressed, the afflicted) correspond to the theme of the Psalmist's personal piety? The term *anawim* (ענוים) is the plural nominal form from the verb ענה = to afflict, oppress, or humble (note here the homonymous verb ענה = to answer, respond). The word appears in the following Psalms: 10:17; 22:27; 25:9; 34:3; 69:33; 147:6 and 149:4. Translations of the expression show certain inconsistencies; so it has been variously translated as to designate those who are *humble, poor* or *oppressed* (that is, persecuted).[9]

---

7. Von Rad, 1:383–84. Now, the renowned scholar Kraus, following Kohler, had stated that it is not the "Hebrew individual," but the "individual in Israel" who is the real subject of investigation. In other words, it is a "question of the relationship of the individual to Israel" (Kraus, *Theology of Psalms*, 138), rather than the individual himself and his relationship to his God. This fully follows Mowinckel's exposition of the position of the individual in Israel. Cf. Mowinckel, *Psalms in Israel's Worship*, and ch. 3, "'I' and 'we' in the Psalms." Von Rad notes that even a personal prayer of the psalmist is a matter of "cultic and conventionalised concepts and phraseology." Von Rad, *Old Testament Theology*, 1:399. Von Rad's conclusion is questionable that the psalmist's petitions or complaints are expressed in only few "typical and often very faded concepts." Von Rad, *Old Testament Theology*, 1:399.

8. Pedersen is listing terms around which he organizes the understanding of the concept of the *tsadik*. Such terms as: תמם (integrity, be complete or innocence, cf. 1 Kgs 9:4); שלם (be complete, cf. 1 Chr 29:19); כון (establish, fix, cf. Ps 78:8); the soul which is complete, innocent and firm is also upright, ישר (leveled upright, being straight up). All of these and more, are concentrated in the very word and concept of *tsedakah* (justice) and the righteous (*tsadik*). See Pedersen, *Israel*, 336.

9. In Ezra 9:5, there is a nominal form תענית in the sense of *humiliation* (by fasting).

Having in mind this ambiguity, as well as the discussion about the identification of *anawim*, it seems that an unequivocal designation of *anawim* is almost impossible.

Several examples of the variety and inconsistencies in translating the term may provide an indication of the problem faced in identifying who the *anawim* really were.

In Psalm 10 we read, "You listen, LORD, to the needs of the poor (עֲנָוִים)" (NAB). The same text, according to the Jewish Publication Society (JPS), translates as, "LORD, Thou hast heard the desire of the humble" (Ps 10:17). In Psalm 25 the JPS translates, "He guides the humble in (his) justice" (Ps 25:9 JPS), while the same text in RSV reads: "He leads the humble in what is right, and teaches the humble his way" (RSV). Though the most frequently consulted translations seem to be unanimous and content to translate *anawim* as the "humble," the text of Psalm 22:27 shows how the translations may vary:

> Let the humble eat and be satisfied; let them praise the LORD that seek after Him (JPS).
>
> The poor will eat their fill; those who seek the LORD will offer praise" (NAB).
>
> The afflicted shall eat and be satisfied; those who seek him shall praise the LORD (RSV).[10]

So, who were the *anawim* (עֲנָוִים) (*poor, meek* or *humble*) of the Psalms? Are there any posible hints in the Psalter that this may refer to an elitist pietistic party? Or, simply a particularly pious sectarian group? But then, who were the enemies who persecute the *anawim*? These issues have been and still are the subject of discussion and interpretation.

There are probably only three possible options left. First, they may have been simply the poverty-stricken, economically deprived, socially ostracized class. Second, the psalmodic texts provide enough grounds for believing that they were the suffering people (through illness, or persecution). Finally, could

---

10. JPS is consistent in translating *anawim* as "'the humble." Other translations are inconsistent. In Ps 25:9, the translators are unanimous in using the "humble" (in LXX πραεῖς "humble"). In Ps 34:3: "My soul shall glory in the LORD; the humble shall hear thereof, and be glad," the translations are inconsistent: *humble* (JPS), *poor* (NAB), *afflicted* (RSV). Similar inconsistencies are found in Pss 69:33; 147:6. The alternative ancient translations have: in LXX πένης (the poor/needy person); the Vulgate gives the adjectival form: "pauper" (the poor).

it be that they were a kind of exclusive, pietistic, sect-like group, perhaps not so well organized, consisting of the humble and the pious?

What arguments are there for any of these suggestions? If for a moment we turn to the New Testament and the teachings of Jesus of Nazareth, especially in the Beatitudes, we will find an echo from Psalm 37:29: "The righteous (צדיקים) shall inherit the land." Jesus then quotes Psalm 37, but he alters it to the "the humble" or "meek" who will "take over" (inherit?) the earth (land) (Matt 5:5; Luke 6:20).[11] This however may sound like a somewhat surreal statement, whether in the context of Psalm 37, or from the mouth of Jesus, or indeed from the point of view of modern outlook. Regardless of alternative readings, that is, the "earth" (as humankind, or natural resources) or the "land" (as a geographical or political entity). It should be borne in mind that in more primitive cultural contexts, the land was/is a fundamental blessing. In the biblical context, the possession of the land is linked to Yahweh who gives its governance and purpose; befitting the perspective and context of Genesis 1:28b (to govern, subdue) and Genesis 2:15 (to cultivate and care for).[12]

Kraus well observes that the *anawim* are also described as those who are the "brokenhearted" (נשברי לב) (Ps 34:18). In other words, whatever it was that brought them to be the *anawim*, it affected their very being, the innermost part, the heart.[13] Others will suggest that the "brokenhearted" are the ones who have lost their self-confidence, and are in deep despair. As a result, they then seek the nearness of God.[14] The context of most of the texts where we meet with the *anawim* aims to show that the poor/humble is confident that God will accept them in their affliction and that only in fellowship with God is their fortune.

---

11. "Blessed are the meek (πραεῖς) for they will inherit the land" ("Μακάριοι οἱ πραεῖς, ὅτι αὐτοὶ κληρονομήσουσιν τὴν γῆν") (GNT) (Matt 5:5). Cf. πραΰς (humble, gentle). Prior to this statement, Jesus utters a similar proclamation: "Blessed are the poor in spirit, for theirs is the kingdom of heaven" (Μακάριοι οἱ πτωχοὶ τῷ πνεύματι) (Matt 5:3). Here πτωχοί clearly has the disposition of being weak in the sense of humble, rather than poor as materially deprived (cf. Gal 4:9).

12. Commenting on the Beatitudes, R. T. France says that the possessing of the land is not so much a matter of territorial possession as the eventual endorsement of the meek and humble. France, *The Gospel According to Matthew*, on Matt 5:5.

13. Kraus, *Theology of Psalms*, 154.

14. See also the expression: "look at my affliction" (ראה עניי), Pss 25:18; 119:153).

7.3 The Pious Man

In analysing Psalm 18, in the section entitled "The Integrity of the Pious Man," Samuel Terrien draws a picture of the pious psalmist where he portrays the psalmist-poet as one who "parades and struts with the indulgence of a pious devotee."[15]

Briggs brings in the variance in the openings between 2 Samuel 22:2 and Psalm 18 (the text of Ps 18 is almost identical to 2 Sam 22); "The Lord is my rock" (2 Sam 22:2), and Psalm 18:2 has it as: "I love you, Lord my strength." He concludes that this line in 2 Samuel 22 was intentionally omitted[16] and maintains that the words for love and strength "are Aramaisms, and the conception of loving Yahweh is post-Deuteronomistic."[17] However, most commentators focus attention on the theophanic elements and aspect of Psalm 18 (8–16).[18] Terrien here emphasizes the integrity of the pious psalmist:

> The pious man is blameless, for he avoids committing an evil that would separate him from divinity. His keeping himself constantly attentive to prescriptions of the Law has freed him from a sense of guilt . . . the pious man is perfect.[19]

It should be noted that this is not so much a matter of the psalmist's moral self-evaluation, but more a case of his reliance on God, confirming and building up his relationship with Yahweh. He waits on the Lord the whole day long (Ps 25:5); he praises God and speaks of his righteousness all day long (71:8, 15). Then, when he is at his lowest ebb, he declares, "I kept faith even when I said 'I am greatly afflicted' (עניתי)" (Ps 116:10), and he then concludes: "And now, LORD, for what do I wait? You are my only

---

15. Terrien, *Psalms*, 200.
16. Briggs, *Critical and Exegetical*, 2:141.
17. Briggs, *Critical and Exegetical*, 2:141.
18. Weiser, *Psalms*, 189; Kraus, *Theology of Psalms*, 38; Brown, *Seeing the Psalms*, 293; Craigie, *Psalms 1–50*, 173. Craigie elaborates and suggests that the whole thing in Ps 18 has taken on "cosmic dimension" and uses language rooted in ancient Near Eastern (ANE) mythology, which has been "transformed to express the Lord's deliverance of his human servant." He parallels the poetic language of Babylonian Marduk and Tiamat, as well as the Canaanite myths of Baal, Mot and Yam. Craigie then concludes that in Ps 18 we are "dealing with adaptation, not simple borrowing." Cf. Craigie, *Psalms 1–50*, 173.
19. Terrien, *Psalms*, 200. Compare Ps 18:23: "All His ordinances were before me, and I put not away His statutes from me."

hope" (Ps 39:8). Such psalmodic language is often, directly or indirectly, a declaration of the innocence of the devotee and clearly points towards his personal and private piety.[20]

---

20. Also Pss 39, 64, 88. The self imprecatory psalms (Pss 6, 7, 16, 38) are fine examples of protestations of innocence.

CHAPTER 8

Cult-Free Psalms

In the chapter entitled "The Collection of Psalms" (sections 10 and 14) in his *Introduction to Psalms: the Genres of the Religious Lyric of Israel*, Hermann Gunkel deals with what he calls "cult-free poetry" or "spiritual, cult-free psalms."[1] These are Psalms or psalmodic sections which belong to the individual's personal pietistic practice. Most often, they are individual complaint songs as Gunkel states:

> Undoubtedly, psalmody held significance for the Temple service. This usage hardly needs proof. But what is the situation with respect to cult-free poetry and with respect to the non-cultic use of psalms originally composed for the cult?[2]

He lists a number of examples of individual psalmodic types who have little or no direct connection to the temple service, such as Jonah, Daniel, Jeremiah and Job. The psalm of Jonah is spoken from the belly of the fish (Jonah 2:2).[3] Daniel went home and blessed the God of heaven, saying, "Blessed be the name of God forever and ever" (Dan 2:20). Although this is

---

1. Gunkel, *Introduction to Psalms*, par. 10–14. Original title: "Einleitung in die Psalmen: die Gattungen der religiosen Lyrik Israels" (Gottingen, Vandenhoeck & Ruprecht, 1933 and 1985).

2. Gunkel, par. 13:10, 342.

3. The actual cause and initial drive for Jonah's psalmodic prayer are curiously explained by rabbinic interpretation of the use of the words "innermost part" (ירך) and "belly" (בטן) in Jonah 1:5 and 2:2: "It was a male fish, and since its insides were quite spacious, Jonah gave no thought to prayer. The Holy One, Blessed be He, gestured to the fish to vomit him into the mouth of a female fish which was heavily pregnant. Jonah was then uncomfortable and prayed. As it is said: And Jonah prayed from the loins of the fish." Rashi, citing Midrash, in Gruber, *Rashi's Commentary*. See also Perry, *Honeymoon Is Over*, 20–36.

presented as an original composition, it has a liturgical format, in common with the liturgy of the synagogue and there is no reason to use that in one's private worship.[4] Later on, Gunkel elaborates the idea of the Psalms which have no direct "relationship to the worship service."[5] What was the purpose of this particular collection of Psalms, which he calls "spiritual cult-free psalms"?[6] He answers: "It was compiled with the intention of creating a devotional and home book for the pious laity."[7] Spiritual songs were to inspire and encourage the pious and the "book" for the pious was not composed for a cultic purpose.

The subject of the psalmist's sudden change of mood, from desperation to exuberance, which we tackled on a few occasions ought to be considered yet again. Wevers here supports Gunkel's explanation that the Psalms were a "book for the pious laity."[8] Wevers points out to two possible explanations of the pious swings in mood. One is the so-called psychological explanation, following Friedrich Heiler.[9]

> In the course of prayer, an unsought and unconscious metamorphosis suddenly takes place. The feeling of uncertainty suddenly disappears to be replaced by the joyous consciousness of being protected and hidden by the hand of a higher power.[10]

The other interpretation for the psalmist's sudden change of mood follows the explanations of Gunkel and Mowinckel, who proposed that after the complaint, the authoritative priestly blessing ushers in the change. And, although there is still complaint in the heart of the complainer, there is a sense of the certainty of being heard. It was an *ipsissima verba Dei*, hence fully efficacious, in the sense that the complaint was heard. So, according to Gunkel:

---

4. See Lacocque, *Book of Daniel*, 43. Compare Ps 41:14; 106:48: "Blessed be the LORD, the God of Israel, from everlasting and to everlasting. Amen, and Amen." Lacocque here gives some good examples of other biblical characters (Joseph, Jeremiah) who in mortal danger, experience the salvific and providential nature of divine actions. Lacocque, 44.

5. At least these nine Psalms: 7; 16; 17; 25; 27; 32; 33; 35; 37.

6. Gunkel, *Introduction to Psalms*, par. 13:14, p. 346.

7. Gunkel, par. 13:14, p. 346.

8. In his study of individual complaint Psalms, John Wevers aptly brings up the theme of the sudden change in the psalmist's mood, from utter discouragement to encouragement and a spiritual song of an individual. Wevers, "Study in Form Criticism."

9. Heiler, *Das Gebet*.

10. Wevers, "Study in Form Criticism," 81.

At the conclusion of the complaint songs, it is not uncommon to be able to observe a very noteworthy, abrupt change in the mood of the one praying. He still complains in a heart rending manner, and petitions importunely that he be heard and liberated. In the next instant he speaks with a comforting and happy soul like a person who no longer needs to petition.[11]

For example, after the fearful and prayerful petitions of Psalm 13:1–4, the crux of the change we find in verse 5 where the psalmist suddenly changes to his confessional mood, "as for me in your faithfulness I trust" (13:5).

Gunkel here asks whether this sudden change of mood is to do with the "internal process of the one praying" or does this change depend "upon an external event"? If it is to be the latter, then it is due to a priestly oracle, for which some commentators believe it is associated with some kind of sacrifical offering of the petitioner. This interpretation then inevitably links the complainer to the cult and public office, rather than a private piety.[12] This can hardly be supported for all the instances of the complaint psalms and the changes of mood.

---

11. Gunkel, par. *Introduction to Psalms*, 6:23, p. 180.
12. Kuchler in Gunkel, par.6:23, p.182.

CHAPTER 9

Silence and the Uttered Cry

9.1 The Psalmist: His Discontent and Strife

The psalmist's discontent has been thoroughly discussed in the context of individual psalmodic laments or complaints. The psalmist's potential strife with God, in the context of his piety, has been dealt with less. In the Psalter, we do not find the legal-judicial trial form, as in prophetic literature, yet the psalmist engages in confrontation and dispute with God in a similar manner. In his disorientation or self-defence (see the imprecatory psalms), the psalmist enters into dispute with his Maker.[1] This is most evident in the imprecatory and self-deprecatory Psalms and/or generally when the psalmist protests his innocence (Ps 35:1, 23; 43:1).

Only a few commentators have examined and recognised the psalmist's contention/striving with God (ריב). There may be several valid reasons for this. First, the root (ריב) with its cognates appears only rarely in the Psalter (Pss 35; 43; 55; 74; 103; 119), and mostly in the context of the psalmist appealing to God to defend him and his cause against his enemies. Thus, "Strive, O LORD, with them that strive with me; fight against them that fight against me" (35:1).[2] Second, court procedures and debate between God and his people

---

1. The majority of studies of the psalmist's discontent focus on the Psalms which are generally categorized as Psalms of lament, "songs of complaint" or the "individual complaint songs." Gunkel notes that affiliating the "I" of the lament Psalms almost exclusively to the community is the "gravest mistake that the psalm research in general could have made." Gunkel, *Introduction to Psalms*, par.6, 1; 122.

2. ריבה יהוה את-יריבי

is linked to prophetic literature, particularly with the Isaianic writings (Isa 1:18; 41:21; 43:26, etc). Third, in the Psalter, the formal trial form of legal process between two parties, marked by lawsuit speeches, with the presence of the root ריב is not found.³ In his disorientation and discontent, the psalmist seems to be in an unenviable position.⁴ Can his faith accommodate strife with his Maker? One typical feature is the psalmist's protestation of his innocence (especially in the self-imprecatory psalms).⁵ There may be a mismatch between "our life experience of disorientation and our faith speech of orientation."⁶ Brueggemann observes that the minimal use of the lament psalms in the "serious religious use" is due to believing that faith "does not mean to acknowledge and embrace negativity."⁷ Setting it all in the context of the psalmist's disorientation and his piety, he then brings in a community of faith:

> The use of these "psalms of darkness" may be judged by the world to be an act of unfaith and failure, but from the trusting community, their use is an act of bold faith, albeit a transformed faith.⁸

---

3. Surveying the lexicons to look for the precise (primary) meaning of ריב, we find some variations and differences, for example, the root ריב in Isa 3, נצב לריב יהוה (3:13): "The LORD standeth up to plead" (JPS); "The LORD rises to accuse" (NAB); "The LORD has taken his place to contend" (RSV). The same translations have different renderings of ריב in the very similar text of the prophet Micah: את-ההרים קום ריב (Mic 6:1). Here, JPS gives "contend", NAB "present your plea" and RSV "plead your case". I follow BDB, that is, that the root ריב has a common denominator, which could include bodily struggle (as in Exod 21: "When men quarrel ריב and one strikes נכה the other." (21:18)) and verbal contention. Koehler and Baumgartner narrow down the meaning of the root almost exclusively to legal court procedures. Koehler and Baumgartner, *Lexicon*, 888. For a detailed discussion and literature on the root, see James Limburg, "Root ריב."

4. See Brueggemann, *Message of Psalms*, 51–122.

5. Compare with Isa 1:18: "Let us reason together" (or "Let us set things right," NAB). The verb here is יכח (decide, settle). NAB is right to translate here "setting things right," as the verb is used in a formal settlement of a matter in a reciprocal sense. See Keil and Delitzsch, *KD*, 7:98. Similarly in Isa 43:25–27, "Let us argue the matter together" – says Yahweh; though here the verb used is שפט but then there is also "woe" for those that want to argue with God: "Woe to him who contends with his Maker" (הוי רב את-יצרו) (Isa 45:9).

6. Brueggemann, *Message of Psalms*, 51. An apt example of disorientation and (re) orientation is Habakkuk's psalm in Hab 3. After Hab 3:3–17, with its terrifying theophanic demonstrations (3:3–15), the prophet is completely disoriented ("My inward parts tremble") (3:16), then comes the full bliss of reorientation ("But I will rejoice in the Lord") (3:18–19).

7. Brueggemann, 51.

8. Brueggemann, 51.

Private piety of the psalmist is not to be divorced from the community of faith. The private and the communal are not exclusive of each other. In every respect, within the Psalter, we find the personal and the communal to be complementary.

9.2 Silence and Personal Piety

Silence is an important factor in the piety of any religion. Though the public worship is rarely silent, silence as a contemplative aspect of the individual's worship, even within a communal liturgical event can be manifest.[9]

Before tackling silence as a means of religious contemplation, other aspects of silence as found in the scriptural text and context must be considered. Silence may be the consequence of divine punishment (divine silence), the avoidance of pagan practices (priestly silence), personal crisis (boiling silence), or personal piety (contemplative silence). In general and in the Bible, silence is often an indication of personal crisis. It is a blockage in communication. But, silence may and usually does, speak more than a thousand words. Mistakenly, silence is often thought of as mere absence of audible sounds or verbal communication. Sometimes, silence or being silent and speechless can be a more powerful means of communication then verbalization. The psalmist says; "I am numb and utterly crushed; I wail with anguish of heart" (Ps 38:9).

In fact, silence can represent the most intense and total communication. It may also enable a person to listen, hear, or simply rest. Deliberate, momentary silence in speech provides an opportunity for clarification or processing what has been uttered.[10] This is why silence should not only be perceived

---

9. In some modern religious traditions, for example, Quakerism, worship is centred around silence, as an expression of waiting upon the Lord as well as touching the mystical. Communion in silence in this particular tradition extends to abstaining from outward religious practices (baptisms, sacraments, etc.). Not only is personal piety fully internalised, but also communal piety and pietistic practice. An illustration is the so-called "inward baptism of the Holy Spirit."

10. Some religious traditions appreciate silence and contemplation as a way towards inner stillness. Silence is not merely an unpleasant absence of sounds, but making room for inner stillness and listening. In other traditions, silence causes discomfort, tension, disagreement, or even hostility and anger. The silence of one party is often filled by another party talking. In the tradition of the Roman church there was a notion of the so-called "silent mass," where a priest, without any presence of believers can say the Mass, silently on his own. This, though, is a long abandoned practice of the church.

as the absence of sound. It can also provide a space for listening. In biblical texts, silence is not a lack of communication, or an absence of speech. On the contrary, it seems that silence in the Bible is a dynamic concept and force. Silence "speaks" loudly, like an internal cry. The psalmist says, "My soul rests (דום) in God alone" (Ps 62:1, 6; Hab 2:20; Job 6:24; 33:1).[11] However, there are challenges and fears when Yahweh goes quiet.[12] In the face of great sufferings, a person may be unable to speak, like Job's friends, who were unable to utter a word for a week, "for they saw how great was his suffering" (Job 2:13).

Walter Brueggemann emphasizes not only the role of the psalmist's personal piety in his discontent, but also his silence, which is broken as the words explode.[13] Such piety is not best exemplified in silence, and Brueggemann continues to argue about the deadly power of silence. He rightly notices that the psalmist's complaint is: "not spoken by one who is a stranger to Yahweh, but one who has a long history of trustful interaction."[14]

9.3 Silence Is a Pressure Cooker

For the psalmist, silence can be a kind of a "pressure cooker," in which the ingredients boil and threaten to explode. While silence is threatening, one of the main terms for it is *dmm*, which is closely related to death. Being brought

---

11. Silence vocabulary: (חסם) in the sense of stopping a traveller or passer-by (Ezek 39:11), also to muzzle an ox (Deut 25:4) or ceasing to speak, being silent (Ps 39:2) (cf. BDB, 340). הס mostly is used as an interjection in the imperative, as a command, such as "Hush!" When the people, gathered at the festive reading of the Law were sorrowfully grieving aloud, Nehemiah hushed them saying, "Be quiet, for this day is holy" ("Hush, for today is holy") (הסו כי היום קדש) (Neh 8:11). The punishment of the idolatrous people, who were then inclined to call upon the name of Yahweh, includes the order: "Hush! We must not mention the name of the LORD." (Amos 6:10) (See KB:239, חשה).

(שקט/שתק in the sense of being calm, quieting down, as the stormy sea may quieten down (Jonah 1:11), also being at rest after the storm has passed (Ps 107:30), or keeping quiet and silent, rather than being afraid (Is 7:4). (דום/דמם) In the biblical vocabulary of silence, the most powerful are derivatives of the verbal root *dmm*. The verb and its nominal derivative (דומה) (silence) almost unequivocally relates to annihilation and death. The nominal form *dumiah* (silence) refers to the place or land of silence, that is, the grave.

12. Paolo Torresan provides a short and introductory but useful study about the silence in the Bible. Torresan, "Silence." Also, see Ernestine Schlant and her analysis of German literature and the silence in reference to the Holocaust. Schlant, *Language of Silence*.

13. See Brueggemann, *Message of Psalms*. Brueggemann, *Praying the Psalms*.

14. Brueggemann, *Message of Psalms*, 54. See Ps 65:2 (לך דמיה תהלה אלהים בציון).

down to silence means descending to destruction and the grave. Tyre will be lamented in the middle of the silence of the sea (Ezek 27:32).

In Psalm 39 and Jeremiah 20, we find an excellent example of personal piety which is not fully lived or expressed in silence, thus as a pressure cooker boiling until it "explodes" in words.[15] The psalmist initially resolves to sit in silence, lest he sins with his tongue and says something that he may later regret. Dahood translates 39:1, "lest I stumble over my tongue."[16] The psalmist muzzles his mouth חסם (39:1), that is, keeps quiet (compare 39:10). But the silence kills him. It becomes unbearable and his heart and innards are like a burning fire (חם לבי בקרבי) (39:4). Then the words start to flow. The NAB here translates, "I broke into speech."[17] The same pattern is found in Jeremiah's inner struggles, especially in chapters 4 and 20, which reflect the characteristic language of the lament Psalms. At the mere mention of God, Jeremiah would rather be silent. "I say to myself, I will not mention him, I will speak in his name no more. But then it becomes like fire burning in my heart, imprisoned in my bones; I grow weary holding it in, I cannot endure it" (Jer 20:9 NAB). Jeremiah 4 contains an even more powerful picture of this internal pressure on the verge of explosion. "My bowels, my bowels! I writhe in pain! The chambers of my heart! My heart moaneth within me! I cannot hold my peace! Because thou hast heard, O my soul, the sound of the horn, the alarm of war" (Jer 4:19). When the silence is broken, speech comes forth, perhaps one of the most powerful laments in the "Jobian" style. "Cursed be the day on which I was born! May the day my mother gave me birth never be blessed! Cursed be the man who brought the news to my father, saying, 'A child, a son, has been born to you!' filling him with great joy. Let that man be like the cities which the LORD relentlessly overthrew; Let him hear war cries in the morning, battle alarms at noonday, because he did not dispatch me in the womb! Then my mother would have been my grave, her womb confining me forever. Why did I come forth from the womb, to see sorrow and pain, to end my days in shame?" (Jer 20:14–18 NAB).

---

15. See "Anger and Fear."

16. אשמרה דרכי מחטוא בלשוני (39:1). Dahood, *Psalms*, I, 238.

17. As Gunkel notes, often in such situations when the pious person seeks to "rouse himself to trust, the connection to YHWH in the form of the prayer is lost. Then the Psalmist speaks of God in the third person." Gunkel, *Introduction to Psalms*, par. 6, 19, 172.

Yet, in all this struggle and distress, the speaking rather than the silence reveals the personal piety of the sufferer. On the other hand, maintaining silence and not speaking is the way to death, or eternal silence. Indeed, the psalmodic texts and biblical poetry recognize the realm of silence as death. Job contends that if he remains silent, it will be the assured way to death. "If anyone can make a case against me, then I shall be silent and die" (Job 13:19).

CHAPTER 10

The Silence of God

10.1 The Silence of God as Punishment

The motif of divine silence and hiddenness is common not only in psalmodic literature, either to portray the psalmist's suffering and Yahweh's distance from his troubles, or to denote divine hiddenness as the punitive action of God who hides from his people in response to their wrongdoings (Deut 31:17–18; Ps 30:8; Ps 89:47). In such situations, the prophet calls Yahweh a "God of hiding" or a "hidden God" (*deus absconditus*).[1] Yahweh is not only proactive in his punitive actions or manifestations of divine terror and majesty, but also simply withdraws (סור), as in Isaiah 2:10 and 3:1: "Get behind the rocks, hide in the dust, from the terror (פחד) of the LORD and the splendour of his majesty!" (2:10); "The LORD of hosts will take away from Jerusalem and from Judah support and staff – all support of bread, all support of water" (3:1).

God goes quiet, in the ultimate retributive action. In prophetic traditions, divine silence is described as a sealed book and a cessation of prophecies and visions. "And the vision of all this has become to you like the words of a

---

1. In "indeed you are a God of hiding" (Isa 45:15), this may be an expression of divine mystery, as many commentators have suggested. But, on the other hand, if God hides himself from his people in times of punishment of sins, why does he hide now in the salvific context of Isa 45? Westermann and others note that the hiddenness of God may well refer to amazement at the way God has acted in choosing Cyrus as his "anointed" (45:1). Westermann, *Isaiah 40–66*, 170. Similarly, Delitzsch comments that the meaning here is that of a God "who guides with marvellous strangeness the history of the nations of the earth, and by secret ways which human eyes can never discern." *KD,* "Psalms," 7:226. The same prophet (Isaiah) elsewhere concludes that God's thoughts and plans may not match human ideas (Isa 55:8).

book that is sealed. When men give it to one who can read, saying, 'Read this,' he says, 'I cannot, for it is sealed.' And when they give the book to one who cannot read, saying, "Read this," he says, 'I cannot read.'" (Isa 29:11–12 RSV).[2]

There are times when a divine order comes to the prophets to keep silent and not prophesy.[3] "As for you, do not pray for this people, or lift up cry or prayer for them, and do not intercede with me, for I do not hear you" (Jer 7:16 RSV).

The silence of punishment denotes God's rejection of his own people. "I will cast you out of my sight" (Jer 7:15).[4] The syncretistic habits of Yahweh's people were now so widespread and customary that there was no point in praying any more. In fact, things had moved so far out of control that the Israelites had (i) started to practise syncretism at the household level and (ii) attempted to disguise idolatrous practices within the walls of the temple (7:2–7). To them, it seemed almost impossible that Yahweh would deny his own temple. But this is exactly what Yahweh intended to do (7:14–15). In other words, this sanctuary would no longer be a sanctuary for his idolatrous people. In effect, God closed both the door of the temple and his mouth, retreating into silence (Isa 29:10). The frightening silence of God was not only present at the national level, but is also reflected in the psalmist's fears in the midst of his suffering, above all the fear of being abandoned by God.

Even more vivid pictures regarding the intensity of punitive silence are given to the prophets, such as that to Ezekiel. "I will make your tongue cleave to the roof of your mouth, so that you shall be dumb and unable to reprove them; for they are a rebellious house" (Ezek 3:26 RSV). The prophetic silence lasted for a long time, and no one knew how long it would continue. The psalmist could only ask himself, "Until when?" (עד אנה) and "How long?" (עד מה) the silence would last before Yahweh would be merciful and show his grace again. He pleads, "God of my praise, be not silent (חרש)." (Ps 109:1; 39:13).[5]

---

2. Compare Dan 12:9, Rev 5:1.

3. Similar examples can be found in the New Testament, particularly the book of Acts, when the apostles were prevented by the Spirit of God from preaching (speaking) the gospel (Acts 16:6).

4. The language is similar when Saul is dethroned; because "you have rejected the word of the LORD, he has also rejected you from being king" (1 Sam 15:23).

5. Dahood translates: "My God, be not deaf to my song of praise." Dahood, *Psalms*, III, 97. An identical phrase is found in Ps 39:13; "Do not be deaf to my weeping."

The punitive silence of God provokes not only the communal, collective desire of "returning to the Lord" (Hos 6:1) but also gives rise to intense, personal pietistic reactions.[6] For the psalmist, the fact that God has gone quiet is even more frightening than his active, retributive deeds.

10.2 The Silence of Death and Suffering

The silence of God is also a perpetual theme of human suffering. The most familiar rationalization follows the pattern, "where is God in my suffering?" For the psalmist, already persecuted or suffering from illness, it is increased by fear of divine silence and the remoteness of God. More than personal disorientation, the absence of the divine voice, imparted through an authoritative prophet, was for the Israelites a religious-legal matter of serious concern in interpreting the Torah. For example, in matters of the temple and altar arrangements, there were times when issues remained unresolved until "a prophet should come and decide" (1 Macc 4:44–46).

The silence of Yahweh in the Psalms mostly denotes a mortal threat or a divine punishment in action. So, if God is silent towards the psalmist and his prayers, he fears he will "go down to the pit" (Ps 28:1). Silence as a response to the psalmist's prayers is a sign of Yahweh being far away, thus he prays, "Be not silent O Lord, be not far from me" (Ps 35:22 RSV). In the crisis of suffering he says, "I am numb (פוג) and utterly crushed (דכה)" (Ps 38:9). This is when the psalmist raises his voice and his prayer acquires an imperative mode. Whether by pleading to be heard: "Hear my voice!" (שמע קולי) (Ps 5:3) or beseeching not to be silent: "Do not be silent!" (אל תחרש) (Ps 83:2; 8:1).[7] In this, he is very persistent and continues: "Listen to my prayer, LORD, hear my cry; do not be deaf (חרש) to my weeping!" (39:13).[8] He cries and moans in the evening, morning and noon: "At dusk, dawn, and noon I will grieve and complain" (55:18) (ערב ובקר וצהרים אשיחה ואהמה).[9]

---

6. לכו ונשובה אל-יהוה (Hos 6:1).

7. "God, do not be silent; God, be not still and unmoved!" (אלהים אל-דמי-לך אל-תחרש ואל-תשקט אל) (Ps 83:2).

8. See Wevers, "Study in Form Criticism," 81.

9. The two cohortatives here relate to the duration of this action as well as his resolution under compulsion. GK, par. 108g; Waltke and O'Connor, *Introduction*, 171.

In his complaining (64:2), he pleads for mercy and awaits an answer. "Hear my voice when I cry to you, have mercy and answer me" (27:7). While Psalm 28 is a personal cry, Psalm 83 is an intercessory, national lament probably led by a priest or temple singer. In the former, the psalmist himself feels abandoned, but in Psalm 83, it is God's own people (83:4–5) who feel the silence of God. Apart from the help they seek for themselves, they raise the cause of God himself. For, these enemies are "your enemies" (v. 2), they are "in league (ברית) against you" (v. 6 NAB). In effect the Psalm says: "your enemies are our enemies and our enemies are your enemies." Therefore, God must not rest (שקט) and be unmoved, or silent (דמי), or pretend to be deaf (חרש).

10.3 Priestly Silence

In discussing the psalmist's sudden change of mood, we noted the interpretation that this was due to priestly intervention (see above: "The Psalmist and His Prayer"). A somewhat different explanation must be faced. Now, instead of priestly intervention, there is priestly silence. Instead of prayer being firmly attached to the temple, it belongs to popular religion.[10] In the place of the psalmist's prayer and the role of the priests in the temple service, Yehezkel Kaufmann and others argue a different case, the so-called "priestly silence."[11] In the case of the psalmist's prayer, Kaufmann et al. argue that the priestly temple is the "kingdom of silence."[12]

This interpretation does not deny the temple activities (liturgy, prayers and hymns), but argues against paganism and pagan priestly practices. In fact, Kaufmann argues that the priestly (temple) cult was performed in total silence.[13] He maintains that not only psalms, but also prayers had no place in the priestly court. The priests wanted to avoid any magical elements associated with paganism, such as magical utterances. So, the Israelite cult became a "domain of silence."[14]

---

10. Knohl, "Between Voice and Silence," 17.

11. Knohl, "Between Voice and Silence." See the works of Yehezkel Kaufmann, Israel Knohl, Menahem Haran, Nahum Sarna and Moshe Greenberg. Cf. Fox et al. *Texts, Temples and Traditions*"; Haran, *"Cult and Prayer"*; Sarna, *Psalm Superscriptions*.

12. Kaufmann, *The Religion of Israel*, in Knohl, "Between Voice and Silence," 17.

13. Knohl, *Sanctuary of Silence*, 148.

14. Kaufmann, in Knohl, "Between Voice and Silence," 17.

> The priestly temple is the kingdom of silence. In Egypt and Babylonia and in the pagan world in general, word and incantation were integral parts of the cult; act was accompanied by speech. The spell expressed the magical essence of cultic activity. In more developed form, pagan rituals might be accompanied by mythological allusions relating to events in the life of the gods. Speech thus articulated the magical-mythological sense of the rites . . . P makes no reference to the spoken word in describing temple rites.[15]

There are some weak points in Kaufmann's argument which deserve rejoinders. First, he fails to account for the psalmist's sudden change of mood. There are more than a few textual examples of priestly speeches set in the cultic context (Lev 16:21; Num 5:19; Num 6:24). Second, following Michael Fishbane's criticism, it is unacceptable that most of the priestly utterances verged on the magical, which is the starting point of Kaufmann's priestly silence thesis.[16] Fishbane points to certain difficulties in Kaufmann's position, taking Numbers 5:11–31 as an example of priestly intervention. There, in the case of a woman accused of adultery, priestly intervention involved a combination of sacred acts (5:16–18, 23–31) and sacred words (5:19–22), which clearly form an example of cultic ritual, from which it may be difficult to conclude that psalmody was exempt from cultic events and accompanying priestly interventions. For example, when the people were ready to move on from an encampment and the Ark of the Covenant had to be made ready, Moses would perform a short ritual. "Whenever the ark set out, Moses would say, 'Arise, O LORD, that your enemies may be scattered, and those who hate you may flee before you.' And when it came to rest, he would say, 'Return, O LORD, you who ride upon the clouds, to the troops of Israel'" (Num 10:35–36).[17] Clearly, Leviticus 16:20–22 (sending the scapegoat into the wilderness) is another example of a priestly ritual, accompanied by the priestly *verba sacra*. Similarly, in 1 Chronicles 15–16, in the story of the bringing of the Ark to its rightful place in Jerusalem, the liturgy was accompanied by a

---

15. Kaufmann, in Knohl, 17.

16. Fishbane, "Accusation of Adultery," 27–28.

17. Fishbane also gives a resume of a number of difficulties with texts, such as here, Num 5:11–31 (see the discussion on pp. 28–29).

psalm (16:8–36). Thus, in his critique of Kaufmann, Fishbane rightly asks, "Were the Psalms totally divorced from cultic events in ancient Israel, in contrast to the rituals of Mesopotamia and the Second Temple?"[18]

---

18. Fishbane, 28.

CHAPTER 11

Silence Will be Broken

The psalmist concludes, "We do not see our signs; there is no longer any prophet, and there is none among us who knows how long" (Ps 74:9 RSV). There were great expectations that the divine silence would be broken by the arrival of a great prophet, as a precursor of the Messiah (though there was a degree of confusion as to how many prophets, or even Messiahs, were to be expected).[1]

However, the Jews of the New Testament days were still waiting for the reappearance of the prophets and prophetic ministry, which would be accompanied by supernatural powers and signs, particularly healing.[2] When Jesus fed five thousand people by the Sea of Galilee and when those present witnessed it, they said, "This is truly the Prophet, the one who is to come into the world" (John 6:14). This reappearing of the prophet of olden days would break the divine silence and be introduced in eschatological terms. The prophet Malachi foretells, "I will send you Elijah the prophet before the great and terrible day of the LORD comes," (Mal 4:6 NRSV). So, the prophet Isaiah portrays God breaking his silence, "For a long time I have kept silent (חשה), I have said nothing (חרש), holding myself back; now, I cry out like a woman in labour, gasping and panting" (Isa 42:14).

Isaiah 61 foretells the arrival of a prophet to "announce a year of favour from the LORD and a day of vindication by our God, to comfort all who

---

1. Silberman, "Two Messiahs"; Brown, "Messianism"; Moore, "Covenanters of Damascus."
2. When a young blind man was healed by Jesus, he declared of Jesus, "He is a prophet" (John 9:17).

mourn" (Isa 61:2).³ Divine favour will return and the prophet's task is to offer long-awaited comfort for "all that mourn"; part of the whole picture that perfectly fits with New Testament prophetic (and sometimes confusing) expectations. Commenting on Isaiah 61, Westermann concludes that

> to the best of our knowledge, this was the last occasion in the history of Israel on which a prophet expressed his certainty of having been sent by God with a message to his nation with such freedom and conviction.⁴

This may conflict with his own remarks in relation to the comforter in question. He notes the unique character of this particular promise and the way it is presented, since it does not resemble the familiar form of a prophetic call, as in Isaiah 6, Jeremiah 1 or similar texts, though it resembles the forms of the Servant songs to a certain extent (Isa 42; 49). Westermann concludes:

> A leading feature in this proclamation made by the messenger of salvation is the accumulation of meditorial functions, and of the qualities for it, that here heaped upon one person. This makes it very apparent that, at the time when these words were spoken, they had lost the clear co-ordination with definite functions which they once had, and in the process had also ceased to be precise.⁵

This particular text poses several questions. Who is the comforter, and is he a prophet figure? Who is the person speaking and of whom is he speaking? Westermann may be right in saying that, at the time, the people "had lost the clear co-ordination with definite functions." In the Isaian context, it can hardly be the prophet himself who speaks of himself in such an all-embracing way. Nowhere in Isaiah does the prophet speak of himself at such length. A similar "accumulation of functions" is only found in such texts as in Isaiah 9 and Isaiah 11, where the prophet is not clearly identified. In 9:5, there is a (prophetic) child, and in 7:14, a "shoot from the stump of Jesse" (11:1).

---

3. Since there is a juxtaposition of "year" and "day," Westermann comments that it shows "no particular event in mind, but a new era." Westermann, *Isaiah 40–66*, 367.

4. Westermann, 367.

5. Westermann, 365.

11.1 Moses or Elijah?

Divine silence will be replaced by divine restoration and renewed communication. This comfort and the cessation of divine silence were expected for generations by the many pious in Israel. The report of the birth of Jesus of Nazareth and the events surrounding it are evidence of their existence.[6] The expected prophet will be some kind of reincarnation of an Old Testament prophet. Popular and religious expectations were expressed in terms of anticipation of Elijah, or Moses who seemed to rank somewhat higher than Elijah. John the Baptist, when cross-examined by the Jewish clergy, resisted being identified with any of the prophets.[7] They asked him, "What then? Are you Elijah?" He said, "I am not." In response to "Are you the prophet?", his answer was: "No" (John 1:19–21 RSV).[8]

There are several dilemmas to address here. One is the popular sentiment regarding John the Baptist's ministry and his prophetic status, publicly supported by Jesus of Nazareth. The other is that while the Baptist resisted being identified as the reincarnation of an Old Testament prophet, he actually acted and spoke in exactly the manner of the awaited prophet. In fact, popular opinion already considered John the Baptist to be a prophet, probably associated with Elijah: "They all thought John really was a prophet" (Mark 11:32). This sentiment was supported by Jesus himself, who when examined about his own identity also spoke about John the Baptist. He endorsed John the Baptist as even "more than a prophet" (Matt 11:9), adding to the mystification regarding which of the ancient prophets was to return. Jesus then answered his disciples, when asked, "Why do the scribes say that Elijah must come first?" with "Elijah will indeed come and restore (ἀποκαταστήσει) all things"

---

6. At the time of the events surrounding the birth of Jesus, there was a certain Simeon in Jerusalem. He was "righteous and devout (εὐλαβής)"; and "awaiting the consolation (παράκλησιν) of Israel" (Luke 2:25). There was also a prophetess, Anna, who "spoke about the child to all who were awaiting the redemption (λύτρωσιν) of Jerusalem" (Luke 2:38).

7. Brown, *The Gospel According to John*, 49, 234. There are interpretations that suggest the Gospel of John emphasizes the Baptist's reluctance to be identified as a prophet because of the Johannine desire to avoid the following of John the Baptist. Richter in Brown, 49.

8. Both Moses and Elijah traditionally appear in the anticipatory context of the coming prophet. On the Mount of the Transfiguration, it is Elijah and Moses who join Jesus (Matt 17:3; Mark 9:2–13; Luke 9:28–36). On another occasion, Jesus asks his followers about popular perceptions regarding him, and they report that the people are divided, so some identify him as John the Baptist, others as Elijah (cf. Luke 9:19).

(Matt 17:10–11).⁹ But then Jesus concludes with the enigmatic: "Elijah has already come, and they did not recognize him but did to him whatever they pleased" (17:12). This probably encouraged popular identification of John the Baptist with Elijah.

John the Baptist himself, in word and deed, identified himself with Elijah and the one to come. While in Matthew and Luke he mainly behaves like a preacher of repentance and righteousness, in John, the words he proclaims identify him as "the voice of one crying out in the desert, 'Make straight the way of the Lord'" (John 1:23). This is clearly a prophetic identification, by which he "declares his own ministry to be the immediate prelude to the great divine Event."¹⁰ Moreover, John the Baptist confirms his prophetic ministry by describing and hailing Jesus of Nazareth in Messianic terms: "Behold, the Lamb of God, who takes away the sin of the world!" (John 1:29).

What then of Moses and his stature? It seems Moses ranked somewhat higher than Elijah. So, in his Jerusalem speech, the apostle Peter, speaking of Jesus, cited the words of Moses from Deuteronomy 18:15, "A prophet like me will the LORD, your God, raise up for you from among your own kindred; that is the one to whom you shall listen" (compare Acts 3:22). In comparing the Israelite prophets with the pagan diviners of the surrounding nations, S. R. Driver concludes that this does not refer to a particular prophet, but rather an office.¹¹

So, while Elijah would "restore all things" and in this way prepare the Messianic way, Moses would play a multiple role, as a reincarnated legislator, judge and interpreter of the Law, who would be able to solve religious legal problems, as in Exodus 18, but also in the office of a prophetic intercessor and mediator (Exod 32:30; Num 11:10–17). Both are very illustrative of

---

9. Here Jesus's words in Matt 17:11, "restore all things" (Ἠλίας μὲν ἔρχεται καὶ ἀποκαταστήσει πάντα), follow LXX from Mal 4:6 of Elijah who will "turn the hearts of the fathers" (ἀποκαταστήσει καρδίαν πατρὸς).

10. Dodd, *The Interpretation of the Fourth Gospel*, 292–93.

11. See Driver, *Deuteronomy*, 227. Following the texts and contexts of Judg 2:16,18 where Yahweh raises up judges over the Israelites as needed, Driver comments and concludes that on the particular passage:"the context shows that no single, or particular, prophet can be intended: it was a constantly recurring need which prompted the heathen to resort to diviners for the purpose of unlocking the secrets of the future; and as the prophet is to supply the place of such diviners in Israel, it must be a similarly recurring need which (so far as Jehovah permits it) he is designed to satisfy. It follows that the reference here is to a permanent institution, not to a particular individual prophet." Driver, 227.

Moses's earthly ministry.[12] But the prophet to come would carry out several crucial functions.

One would be to help construct an authoritative interpretation of religious legislation and the Torah. In that sense he would assume Moses's judicial functions (e.g. 1 Macc 4:44). Second, even more importantly, he comes to break the silence between God and his people. By restoring real faith and understanding, thus making sure that the coming Messiah would not arrive among an unprepared people.[13] In that, the prophet would resemble Elijah.

11.2 How Many Messiahs?

In the early Christian and Jewish communities, there were further uncertainties and confusion regarding who would be the mediator in breaking the long-standing silence between God and his people. Who should they expect to come first, Elijah or Moses, or both at the same time? Some sectarian religious communities apparently awaited more than one Messiah.

Examination of the spirituality of the Qumran community has revealed perplexity about the number of Messiahs expected. In his short but important work, Millar Burrows pursues the discoveries of Solomon Schechter.[14] Schechter found another Jewish sect (*Damascus Covenanters*), and thus opened a discussion regarding various references to the "messiah of Aaron and Israel" or to "lay and priestly messiahs" in a writing known as the *Zadokite Document*.[15] This confusion was brought about while analysing the Qumranic *Manual of Discipline* (DSD) (IX:10–11), and comparing it with the *Cairo Manuscript of the Damascus Covenanters* (CDC). From these documents, it

---

12. Brown, *Gospel of John*, 49.
13. Hill, *The Gospel of Matthew*, 269.
14. Burrows, *Dead Sea Scrolls*.
15. Solomon Schechter (1847–1915), a Jewish rabbi and scholar, unearthed manuscripts of a Jewish sect in Cairo (*Damascus Covenanters*) also known as the *Zadokite Document*.

George F. Moore reports comprehensively on the findings of S. Schechter from 1896–97 in a text published in the *Harvard Theological Review* (1911): "Among the Hebrew manuscripts recovered in 1896 from the Genizah of an old synagogue at Fostat, near Cairo, and now in the Cambridge University Library, England, were found eight leaves of a Hebrew manuscript which proved to be fragments of a book containing the teaching of a peculiar Jewish sect; a single leaf of a second manuscript, in part parallel to the first, in part supplementing it, was also discovered. These texts Professor Schechter has now published, with a translation and commentary." Moore, "Covenanters of Damascus," 330.

appeared that these spiritual communities were awaiting one or two Messiahs. The Covenanters believed they were the real, faithful remnant of Israel. They declared that after Israel went astray by being unfaithful to God, there were men of both the priesthood and laity who had to secede and leave Judah:

> The land was laid utterly waste. Nevertheless, God still remembered the Covenant which He had made with their forbears and raised from the priesthood men of discernment and from the laity men of wisdom, and He made them hearken to Him. And these men "dug the well" – that well whereof it is written, "Princes digged it, nobles of the people delved it, with the aid of a mehoqeq" [Num. 21.18]. The "well" in question is the Law. They that "digged" are those of Israel who repented and departed from the land of Judah to sojourn in the land of Damascus.[16]

In more than one place, the Covenanters' eschatological language speaks of the times "until the lay and priestly messiah(s)" assume their office."[17] Without going into detailed analysis, Millar Burrows concludes that the texts could mean (1) "the coming of a prophet and of his Messiah, Aaron, and of Israel"; (2) "the coming of a prophet and of his Messiah, Aaron-and-Israel"; or even (3) "the coming of a prophet and of his Messiahs, Aaron and Israel."[18]

---

16. Zadokite document, "Of the Remnant"; V, 17.

17. Zadokite document: "Of the future requital of the disobedient" (VII–VIII) and "Prologue" (XII–XIII).

18. Burrows, *Dead Sea Scrolls*, 202–6.

CHAPTER 12

Realms of Piety and Privacy

It has already been noted that there can be no sharp demarcation between personal and private piety on the one hand, and the public, liturgical aspect and participation on the other.

However, in terms of Judaic religious typology and the record of Scripture, personal dedication is not only a matter of personal devotion, it is a prerequisite of the full value of the cultus. This is why piety, personal and private, ought to be taken seriously into account and examined.

12.1 Solitude Vocabulary

The verb בדד refers to loneliness and appears in the biblical text in various verb or noun forms. Its original meaning is "to separate, to isolate." It also appears as a noun (בדד) (*solitude*) (Lam 1:1); but most frequently as an active participle (בודד). The psalmist, during his sleepless nights, tosses and turns as an insomniac, feeling alone (בודד) "like a bird on the roof."[1] "I lie awake, I am like a lonely bird on the housetop" (Ps 102:7 RSV), while in the preceding verse he compares himself and his loneliness to a pelican or owl in the deserted places (102:6).[2] The opening of Lamentations of Jeremiah (Lam 1:1) begins with an introductory clause of a dirge, proclaiming the tormenting condition of the lone and abandoned city of Jerusalem: "How doth the city sit solitary, that was full of people!" (Lam 1:1 JPS). The איכה (where?, how?) would be better rendered as 'alas!'; that is, "Alas, how the city is solitary," with

---

1. Alter, *Book of Psalms*, 354.
2. On the verb *bdd* see Zobel, "Bdd," 473–79.

the "alas" as an opening interjection to the sorrowful dirge (see also Deut 1:12; Isa 1:21; Lam 2:1).

Separation and solitude for many biblical characters was a prelude to major emotional and religious experiences.

12.2 Solitude Narratives

Many biblical characters had their deepest emotional and religious experiences in different forms of solitude, most of which were theophanic in nature. Solitude may be voluntary, or externally imposed isolation from human community.[3] Solitude and loneliness may be terrifying (1 Sam 21:2; 2 Sam 17:2). From the very outset of creation it is said that it was not good for man to be alone (לא טוב היות האדם לבדו) (Gen 2:18).

Biblical texts present a great number of what we shall call "solitude narratives" that contribute greatly towards a better understanding of personal and private piety. These are stories and narratives in which a pious individual in his solitude seeks the divine presence. Two brief questions are necessary here. First, how does a narrative connect or relate to poetry? Second, how do solitude narratives relate to the subject matter of piety in privacy?

We cannot go into a detailed analysis of the literary structure of narration and narratives. Their connection has been presented earlier in this work, examining how narrative elements are evidently present in psalmodic poetry (see "Narrative Elements and Poetic Imagination"). Alter's exposition is particularly useful here on how parallelism, a typical poetic device, is not mere repetition, but can be seen as a constituent part of a *narrative poem*. Poetry indeed tells a story, in its own way, using a distinct literary instrumentary. On the connection between poetic parallelism and narration, Alter says,

> The parallelism of biblical verse constituted a structure in which, through the approximately synonymous half-lines or verses, there was constant repetition that was never really repetition ... so that every restatement is a new statement.[4]

---

3. The Torah commands that for some human diseases, particularly infectious ones, the person "shall dwell alone in a habitation outside the camp" (ב........יש בדד הוא) (Lev 13:46).

4. Cf. Alter, *Art*, 122. Cf. Broyles, *Conflict of Faith*; Bar-Efrat, *Narrative Art*.

Second, such biblical solitude stories provide a "precondition for the reception or transmission of a divine revelation,"[5] also most certainly true in the context of the pious man of the Psalms. Bar-Efrat aptly remarks that Hebrew Bible narratives are of "the highest artistic quality,"[6] which is even truer of the solitude narratives. In these narratives, apart from the wider context of each particular one, there is a detailed description or portrait of the character in question. The narrator is inside the narrative as an integral part of the narration. At times, the narrator is obvious and palpable; as in first-person narratives, which frequently occur in the psalmodic material. At other times, he is less apparent.[7] In some solitude narratives, solitude is of the narrator's own choosing, preliminary to impending events or expectations (Moses, Daniel). For others it is a somewhat traumatic experience, an isolation of sorts, filled with resentment and depression (Jeremiah), even with suicidal feelings (Elijah, Jonah). For yet others, it is filled with fear and encountering the unknown (Jacob).

Moses had solitude and times of privacy with YHWH in the *meeting tent* (אהל מועד) (Exod 33:9.). There he conversed with God "face to face" (פנים אל-פנים) (33:11). As opposed to the somewhat enigmatic theophanic experience of the burning bush story of Exodus 3, now Moses's privacy and familiarity with YHWH is elevated as described in Numbers 12:8, where he speaks with God "mouth to mouth" (פה אל-פה). In the incident of the rebellion of Mirian and Aaron against Moses, the heavenly arbiter intervenes in favour of Moses, "face to face I speak to him, plainly and not in riddles. The likeness of the LORD he beholds, why, then, do you not fear to speak against my servant Moses?" (Num 12:1, 8). This unparalleled relationship is confirmed in the New Testament (Heb 3:1–6) where Moses, the keeper and mediator of the covenant, is uniquely compared with Jesus Christ.[8] Solitude narratives continue throughout the Old Testament with a diversity of experiences. The common denominator in them all is a theophanic element.

---

5. Zobel, "Bdd," 477.

6. Bar-Efrat, *Narrative Art*, 9.

7. The relationship between the narrator and the characters is well presented in Bar-Efrat's study. Bar-Efrat, *Narrative Art*, 9, 13, 47.

8. Moses was superior to the subsequent prophets in the way that they continued to build upon the foundations which were set by Moses. New foundations were laid down, and a discontinuity came with Jesus of Nazareth.

Daniel. Another example of privacy is exemplified in Daniel's experience of separation (בדד) from others, in his solitude episode in Daniel 10:7–8 "So I was left alone," (נשארתי לבדי ואני). Though surrounded by people; "people who were with me did not see the vision" (10:7b), in the face of this unique event Daniel is a lone witness. There follows a private trance-like experience with clearly psychosomatic manifestations. These are frequently found in the solitude experiences of the pious psalmist, as well as other biblical characters.[9] In crucial situations, Daniel's custom was to go to the seclusion of his room in prayer, facing the direction of the city.[10] We find another example of personal, yet very private experience in King David's mourning over his son Absalom, when the king "went up to the room" and wept (2 Sam 19:1). In his privacy, David wept over his son, though he betrayed his father,

> The king was shaken, and went up to the room over the city gate to weep. He said as he wept, "My son Absalom! My son, my son Absalom! If only I had died instead of you, Absalom, my son, my son!" (2 Sam 18:33)

Jacob. One of the first Old Testament solitude narratives is Jacob wrestling with a "man." Again, Jacob "was left alone" (ויותר יעקב לבדו), but a man "wrestled with him" (Gen 32:25). This solitude narrative of Jacob seems to be archetypal as a major turning-point in the lives of so many biblical characters. For Jacob, this was neither a voluntary decision, neither a pleasant experience, yet somewhat of a pattern in the biblical solitude narratives.

Elijah. The prophet's experience is in a way unique. But this is not the only example of depression which led to solitude and even suicidal attempts and feelings (e.g. Jonah). Elijah, after all he had been through, felt abandoned, forsaken and yet again joined the club of all those who felt abandoned and "left alone" (אני לבדי). He was begging for his life to be taken, "take away my life" (1 Kgs 19:4), even though there were those who already sought his life to be terminated (ויבקשו את נפשי לקחתה) (1 Kgs 19:10). However, as a matter of pattern, there follows an exceptional theophanic experience and

---

9. Similar to these is Paul's experience on the Damascus road in the New Testament. In his Damascus road experience, Paul, though accompanied by others, was the sole witness of the vision (Acts 9:7).

10. The first mention of this practice of facing Jerusalem in private prayer may be found in 1 Kgs 8:44. Cf. Lacocque, *Book of Daniel*, 114. On this custom, see Young, *Daniel*, 135.

an outcome to his solitude experience, "go and return" (1 Kgs 19:15), that is, get up and get on with it.

Jeremiah is not quite sure whether he really enjoys his solitude. Initially, God's word is a joy to him, when he sits alone (בדד) (Jer 15:16–17), but then YHWH fills him with indignation (15:17). His lamentation is then clearly also a protestation of innocence ("I did not sit in the company of merrymakers," (15:17 RSV)). The phrase "O Lord, you know," as in Jeremiah 12:3 and elsewhere, is a protestation of innocence formula (Isa 45:4–5). Jeremiah then indirectly proclaims his solitude as being cast out in some way,

> O LORD, thou knowest; remember me and visit me (זכר), and take vengeance for me on my persecutors. In thy forbearance take me not away; know that for thy sake I bear reproach. Thy words were found, and I ate them (אכל), and thy words became to me a joy and the delight of my heart; for I am called by thy name, O LORD, God of hosts. I did not sit in the company of merrymakers, nor did I rejoice; I sat alone (בדד), because thy hand was upon me, for thou hadst filled me with indignation. (15:15–17 RSV)

Jonah. All these biblical characters found themselves in very private places of personal emotional and religious experiences. However, perhaps the most unusual place of seclusion and privacy was that whale's belly where Jonah ends up and sends up his prayer (Jonah 2:2). The scenography of Jonah's psalm and experience is portrayed by some unusual expressions. It is also issued from an unusual place, from the *belly of Sheol*, that is, from the gates of death: "I called to the LORD, out of my distress, and he answered me; out of the belly of Sheol (מבטן שאול) I cried" (Jonah 2:2 RSV). His seclusion is finalized by an unusual word, by closing of the "bars of the netherworld" – "the land whose bars closed upon me" (הארץ ברחיה בעדי) (2:6 RSV).

As the "belly of Sheol" is being mentioned here, we ought to note the significance of the abdominal organs (here: *belly*, בטן) in general, as far as the personal and private emotional and religious experiences appear in biblical texts. Theodore Perry rightly notes that the biblical belly is "a conceptual merism."[11] That is, it is an ambivalent word, with two opposite meanings

---

11. Perry, *Honeymoon Is Over*, 31.

which then form a whole. In the biblical (con)text, *belly* may denote either death or birth (see here: "Biblical Gastroenterology"). There are two primary meanings. That of *absorption* and ingestion, thus destruction and *death*; or as the womb, thus the place of birth and *life*. The two aspects of belly, repeatedly occur and alternate in biblical texts. In Jonah's psalm (Jonah 2), we find the engaging usage of anthropological terms, like: "belly of Sheol" (2:3) or the "heart of the seas" (2:4). Although these may appear to be somewhat unusual, they are not so surprising. That is, bearing in mind that Jonah in his loneliness is facing a near-death experience. At the same time as wanting to die, he nonetheless chooses and seeks life (Jonah 2).[12]

Another term designating privacy (or secrecy) is denoted by the verbal root סתר, with its primary meaning to *hide* or alternatively to lie in wait to attack, hiding in an ambush. The nominal form סתרה denotes a hiding place (Deut 32:38) or a place of secrecy (Ps 9:17).[13] The wicked waits in ambush to kill the innocent in secret (Ps 10:8). Jeremiah decides to cry, appeal and pray to God in privacy, "My soul will weep in secret" (Jer 13:17 RSV).[14] However, there is neither a hiding or a private place where God will not be able to see and find, "'Can a man hide himself in secret places so that I cannot see him?' says the LORD. 'Do I not fill heaven and earth?' says the LORD" (Jer 23:24 RSV).

The pious psalmist is aware that there is nowhere to hide from God (Ps 139:7); he can only go to a place of "hiding" in order to open his soul to God in privacy.

12.3 Solitude or Conventions

In this section, an examination of situations and texts regarding the pious psalmist's personal religious experience exercised in solitude and privacy will be presented. The emotional dimension plays an important role in understanding the private piety of the psalmist. On the other hand, some commentators suggest that particular phrasemes found in what appears to be a

---

12. Theodore Perry elaborates on Jonah's psalm, helpfully explaining its anthropological dimensions. Cf. Perry, 20–36.

13. "Let them be your protection" (יהי עליכם סתרה) (Deut 32:38).

14. Here a denominative, from סתר, formed with the prefixed מ is מסתר, the hiding place or secret place. Cf. Pss 10:8; 17:12; 64:5, etc.

personal prayer are simply a conventionalised body of formulae chanted by the pious. Should that be the case, it would weaken our case for the personal and private piety of the faithful Israelite. The proposition should be seriously considered, but one wonders how realistic it is, bearing in mind the average person's level of literacy and the accessibility of written material at the time.

One cannot disregard the fact that in the wider range of biblical psalmodic literary types, a number of songs are put into the mouths of ordinary people (Jonah, Hannah, Mary, etc), who appropriate them for their personal and private devotion. One also cannot overlook the extreme frequency with which YHWH is designated as "my" (my God, my shepherd, my rock, my salvation). These utterances, in the first person singular, cannot be simply ascribed to corporate anthropology, the collective person or poetic convention.[15]

Psalm 18 is a good example. It is one of the longest psalms in the Psalter (only Pss 78 and 119 are longer).[16] The Psalm opens with a profound personal statement, "I love you Lord" (18:2), expressed by using the root "rhm" (רחם), which is clearly a very suggestive personal term of intimacy. Perhaps the phrase: ארחמך יהוה would be better translated as, "Lord, you are my love."[17] After that comes an unusual series of "my" expressions verbalizing deeply personal devotion:

> LORD, my rock, my fortress, my deliverer, My God, my rock
> of refuge, my shield, my saving horn, my stronghold! . . . The
> LORD lives! Blessed be my rock! Exalted be God, my savior!
> (Ps 18:3, 47)

This personal, even intimate declaration of piety is conveyed by a progression in *anthropological* terms, particularly referring to the internal organs, intestines and digestive system. On the other hand, powerful *anthropopathic* expressions convey YHWH's personal and intimate allegiance to *Ephraim* his "dear son." The biblical poet declares that it arises in the divine intestines; "'Is Ephraim my dear son? Is he my darling child? For as often as I speak against him, I do remember him still. Therefore my heart yearns for him; I will surely have mercy on him,' says the LORD." (Jer 31:20 RSV). Although

---

15. Compare, Mowinckel, *Psalms in Israel's Worship*, 1:44.
16. Ps 18 is almost identical to 2 Sam 22.
17. The root רחם means *deep love, mercy, womb*.

the translators here, no doubt for the stylistic reasons, speak about the "heart," we have here in the text the "innards" and "womb" (mercy).

It is YHWH's bowels (מעה) which are in tumult here. Eugene Peterson (The Message) translates verse 20c as "Everything in me cries out for him" (המו מעי לו). God's merciful action to come and his yearning for Ephraim are expressed using the root רחם (womb), and another strongly anthropopathic expression, רחם ארחמנו ("I will surely have mercy on him"). Unfortunately, most translators ignore the vital difference between the heart and intestines, as used by the biblical poet, so most frequently the entire array of internal organs is simply translated as the heart. This is not only an injustice to the writer, but surely weakens the intimation of the original text.

CHAPTER 13

Realms of Privacy

Very personal expressions may incorporate or relate to statements concerning piety in privacy. We shall examine three biblical aspects of piety in privacy, that of: *spatial, temporal* and *anthropological* dimensions. In many Psalms, all three aspects of piety in privacy may appear (for example, Pss 77 and 88). Or, in an example from Psalm 25, "My eyes are ever toward the LORD, for he will pluck my feet out of the net," (25:15 RSV) the psalmist's continual confidence in God is expressed in anthropological (*eyes*) and temporal (*always*) terms.

The *spatial* dimension is concerned with the fact that it is not strictly *localized* (the temple) as might be expected. From this, the *temporal* outlook emerges, that is, the duration of the psalmist's personal and private devotion and the fact that it is not bound to a place or is limited by time. Finally, the *anthropological* aspect shows that expressions of piety are linked to tangible, bodily concepts, expressed by gestures and movement, and/or indicative of psychosomatic phenomena.

13.1 Anthropological Dimensions

Anthropology and anatomical idioms shed a particular light on the nature of the psalmist's personal and private, religious and emotional experience. A careful examination of the texts shows that his physical condition also changes.[1] What makes for more intricacy is the variety of homonymous

---

1. We shall examine aspects of psychobiology and physiology as related to the psalmist's emotional condition. Some commentators, who have addressed those issues, ought to be noted: Collins, "Physiology of Tears," Gruber, "Many Faces of Hebrew," Driver, "Some Hebrew," Boyle, "Law of Heart," and Kruger, "Cognitive Interpretation." Noteworthy contribution is published

anatomical idioms,[2] as it has already been mentioned in the case of *belly* (בטן). It has been frequently suggested that the use of anthropological and anatomical terms in biblical poetic texts are mere literary devices used as *synecdoche*. That is to say, any single part of the human body or anatomy can represent the whole person, the "self."[3]

This may be true for some more frequently used anthropological and anatomical terms but not for all. For example, the use of נפש (neck, soul) or ראש (head), even עצם (bones) may be synecdoche for a whole person. In Psalm 6, the psalmist declares, "my bones are troubled," meaning, "I am troubled." Nonetheless, there are texts where body parts cannot be considered as synecdoche, and simply as literary devices, but rather expressions denoting an emotional or physical state. We find an apt example in Psalm 22, where the psalmist describes his sufferings and anxieties.

> I am poured out like water, and all my bones are out of joint; my heart is like wax; it is melted within my breast; my mouth is dried up like a potsherd, and my tongue sticks to my jaws; you lay me in the dust of death. (Ps 22:14–15 NRSV)

Commenting on the expressions, Artur Weiser suggests that we should assume "various phrases are mere figures of speech."[4] Though he immediately concludes that the psalmist means that his limbs, actually his body "fails him."[5] It is surely unconventional that a phrase be both a figure (of speech) and an objective description of a physical state all at the same time.

Other authors like Mayer Gruber focus on the issue of anatomical idioms in biblical texts and successfully demonstrates that their use is not only a

---

PhD dissertation (2014) by Angela Thomas where she examines anatomical idioms and related emotional expressions in biblical texts.

2. Gruber, "Many Faces of Hebrew," 252.

3. Synecdoche, as a figure of speech is a kind of metonymy. That is to say that a part denotes and represents a whole. For example, in biblical texts the "soul" (נפש), as a "part" of a human being, denotes a whole "person." While metaphors operate on the basis of *similarity* ("love is strong as death," Sol 8:6) (metaphor), synecdoche is a matter of *association* ("sing aloud, O daughter of Zion, shout, O Israel," Zeph 3:14) (synecdoche); in the latter case, Zion being an association for the whole of Israel.

4. Weiser, *Psalms*, 223.

5. Weiser, 223.

matter of conventionalized poetic literary forms or figures of speech.[6] In their arguments, they successfully attest to the psychosomatic and physiological conditions of the psalmist. We can say that the psalmodic use of body parts and anatomy often go beyond poetic erudition, conventions and literary embellishment. At times it can be a prop to literary style, but it also reveals the vigour of the psalmist's experience in terms of psychobiology.[7] His internal organs, particularly the abdominal organs, like stomach, kidneys, liver, bowels or womb become extraordinary instruments of religious expression and no doubt, a superb source of insight into his emotional predicaments.

The juxtaposition of body parts, which often come in pairs within a single verse, is not unusual in the Psalter. The reason behind such pairings lies in literary patterns, particularly in respect of the rules of *parallelisms*, which undoubtedly is the cornerstone of Hebrew poetry. Following the initial work of the Anglican bishop Robert Lowth (1710–87), numerous studies of Hebrew poetic and psalmodic parallelism have been produced.[8] Harshav introduces a prosodic system which he calls *semantic-syntactic parallelism*. Fundamentally, it is the building up of *semantic momentum* based on development from the more general to the specific, accompanied by mounting suspense. For example:

Be gracious to me, O LORD, for I am languishing (אמל);

O LORD, heal me, for my bones are troubled. (Ps 6:2 (3) RSV)

The first line is a general plea (*have mercy!*) while the second line is physically specific (*heal me!*). It would be a mistake to think that the poet is merely repeating the same thing in different words, or stringing together

---

6. Gruber, "The Tragedy of Cain and Abel"; Gruber, *Aspects of Nonverbal Communication*; Gruber, "The Many Faces of Hebrew"; Gruber, "Hebrew 'Daabon Nepeš.'"

7. There is communal biblical anthropology articulating the experience(s) of Israel as a living corporate personality. In that respect "I" and "we" may alternate within the same psalm. However, in a great number of texts, the reference is clearly to the individual and his anatomy, and cannot be mistaken for the collective anthropological sayings or figuration.

8. The contributions of Robert Alter and Benjamin Hrushovski (Harshav) in modern times, building upon Lowth, on the subject are particularly worth noting. Since the investigation of Hebrew poetic parallelism has been an insistence on looking for rhyme or regularity of meter, Robert Alter suggested that this insistetnce might be misguided. Harshav's approach brought a fresh impetus to studies in Hebrew poetry and parallelisms. Both Alter and Harshav contributed greatly in emphasizing that there is more dynamic aspect, beyond the structural one, to the psalmodic poetry. See further: Alter, *Book of Psalms*; Harshav, *Prosody, Hebrew*.

psalmodic cliches and formulas.⁹ Martin Noth is right in alerting us that the study of forms (*Formgeschichte*) should not become *formula criticism* (*Formelgeschichte*). Robert Alter also rightly comments, saying, that there is more to it than stereotypical language:

> Although some psalms are laden with stereotypical language in which both the parallelism within the line and the poem as a whole are relatively static, the strong forward thrust in many of these lines of poetry as well as from line to line means that this is by and large a highly dynamic poetic system in which ideas and images are progressively pushed to extremes and themes brought to a crisis and a turning point.¹⁰

Alter and Harshav's explanations of the concept of semantic-syntactic parallelism is a great contribution to a better understanding of the anthropological dimension in the Psalter. Particularly in pointing out and in highlighting the place of anthropological pairings. For example, such anthropological pairings will include pairs like

1. heart-face: "my heart says, 'seek his face!' Your face, LORD, do I seek" (Ps 27:8 NRSV)
2. heart-soul: "my heart is glad, and my soul rejoices" (Ps 16:9 NRSV)
3. heart-eyes: "rejoicing the heart; the commandment of the LORD is clear, enlightening the eyes" (Ps 19:8 NRSV)[11]
4. hands-feet: "the works of your hands; you have put all things under their feet" (Ps 8:6 NRSV)
5. eyes-hands: "my eye grows dim through sorrow . . . I spread out my hands to you" (Ps 88:10 NRSV).

In these pairings and in the light of semantic-syntactic parallelism, it is fascinating to observe the pairing of human anthropology with divine anthropomorphism and anthropopathism.¹² There is frequent anthropomorphic

---

9. Alter, *Book of Psalms*, XXII–XXIII.
10. Alter, XXIV.
11. See Psalm 19:3, 38:11, 73:7.
12. Anthropopathism, in biblical texts, a frequent manifestation of human emotions and feelings, is attributed to a divine subject.

and anthropopathic pairings, particularly in biblical poetic parallelisms. We often find human and divine intents or yearnings paralleled; as in Psalm 27: "My heart says, seek his face" (Ps 27:8). In Psalm 10, the pairing is the human *heart* and the divine *eyes* (face), the psalmist thinks "in his heart, 'God has forgotten, he has hidden his face, he will never see it'" (Ps 10:11 RSV). How is it that the psalmist commends his *spirit* and his life into God's *hands* (Ps 31:5)? How does this pair: *hands-spirit*, perform?

The Genesis flood narrative is another case in which hearts, divine and human, and God's eyes are paralleled. God was deeply grieved (עצב) in his heart, even regretted (נחם) that he created man, when he saw what prevailed in human hearts (Gen 6:6).[13] In all this, gestures (hands, eyes, face) is another important aspect in the non-verbal communication of the psalmist's piety, through which a diverse range of religious and emotional experiences are expressed.

13.2 Location

A number of psalmodic passages show that the devotee's piety is not undividedly attached to the public place of worship or collective self-identification. His piety in solitude is clear in the texts. It can be exercised in one's house, and for the pious psalmist, in the privacy of his bed. The latter often being not only the deepest experiences but often a traumatic sleepless night with laments. Then "enter your chambers and shut your doors behind you; hide yourselves for a little while until the wrath is passed." (Isa 26:20 NRSV) It will be a frightful time of hiding.[14]

13.3 Privacy and Prayer

The demarcation between religious experience – which is *personal* and that which is *private* – has already been examined. The former clearly incorporates

---

13. The description of the divine-human relationship preceding the deluge in Gen 6 is intriguing. There the human and divine hearts are intertwined, "The LORD saw that the wickedness of man was great in the earth, and that every imagination of the thoughts of his heart was only evil continually. And the LORD was sorry that he had made man on the earth, and it grieved him to his heart" (Gen 6:5–6).

14. Cf. Matt 24:26; Luke 12:3.

manifestations of public and institutional religion. The latter is assigned to the pious man and the privacy of his solitude (see here: "Solitude Narratives"). However, an additional note on this section is desirable. In *The Varieties of Religious Experience,* William James, fundamentally following the dichotomy between the *numen locale* and *numen personale* of religious typology, expounds on external religion and internal experience:

> At the outset, we are struck by one great partition which divides the religious field. On the one side of it lies institutional, on the other personal religion. As M. P. Sabatier says, one branch of religion keeps the divinity, another keeps man most in view. Worship and sacrifice, procedures for working on the dispositions of the deity, theology and ceremony and ecclesiastical organization, are the essentials of religion in the institutional branch. Were we to limit our view to it, we should have to define religion as an external art, the art of winning the favour of the gods. In the more personal branch of religion, it is on the contrary the inner dispositions of man himself which form the centre of interest, his conscience, his deserts, his helplessness, his incompleteness.[15]

The internalization of the devotee's faith and private manifestations result in deeply intimate personal experiences. In the Psalter, it most probably has a basis in real events. The text shows that some kind of change has happened, with the concomitant emotional reaction to the event(s). As for the structure of these emotions, this will also have to be examined. Who or what were the agents that caused the affective reactions of the psalmist? Were some of these perhaps only construals about the things that happened? We can only guess.

In all this, the individual transacts religious "business" by himself. The relationship between him and God is conducted personally and privately in solitude, between the devotee and his God, from heart to heart, and from soul to soul. How the psalmist's solitude and private religious experience are forcefully manifested in many aspects and texts within the Psalter will be shown. Yet, his personal piety in solitude is not dissonant with public worship. The connections can easily be established and are beyond any reasonable doubt.

---

15. James, "Varieties," 36.

On the other hand, whether there were any devotional books for the pious laity to use at home, beyond the cultic public worship service, is another matter. There are suggestions that there was a peculiar collection of "spiritual, cult-free psalms" in circulation, strictly for personal and private use. Though the privacy of the psalmist's personal piety is beyond any reasonable doubt, the alleged existence of a personal prayer book is a highly unlikely, speculative interpretation.[16]

13.4 Ritual Acts and Private Piety

It has already been highlighted that public worship and ritual acts do not preclude the personal and private piety of the devotee. In fact, it is precisely the individual's personal and private piety that gives meaning to ritual acts of worship,[17] just as personal or individualistic piety cannot dispense with ritual acts. The two are complementary. H. H. Rowley notes well that "where the ritual act was prescribed, sincerity of penitence could not dispense with it. Neither could the act dispense with the spirit."[18] The prophets noted more than once that ritual acts which did not involve the heart and action were futile. When the people "delight to draw near to God," but their hearts are not in tune with their rituals, their worship becomes hateful to God.[19]

> Because this people draw near with their mouth and honour me with their lips, while their hearts are far from me, and their fear of me is a commandment of men learned by rote. Therefore, behold, I will again do marvelous things with this people, wonderful and marvelous; and the wisdom of their wise men shall perish, and the discernment of their discerning men shall be hid. (Isa 29:13–14 RSV)

The prophets continually confronted such dichotomous situations, where the visible (acts of worship) was in dissonance with the invisible (personal

---

16. Gunkel suggests that a number of psalms which, according to him, have no place in any tradition within the Psalter, are probably a compilation "with the intention of creating a devotional and home book for the pious laity." Gunkel, *Introduction to Psalms*, 346.

17. See "The Psalmist and His Prayer."

18. Rowley, *Worship in Ancient Israel*, 246.

19. Isa 58:2, קרבת אלהים יחפצון "They delight to draw near to God" (see also Ps 73:28).

piety). We are back in the sphere of religious typology and its constant tensions between the *personal* and *localized* God. Superficial religiosity cannot "localize" God's freedom (2 Sam 7:5–7). The false reliance of the *numen locale* type of institutionalized religion, without the full integrity of the faithful, carries no warranty of divine presence, therefore they are to,

> Amend your ways and your doings, and I will let you dwell in this place. Do not trust in these deceptive words: "This is the temple of the LORD, the temple of the LORD, the temple of the LORD." (Jer 7:3–4 RSV)

The holy ground of the temple was considered to be sufficient guarantee for security. It is a peculiar type of extortion. The implication is that since the temple is so important to God, he would be obliged to assure them safety.

Probably the most cynical, even sarcastic prophet who addressed this issue was Amos. Of course he did not refute the need to approach God. This is evident in his frequent use of the verbs "to draw near" (that is, "in the midst") (קרב) and "to seek" (דרש). The prophet's criticism of ritual acts of worship divested of the "heart" content is unique and at times, scathing. He calls their songs mere "screaming" (המה) (Amos 5:23), while their festivals and feasts are "hateful" (שנא) to YHWH (Amos 5:21).[20] It has been already noted that psalmodic piety cannot be fully grasped apart from Hebrew anthropology of the individual which places the human heart and innards at the centre of events. In terms of religious typology, Judaic religion should be viewed primarily as a "religion of the heart of flesh," whereas the institutional aspect is in service of personal piety. The heart here is more than the seat of decision-making; and this is why the texts so frequently call upon a "clean" and "fleshy" heart.[21] The more discerning religious leaders of Israel were fully aware that "it was the spirit that gave meaning to the act and that the spirit was more important than the act."[22]

---

20. Similarly in Isaiah (1:11–15).

21. In its psychophysiology, the heart in Hebrew anthropology is more than merely a physical organ. Its metaphorical use is marked by comprehension and emotive response. Particularly suggestive is the phrase the "heart of God" which clearly indicates God's relationship with man (Gen 6:6; 1 Sam 2:35), just as the "heart of man" indicates his personal relationship with God. Wolff, *Anthropology of Old Testament* 44, 55.

22. Rowley, 246.

Yet there are reservations, even resistance towards allowing the psalmist to exercise his piety in private prayer. The proposition against private piety has been argued on several grounds. Some will argue that the cult/liturgy was sufficiently dynamic in itself, so that taking refuge in private prayer was not really needed. Walther Eichrodt, argues against private piety on the basis of the vigour of the official cult: "Because the official cult is not dominated by lifeless formal trumpery and degrading incantations, there is no need for a real and living piety to take refuge in private prayer."[23] He then declares that there is no disparity between the prayer of the cultus and the prayer of the private individual, allowing for the private piety of a worshipper. He also suggests that the prophets' assault on the formalism of the cultic practices "resulted in the introduction of the true spirit of prayer" (Isa 1:15; 29:13; Amos 5:23).[24]

Prayer (personal or corporate) is the very essence of any religion, building a highway for the "traffic" between a believing individual and their God. William James summarizes prayer as "religion in act," also saying that "prayer is real religion." He continues by confirming that real prayer is not a formal religious exercise or procedural technique.[25] In James's words, prayer is

> no vain exercise of words, no mere repetition of certain sacred formula, but the very movement itself of the soul, putting itself in a personal relation of contact with the mysterious power of which it feels the presence.[26]

In direct contrast to what is advocated by Williams, others will view prayer in a more speculative manner. A good example is that of H. H. Rowley. He proposes that prayer can be thought of as,

> a technique for imposing one's will on God, or for extracting something from him. It may be merely the expression of one's selfish desires. There is nothing very exalted in this, and if the prayers of the Psalter were no more than this, there would be

---

23. Eichrodt, *Theology of the Old Testament*, 175.

24. Eichrodt, 174–76.

25. William James (*The Varieties of Religious Experience*, New York, 1936) in his 19th, penultimate lecture, focuses on the act of prayer as the essence, and the relationships between prayer, religion and the worshipper.

26. James, *Varieties of Religious Experience*, Lecture XIX.

nothing rewarding in the effort to understand the spirit with which they sought to infuse worship.[27]

However, the psalmist's prayers are highly emotionally charged, as might be expected, since religion and emotions are closely intertwined.[28] The underlying emotional structure of the psalmist's religious experience ranges widely, even within the same Psalm, from *confidence* and *thanksgiving* (for example, Pss 16, 23, 27) to *complaint* and *desperation* (for example, Pss 6, 7, 38), or simply general disorientation.[29]

---

27. Rowley, *Worship in Ancient Israel*, 250–51.

28. Hans Schilderman, "Religion and Emotion," 85–96.

29. According to the traditional classification of the psalms, following Gunkel's categorization (Gattungen), as well as Westermann's evaluations, the lament psalms are not only present in most of the Psalter, but shape a fundamental design of the entire Psalter. Gunkel reckons that, "The individual complaint songs form the basic material of the Psalter." Gunkel, *Introduction to the Psalms*, par. 6/2, 122.

With regard to the psalmist's oscillations, Walter Brueggemann uses a scheme: *orientation – disorientation – reorientation*. Brueggemann, *Message of Psalms*. He also explicitly states that his work addresses "the pastoral use of the Psalms"; though his analysis certainly has a theological application. This can be seen in his "attempt to be 'postcritical.'" Brueggemann also states that he does follow Gunkel's form analysis, but "have also tried to pay attention to the emerging methods of sociological and rhetorical analysis that are latent in Gunkel's work but only now coming to full attention." Brueggemann, 9–10.

CHAPTER 14

The Temporal Aspect

The psalmist's personal, private piety is enhanced by several temporal designations – *always, day and night, all the days.* Some of these may denote the constancy of cultic duties, in reference to communal and public temple practices. They may also refer to his own desires, as in Psalm 27: "One thing I ask of the LORD; this I seek: to dwell in the LORD's house all the days of my life" (27:4). If taken literally, for a layman this prayer was unrealistic and impossible to accomplish.[1] It is more than unlikely that the lasting nearness of God alludes to dwelling permanently in the temple.[2] Rather, it is referring to the permanent presence of the Lord with the psalmist as an individual in his privacy. Though the pious man "offers in his tabernacle sacrifices with trumpet-sound" (27:6), his piety is not fully conditional on public worship. Even if he would attend temple worship, on the daily basis, it will not account for what happens in the middle of the night, as he continues to feel the divine presence, as in his rationale it says, even in the night "my heart instruct me"(Ps 16:7b RSV).

> By day the LORD commands his steadfast love,
> and at night his song is with me,
> a prayer to the God of my life. (Ps 42:8 RSV)

Indeed, the night seems to be reserved for privacy and private piety. It is the time when the psalmist prays and praises God.

---

1. Weiser, *Psalms*, 231.
2. Weiser, 231.

14.1 Always

14.1.1 Always (תמיד)

The psalmist continually concentrates his thoughts on God without being restricted by place or time. His contemplation of God is day and night, and even at night God dictates his desires (Ps 16:7).[3] He calls out by day or by night (Ps 22:3), his praises are always on his lips (Ps 34:2). The psalmist seems to be in a prayerful mood and always hopeful even in the middle of the night (Ps 71:14).

Of all the Old Testament occurrences of the adjective תמיד (always), approximately one third appear in the Psalter. This occurrence is almost exclusively in the context of the nearness and reliability of God.[4] And although the psalmist is exhausted by his pain (כאב) and sin (חטט), which is *always* before him (Ps 38:18; Ps 51:5), yet in the majority of cases the adjective תמיד (always) is used in the context of the psalmist's unequivocal confidence. He personally and privately seeks God's face continually (Ps 105:4) and urges others to do the same (Ps 40:17): "But may all who seek you rejoice and be glad in you; may those who love your salvation say continually, 'Great is the LORD!'" (Ps 40:16 NRSV).

14.1.2 Always (עולם)

Another biblical term regarding duration and temporality or futurity is the polysemous עולם.[5] Its primary meaning signifies perpetuity, often in reference to the *everlasting* or ancient past as "days of old" (כל ימי עולם, Isa 63:9), which is also found and translated as the "world" (Eccl 3:11).[6] Clearly, עולם (*olam*) has eschatological overtones (Pss 21:5; 61:8; Eccl 1:4).[7] The majority of appearances of this term either refer to the eternal nature of God who is

---

3. "Even during the night he dictates my desires" (Ps 16:7). Terrien, *Psalms*.

4. Koehler counts 103 appearances of the same adjective. Koehler and Baumgartner, *Lexicon*, 1031.

5. Jenni, *Das Wort*, 761–62.

6. "He hath made every thing beautiful in its time; also He hath set the world in their heart" (Eccl 3:11 JPS).

7. For example, in the royal Psalm (Ps 21) referring to the relationship between the Messianic king and YHWH; Dahood translates, "Life eternal he asked of you, you gave it to him. Length of days, eternity, and everlasting" (ארך ימים עולם ועד) (Ps 21:5). The word עולם would be also used in the blessing/greeting for a king, "Let the king live for ever" (Neh 2:3; Dan 2:4). Jenni, *Das Wort*, 5

אל עולם, the "Everlasting" (cf. Gen 21:33, etc.), or as in the book of Daniel, the "Ancient of Days" (Dan 7:9, 13, 22) who abides in the "mythical distance" or in reference to the messianic king (cf. 1 Kgs 1:31; Ps 21:5); and it seems that it is not used in the personal piety context.[8]

14.1.3 Psalm 16

The adverb *tamid* (always) frequently presents "the impression made on him (the psalmist) by God's presence."[9] Psalm 16, along with Pss 23 and 27, are illustrations of piety which exemplifies personal devotion and private piety. Psalm 16 is riddled with difficulties in terms of structure, content and context, all of which have been variously interpreted.[10] However, it is of primary interest in relation to this work to follow the personal, private devotion of the worshipper.

> I will bless the LORD, who has given me counsel;
> yea, in the night seasons my reins (כליה) instruct me.
> I have set the LORD always before me;
> surely He is at my right hand (ימין), I shall not be moved.
> Therefore my heart (לב) is glad, and my glory (כבוד) rejoiceth;
> my flesh also dwelleth in safety (16:7–9). (JPS)[11]

The poet clearly wishes to accentuate the nature of privacy and intimacy of his experience. Though most translations render "the heart" that directs instruction in verse 7b, the original text has "kidneys" (כליה). Translators often needlessly render "the kidneys" with the more general term "heart." Whether this is literary convention, convenience or for stylistic reasons, equating the heart with the internal organs diminishes the original author's intent and the intensity of his deep-seated experiences. It is these (lower body) parts which

---

8. Pope, *El in Ugaritic Texts*, 73.

9. Weiser, *Psalms*, 176. See Pss 16:8; 25:15; 34:2; 38:18; 40:17; 51:5; 70:5; 71:3, 6, 14; 73:23; 105:4; 109:15 (always).

10. The somewhat dubious proposition is that it was written by a Canaanite convert to Yahwism. Dahood, *Psalms*, I, 87. Others suggest that its "spiritual" content is only due to God's presence in the temple. Weiser, *Psalms*, 173.

11. In the extraordinary and widely recognized translation of the Old Testament by Andre Chouraqui, this passage reads, "Je bénis IHVH-Adonaï qui me conseille. Même les nuits, mes reins me corrigent. Je situe IHVH-Adonaï contre moi toujours; oui, à ma droite, je ne chancellerai jamais. Aussi, mon coeur se réjouit, ma gloire s'égaye; même ma chair demeure en sécurité."

express the depth of human personality more profoundly than the preferred term in Hebrew anthropology, the "heart." For the biblical poet, the internal organs reflect the "obscure instincts of human personality,"[12] and actually become the objects of the divine searcher and creator (Ps 139:13; Jer 11:20).[13] In Psalm 16, Robert Alter translates "kidneys" as "conscience," as: "I shall bless the Lord Who gave me counsel, through the nights that my conscience would lash me" (Ps 16:7a).[14]

Alter, also and correctly, comments that the Hebrews primarily thought of kidneys as the seat of conscience, this being in common with other peoples of the ancient Near East.[15] Ergo, the *heart* and *innards* may only be just partially synonymous in the biblical texts. The distinction is even clearer in connection with sacrificial regulations. The kidneys (and liver), not the heart, were special parts of the sacrificial animal and had to be burned on the altar (Exod 29:13; Lev 3:4). It is thought that this was due to the belief that the kidneys were particularly important centres of psychic life.[16] However, in Psalm 16:7a it is not quite clear who gives the psalmist counsel, his own *heart* (innards), or the Lord's (innards)? Most translators opt for the former. Others suggest the latter, for example, "I will praise YHWH who counsels me, and whose heart instructs me."[17] YHWH is the one who instructs the pious, even in the privacy of the night. Similarly, Terrien translates, "Even during the night he dictates my desires."[18]

On the other hand, the psalmist continually sets (שוה) the Lord before him (Ps 16:8). The previous line, "I bless the LORD who counsels me; even at night my heart exhorts me," (16:7) also shows his understanding that personal prayer is more than an act of cultic duty.[19] It means communion with

---

12. Terrien, *Psalms*, 178.
13. Here (Jer 11), most translations again give "heart" for "kidneys."
14. Alter, *Book of Psalms*, 46.
15. Alter, 46.
16. Dentan, "Kidneys," 9–10.
17. Dahood, *Psalms*, I, 86.
18. אף־לילות יסרוני כליותי (16:7a), here the verb is *vpp 3pl* that goes with the noun כליות which is *nf pl* with the 1st person suffix. Terrien argues here that by blessing the Lord there will be divine remuneration, for which the psalmist shows his gratitude. Cf. Terrien, *Psalms*, 174–78.
19. The verb שוח indicates the psalmist's deliberation, a proactive action, rather than a religious fortuity, or mere chance. The verb has two distinct meanings: the *shawa* (I)=level, become like, compare (Isa 40:25) and *shawa* (II)=set, place (Ps 16:8). There are suggestions that etymologically the verb is a form of haya. Labuschagne, *Incomparability of Yahweh*, 29.

God; a personal and private dialogue, face to face. Thus, his *eyes* are *always* turned towards the Lord "My eyes are ever toward the LORD" (25:15 RSV), and praise is always in his *mouth* (34:1).[20] Even at the public worship services, the gathered people are exhorted, beyond their participation in the cultic ceremony, to "seek his presence continually" (Ps 105:4 RSV).[21] Is this an encouragement to constancy and regularity in the worshippers' cultic duties, or is it also a stimulation for personal and private devotion? The personal dimensions, the anthropomorphic and anthropopathic elements of God's anatomy (face) clearly designate personal presence, a meeting face-to-face, with both individual and communal aspects. Further, it is in the realm of the individual as well as the community to "keep His statutes, and observe His laws" (105:45 RSV).

It is not always the presence of the Lord, prayer and praise that occupies the psalmist. He also seems to be burdened *always* by his *pain* (Ps 38:18) and *sins* (Ps 51:5), which are continually before him. This can also be understood as an aspect of his personal and private piety.

14.2 Day and Night

Another expression, time related, in reference to the psalmist's is: "day and night" (יומם ולילה).[22] The pious man seeks the Lord or cries to him, or meditates upon the Law "day and night" (Ps 1:2).[23] He also blesses "the LORD who counsels me; even at night my heart exhorts me" (Ps 16:7). Perhaps we can read here with Dahood, "whose heart instructs me." This would agree with a similar text in Psalm 33, "the thoughts of His heart" (33:11). The everlasting counsel of YHWH stands against the counsel of the nations, but for the psalmist, he counsels from the depth of his being, from his inward parts (*kidneys*).[24]

---

20. עיני תמיד אל-יהוה(Ps 25:15).

21. Literally, "seek his face constantly." Dahood, *Psalms 101–150*, 52.

22. יומם ולילה Cf. Pss 16:7; 22:3; 42:8; 77:3, 7; 88:1; 119:55 (day and night).

23. In the Qumran community it was decreed that, "There is not to be absent from them one who can interpret the Law to them at any time of day or night. The general members of the community are to keep awake for a third of all the nights of the year reading books, studying the Law and worshiping together." Cf. 1QS 6: 6–8.

24. Here (16:7), Dahood suggests amending "my heart instructs me" to "his kidneys" אף-לילות יסרוני כליותי. It would be clumsy to translate it as "whose kidneys instruct me." Dahood, *Psalms 1–50*, 90.

Old Testament texts abound with word pairs (heaven and earth, father and son, light and darkness). The word pair *day and night* commonly appears in the Psalter frequently in reference to God's creation (Gen 1:3–5). God the Creator,

> made the great lights, for his steadfast love endures forever; the sun to rule over the day, for his steadfast love endures forever; the moon and stars to rule over the night, for his steadfast love endures forever. (Ps 136:7–9 RSV)

One of the most familiar of the Psalms using the pair *day and night*, in declaring the Creator's powers is Psalm 19:

> The heavens are telling the glory of God; the firmament proclaims his handiwork.
> Day to day pours forth speech, and night to night declares knowledge.
> There is no speech, nor are there words; their voice is not heard;
> yet their voice goes out through all the earth,
> and their words to the end of the world.
> In the heavens he has set a tent for the sun. (Ps 19:2–5 RSV)

On the other hand, the pair *day and night* is human's common experience of the continual alteration between night and day. For the psalmist in his good days, he declares: "I will sing to the Lord as long as I live" (Ps 104:33). But then, when things are not so bright for him and he feels as if the darkness covers him,

> Surely the darkness shall cover me, and the light around me become night, even the darkness is not dark to you; the night is as bright as the day, for darkness is as light to you. (Ps 139:11–12 NRSV)

The day and night become his continual cry for help, with almost a template like pattern; he cries to God for help and there is no help coming, as if God does not want to hear him. In fact, as we shall see in Psalm 88, the psalmist in his prayer files an objection to God feeling abandoned, saying: "Why do You hide Your face from me"? (88:15) (transl.R. Alter). Distinctly, the psalmist expresses his disapointment in the well-known lament of Psalm 22: "I cry by day, but you do not answer; and by night, but find no rest" (Ps 22:2 NRSV).

14.2.1 Psalm 42

This Psalm, described by Dahood as the "dark night of the soul," sets the psalmist in the context of exile, surrounded by enemies, a situation which compels him to seek intimate communion with God "day and night":

> By day the LORD commands his steadfast love;
> and at night his song is with me,
> a prayer to the God of my life. (Ps 42:8 NRSV)

The expressions "day and night" or "by day" and "by night" are not only formulaic, poetic ways of saying "constantly"[25]; it is in the privacy of the night that the psalmist is able to worship and study (Pss 1; 42; 119), weep and soak his bed with tears (Ps 6:7), or even staying awake crying to God (Pss 22; 32; 42; 77; 88). This section is one of the finest examples of personal and private demonstration of the psalmist's religious experience, although somewhat ambivalent as well. Namely, it is either that the speaker (psalmist) hears God's song in his heart of hearts, or it is the psalmist being "mindful of God's kindness, responds in the night with song – such as the song of this psalm."[26] One way or the other, whether it be a "cosmic sound" of a song from above, or a personal response of the psalmist, it provides sufficient evidence that there must be a "psalmist" as an individual in his personal, and here, a very private religious experience.

14.2.2 Psalm 77

In the privacy of the night, there are periods of insomnia when he seeks the Lord with outstretched hands (Ps 77:2).

> In the day of my trouble I seek the Lord;
> in the night my hand is stretched (נגר) out without wearying;
> my soul refuses to be comforted (Ps 77:2 NRSV)

---

25. Dahood, *Psalms*, I, 259.
26. Alter, *Book of Psalms*, 150.

Alter translates for "in the night my hand is stretched out without wearying" (ידי לילה נגרה ולא תפוג) as "My eye flows at night, it will not stop."[27] This is based on the meaning of the verb נגר (pour down, flow, spill).[28] A very similar phrase is found in Lamentations 3:49, "My eyes will flow without ceasing" (עיני נגרה ולא תדמה). Here, JPS assumes that a word is missing (*eyes*) and offers the following solution: "In the day of my trouble I seek the Lord; with my hand uplifted, mine eye streameth in the night without ceasing" (77:2).

14.2.3 Psalm 88

This Psalm is one of "the darkest, gloomiest, of all the plaintive Psalms";[29] the psalmist is fearful and on the brink of death. His experience in this Psalm resounds as being in the near-death experience (88:5). The Psalm is also a fine example of personal piety exercised in the privacy of his home – struggling every day, and night and day. In his distress and dispirited dissapointment of God's absence of intervening to help him, the psalmist declares: "Every day I call on you, O LORD; I spread out my hands to you" (88:9 NRSV). The first thing he does in the morning is he calls upon God, "and in the morn my prayer would greet you" (קדם) (ובבקר תפלתי תקדמך) (88:13) (transl. R. Alter).

In his morning prayer, the psalmist expects and wishes to have an encounter with his God (88:14). But in this קדם of the תקדמך (meeting you) represents the psalmist's morning "going forth on a journey to meet Yahweh."[30] Unfortunately, it seems that God turns his back on him: "why do you cast me off? Why do you hide your face from me?" (88:14 NRSV). Although it seems to be a common practice to understand such texts as a collective declaration of affliction,[31] we cannot perceive why this cannot be a confession and an experience of the psalmist as an individual in his personality and individuality?

---

27. Alter, 268.
28. BDB, 620.
29. Delitzsch, *Psalms*, III, 23.
30. Briggs, *Critical and Exegetical*, 2: 247.
31. Briggs, 247.

14.3 All the Days

The expression "all the days" (כל ימי), clearly refers to all of one's life.[32] God's goodness and mercy will be with the psalmist throughout his life (Ps 23), and he declares his devotion in the desire and prayer to remain in God's presence throughout his earthly life (Ps 27). YHWH and his blessing will be upon those who fear the Lord (Ps 128).

14.3.1 Psalm 23

As we might expect, the psalmist's piety focuses on the lasting *protection* and *nearness* of God. He claims God's goodness all the days of his life (כל ימי חיי) and concludes that he will "dwell in the house of the LORD for ever"(לארך ימים) (Ps 23:6 RSV). Abundant, divine blessing will follow (ירדף) the psalmist (Ps 23:6a),[33] reaching its culmination as he arrives at his eternal rest (23:6b).

14.3.2 Psalm 27

The pious declares his deep desire to spend all of his life in the temple. As noted before, this should be taken literally. Here, the worshipper's craving for the continuous presence of God is expressed in particularly unambiguous language, as other psalmodic texts (Ps 18:1). Here, it is the "one thing" (27:4) he asks:

> One thing have I asked of the LORD, that will I seek after:
> that I may dwell in the house of the LORD all the days of my life.
> (Ps 27:4 RSV)[34]

The wording is unusual in biblical numerical sayings,[35] the "one thing have I asked of the LORD" (אחת שאלתי מאת יהוה), refers to his request to dwell in the house of the Lord for the rest of his life. This of course cannot be taken literally, as if he would permanently live in the temple court. This

---

32. (כל ימי) See: Pss 23:6; 27:4; 61:5; 63:3 (all the days).

33. Dahood translates here: "Surely goodness and kindness will attend me, all the days without end." Dahood, *Psalms*, I, 145.

34. Gunkel here translates: "to see YHWH's friendliness and to observe his temple." Gunkel, *Introduction to Psalms*, 127.

35. Craigie, *Psalms 1–50*, 232.

refers to his wish to live in the presence of God always (see here on: *numen locale* and *numen personale*).[36]

However, the contexts of Psalm 27 and Psalm 73 may be different. One describes an external threat (27), while the other is about envy (73). Both resolutely retract to personal and private devotion and pleas for the presence of God. Some commentators believe that these are not necessarily spiritual cravings, but rather the result of awe-inspiring impressions made by temple worship while others recognize no relationship to the worship service.[37] However, there are suggestions that "the house of the LORD" in Psalm 27:4 does not refer to the temple but to eternal rest in the celestial abode. So, Dahood prefers here to interpret it as of eternal rest and happiness, "after a peaceful life under the guidance and protection of Yahweh"[38] (Ps 29:10 as God's celestial habitation; especially Ps 27:4).

Other commentators, like Craigie, give a stimulating interpretation of this text. Craigie places it in a royal-military context. Namely, it is the sovereign, the king, before departing to a battle, who will approach a divine presence and inquire in the temple about the outcomes of the forthcoming battle. In fact, a special temple liturgy for such occasion may have taken place with a sacrificial act, with the sovereign taking a major part in it.[39]

After we examined different aspects of the psalmist's personal and private religious experiences; the realms of privacy (Chapters 11–12) and the temporal aspects of the psalmist experience (Chapter 13), we will now look into one crucial element of our study, that of personal anthropology which is also one of the fundamental assertions of this thesis.

---

36. There is a similar affirmation in Ps 73. There, the ultimate wish of the psalmist is to be in "the nearness of God" (73:25–26).

37. Gunkel, *Introduction to Psalms*, 346. "The privilege of enjoying God's presence in the Jerusalem sanctuary is a consequence of having followed the ways that God dictates to man. And the temple itself, within the walled city, is repeatedly seen as a sanctuary in the political sense – a place of secure refuge from threatening foes." Alter, *Book of Psalms*, 92.

38. Dahood, *Psalms*, I, 148–49.

39. Craigie, *Psalms 1–50*, 232.

CHAPTER 15

Anthropology

15.1 Four Domains of Anthropology

For a better perspective and more concise presentation of the anthropological dimension in reference to the psalmist's piety, we shall identify four areas of human anatomy, the *limbs*, the *abdomen*, the *head* and the *chest*.

First is the area to do with *limbs* (hands, feet, legs). Of course, this involves motion vocabulary (verbs of motion).[1] Next comes the abdominal region (kidneys, liver, womb, bowels and belly), where deep-seated emotions, often negative, are portrayed. Third is the area of the *chest* (heart, lungs). Israelite anthropology has predominantly been researched in relation to the heart, perhaps unjustifiably so in relation to other parts of the human anatomy. So we shall not go into an in-depth study of the heart. Finally, the fourth area is that of the *head* (eyes, ears, mouth, nose). We will not attempt to deal in detail with all of these. The view that any one part of the human anatomy in the biblical context may be taken as a synecdoche, whereby one part denotes the whole, representing the whole self (person) or body is true up to a point.[2] We find an illustration of desperation in defeat in Psalm 44,[3] as in: "our soul (נפש) is bowed down to the dust; our belly (בטן) cleaves to the ground"

---

1. Verbs of motion are not exclusive to the limbs, hands, feet or legs; this grammatical aspect of the texts is also present in other aspects of anthropology and anatomy (heart, soul), particularly in presenting the emotional condition of the psalmist.

2. Johnson, *The Vitality*, 73.

3. The context and the dating of Ps 44 is sometimes set in the Maccabean revolts and battles. See, Weiser, *Psalms*, 354.

(Ps 44:25).[4] Most modern (English) translations render "belly" as "body" (RSV, NAB, ASV). Older English translations correctly render belly" (KJV, GNV). The Jewish Publication Society (JPS) has it as: "For our soul is bowed down to the dust; our belly cleaveth unto the earth" (44:25).

In profound emotional disturbances, parts of the body should not readily be rendered as synecdoche. There are frequent indications that emotional or spiritual distress gives rise to physical and psychosomatic changes, particularly to the digestive tract and abdominal organs. So synecdoche is not always a viable option, nor should synonimity be assumed between various parts of the anatomy.

15.2 Biblical Gastroenterology

As we set about tackling the issues of the personal and the private, in the Psalter, questions of anthropology cannot be put aside. A peculiar aspect of anthropology will crop up – that of the abdominal domain and the gastric area of human anthropology, as we find it in the Psalter. The importance of anthropological features in relation to the internal body parts, particularly the abdominal region, in the Psalms seems to be quite prominent, yet quite unfairly neglected.

Aubrey Johnson endorses that "by far the most important organ is the heart"[5] and Hans Walter Wolff notes that the most important word in Old Testament anthropology is "generally translated 'heart.'"[6] This, one wishes to believe, is not just a passing remark, although Wolff does not seem to expand on this major issue of the Psalter anthropology. That is to say that in many Old Testament translations, we find abdominal organs rendered as "heart."

The prime example of false synonymy can be found in many biblical translations where a translator will make a synonymy between the gastric organs and the heart. An example, outside the Psalter, can be found in Solomon's Song of Songs. There the feeling of love and the emotions were stirred in the guts, not the heart! Most translations will render the מעה (guts, bowels) as

---

4. כי שחה לעפר נפשנו דבקה לארץ בטננו
5. Johnson, *The Vitality*, 75.
6. Wolff, *Anthropology of Old Testament*, 40.

"heart." For example, "My beloved put in his hand by the hole of the door, and my heart was moved for him" (Song 5:4) (JPS, NAB, RSV). It should read:

> My beloved put in his hand by the hole of the door,
> and my bowels (מעה) were moved for him
> (דודי שלח ידו מן החר ומעי המו עליו) (Song 5:4)

Making the abdominal organs in translations synonymous with the heart is frequent, which not only impairs the integrity of the original text for stylistic reasons, but it also corrupts the context and the message of the original biblical author. This is particularly true in relation to expressions of intimate personal and private emotions, such as love or anger, or general emotional disturbance. Most often, the occurrence of such abdominal vocabulary in the original text, appears within intensely private contexts. The role and importance of other body parts, apart from the heart, in Hebrew anthropology, need to be recognized, particularly the abdominal organs (kidneys, liver). The intestines (innards) in biblical anthropology require more extensive treatment. It is important that we ask why these parts of anatomy are so obviously important in Israelite piety?[7] The reasons surely run deeper than a mere poetic embellishment.

15.2.1 Intestines and Religion

From its very beginnings, the history of religion and medicine devoted particular attention to the organs of the abdomen. A number of ancient documents testify to advanced medical practices of the time. Dissections and autopsies were common. For example, some excerpts from the Ebers Papyrus reveal interesting diagnostics relating to the abdominal organs, and also certain psychosomatic aspects of human life and health.[8] Moreover, the abdominal parts of animal anatomy played an important role in religious practices, sacrificial systems and divination.

In divination, these organs were crucial to decision making. During invasive campaigns, the king of Babylon had to decide where to go next, and consulted the abdominal organs of a sacrificial animal: "The king of Babylon stands at the parting of the way, at the head of the two ways, to use

---

7. Smith, "Heart and Innards," 430.
8. Smith, 430, fn. 14. Cf. Ghalioungui, Paul. *The Ebers Papyrus.*

divination; he shakes the arrows, he consults the teraphim, he looks at the liver" (ראה בכבד) (Ezek 21:21 RSV). Apart from this necromancy practice, widely endowed, the human intestines clearly refer beyond personal emotions; it is also referential to conscience and integrity of a person. In Psalm 26, the psalmist demands that his heart (לב) and his kidneys (כליה) be tested: "Examine me, O LORD, and try me; test my reins (כליה) and my heart" (Ps 26:2 JPS).[9]

15.2.2 Stomach, Womb and Guts

15.2.2.1 *Stomach and womb*

The central part of the lower abdomen is the belly (בטן), or stomach, which is obviously linked to the digestive tract and acts as a food processing centre. "The righteous has enough to satisfy his appetite, but the belly (בטן) of the wicked suffers want" (Prov 13:25). In a powerful metaphor, the prophet Ezekiel was given an unusual item to eat and digest.

> Son of man, cause thy belly to eat (בטנך תאכל),
> fill thy bowels (ומעיך תמלא) with this scroll that I give thee.
> (Ezek 3:3 JPS)

This suggests that as it enters his body, the prophet will have the most intimate, personal and private experience of the word given to him. It will become part of him. Much of the prophet's account is characterized by events involving bodily experiences,[10] and in that, he has much in common with the psalmist. Almost as a parallel it echoes Psalm 17, where the psalmist acknowledges the needs of the belly (for food), but declares that it is only communion with God in his heart that will satisfy his hunger:

> From men, by Your hand, O LORD, from people of the world,
> whose portion is in this life, and whose belly You fill (תמלא בטנם)

---

9. The expression for "remorse of conscience" in modern Hebrew, the מוסר כליות (musar kaliyot) (literally "contrition of the kidneys") is Indicative.

10. For Ezekiel, his service and spiritual experience were a large part of his life, "in such a way as to invade the physical sphere; he more than intensively than any other prophet, finds his experience as a prophet claiming and controlling his body." Eichrodt, *Ezekiel*, 6. In the introductory section ("The person and message of Ezekiel") Eichrodt elucidates further the nature of Ezekiel's experiences which clearly "grow passionate," while at the same time, being amid the strict traditions of priesthood, he "held back all expressions of passion or self-will." Eichrodt, 22–23.

with Your treasure. They are satisfied with children, and leave their abundance to their babies. As for me, I shall behold Your face in righteousness; I shall be satisfied with Your likeness when I awake. (Ps 17:14–15 NASB)

In one of his speeches, Job claims of the godless that "they conceive mischief, and bring forth iniquity, and their belly (בטן) prepareth deceit" (Job 15:35 KJV). The NAB translator renders this as, "they give birth to failure." The female reproductive system is also located in the abdominal region. The womb (רחם) is primarily a reproductive organ and the seat of life and futurity. In a prophetic word for Rebekah, Isaac's wife, it was said that: "Two nations are in thy womb (בטן), and two manner of people shall be separated from thy bowels" (מעה) (Gen 25:23 KJV).

Sometimes רחם relates to emotional disturbance (Job 32:18; Hab 3:16), deep compassion, or simply the inner life. Compassion (רחמים) has a linguistic connection as well as physical association with the womb (רחם). Another term which corresponds closely to רחם is קרב (inside, the innermost part of one's body and person), though not in strict terms of anatomy.[11]

15.2.2.2 Bowels

The bowels (מעה) refer to viscera (the guts, intestines) that fill the muscular, hollow, dilated part of the digestive system. The biblical text often associates the bowels with passionate feelings, as in the lament over Moab in Isaiah 16:

> Therefore for Moab my breast (מעה) moans like a lyre,
> and my heart (קרב) for Kir-hareseth. (Isa 16:11)

Here is another example of translators unnecessarily equating the bowels (מעה) with the heart (JPS) or even the soul (RSV). The NAB gives the translation as *breast*, which is better. Understandably, it would be unappealing to render "for Moab my intestines moan." Yet, any solution which neglects the fine distinction in Israelite anthropology between the chest organs (heart, soul?) and the abdominal organs is unsatisfactory.

Another instance of dubious translation, where the bowels are the seat of passion, is in Isaiah's account of his appeal to YHWH for compassion

---

11. The term קרב has been dealt with in the previous chapters.

towards his inheritance, his people. He asks God about his "yearning of Thy heart (מעה)" (JPS), or "Where is your zealous care?" (NAB). These most probably follow the Vulgate, "Ubi est zelus tuus et fortitudo tua?" (VUL) (Isa 63:15). Peterson comes closer with, "Whatever happened to your passion?" (The Message).[12] Interestingly, there seems to be no problem in the classic example of Jeremiah's passion (Jer 4:19) where most translators are faithful to the source text and render מעה as *bowels* (JPS), *breast* (NAB) or *anguish* (RSV). The bowels also reflect despair. In his turmoil, Job describes his intestines (bowels) being at the boiling point (רתח), "Mine inwards boil, and rest not; days of affliction are come upon me" (Job 30:27 JPS) (מעי רתחו ולא דמו קדמני ימי עני).

15.2.2.3 Kidneys

Of all the internal organs, the kidneys (כליות) rank next to the heart in the Old Testament. The kidneys are related to the innermost part of existence and are identified as the deepest centre of experience. If the heart is a "reasonable man,"[13] the kidneys serve to portray a specific array of emotional states or the conscience (Ps 16:7). Jeremiah reminds God that the wicked have God on their lips, but he is "far from their kidneys" (רחוק מכליותיהם) (Jer 12:2). Or, he is "far from their inmost thoughts," as NAB has it; other translations, again apparently for stylistic reasons, have this as far from "their hearts" (see here: *Biblical Gastroenterology*).

Kidneys often appear in the context of utter vulnerability and pain. Feeling punished by God, Job feels as though arrows are piercing his kidneys, not his heart. His gall (מררה) is being "spilt on the ground" (ישפך לארץ מררתי) (Job 16:13).[14] But, piercing the kidneys with arrows (רב) may also designate divine disciplining, "He pierces his arrows into my kidneys ... He has sated me with bitter food" (Lam 3:13, and see also Ps 73:21).[15] Deep intensity or passionate longing are also set in the kidneys. In the Old Testament, there are longings

---

12. Similar renderings of "bowels" with "heart" are found in numerous other places, including Jer 31:20 where clearly it is God's passionate love that stretches out towards Ephraim.

13. Wolff, *Anthropology of Old Testament*, 40–41.

14. מררה (gall), as a noun appears only here; etymologically comes from מרר (being bitter). The wicked throw "bitter words" (דבר מר) (Ps 64:3).

15. "His arrows strike me from all directions, He pierces my sides (kidneys) without mercy, he pours out my gall upon the ground" (Job 16:13 NAB).

in the heart (Job 17:11) or meditation of the heart (Ps 19:14; 49:3), but the kidneys indicate a much deeper urge, and there is no meditation there. Job's deep desire to see God is set in his innards (חיק) and kidneys.

> Whom I, even I, shall see for myself,
> and mine eyes shall behold, and not another's.
> My reins are consumed within me. (Job 19:27 JPS)

Job 19:27c – כלו כליתי בחקי – is difficult for translators. Some suggest it means Job's utter exhaustion after all his suffering, so the JPS puts this as: "My reins are consumed within me"; other translations again replace "kidneys" with the "heart." So, Meek concludes: "Job is so astounded by the prospect of coming face to face with God that he is completely exhausted emotionally,"[16] and translates this as: "Whom I myself shall see, And my own eyes shall behold, and not some stranger; My emotions are spent within me."[17]

However, bearing in mind the immediate context, it seems beyond any serious doubt that the text portrays Job's longing, rather than monumental suffering. Following David Clines's translation: "to see him for myself, to see him with my own eyes, not as a stranger, my inmost being is consumed with longing."[18] This also fits well in the wider context of the book. Namely, the concluding remark of Job at the end of the book displays his deep longing in very similar wording (Job 42:5): "I had heard of you by word of mouth, but now my eye has seen you" (NAB).

On the basis of Job 19:27, and the phrase, כלו כליתי מחקי, Mark Smith suggests that kidneys may simply be understood metaphorically as representative of all the innards. Job 19:27 locates כליות in the חיק normally translated "bosom." If correct, כליות would refer not specifically to kidneys, but innards.[19]

Though this may be true, anatomical precision may be subject to a degree of metaphoricity or the actual psychosomatic condition of the person. On the other hand, kidneys, very particularly, were recognized and quite familiar in sacrificial practices.[20]

---

16. Meek, 103.
17. Meek, 103. Vulgate has here: *"quem visurus sum ego ipse et oculi mei conspecturi sunt et non alius reposita est haec spes mea in sinu meo"* that is, "this is my only hope that I desire."
18. Clines, *Job 1–20*, 428.
19. Smith, "Heart and Innards," 430.
20. See here: "Intestines and Religion."

15.2.3 Kidneys, Liver and Bowels

The biblical use of abdominal organs to express the symptoms of deep emotions and distress goes far beyond the commonly rendered translation, the "heart." In his personal and private emotional and religious experience, the writer of the Psalms shows that physical manifestations are often descriptions of inner commotion. He frequently focuses on the lower abdominal region, which seems to be more representative of strong and not so positive emotions. Mark Smith concludes, "The innards, including the digestive tract, react strongly in negative situations. More specifically, strong negative emotions are felt in the lower abdominal region."[21]

The human psychosomatic system reacts to negative emotions with several symptomatic changes, including:

> dilation of pupils; inhibition of tear glands and salivation; opening of respiratory passages; increase in heartbeat and blood pressure, release of sugar into the blood for energy . . . inhibition of digestive secretion and stomach contractions.[22]

Jeremiah bursts into a fit of emotional outpouring, crying:

> My bowels, (מעה) my bowels! I writhe in pain!
> The chambers of my heart!
> My heart moaneth within me! (Jer 4:19 JPS)

A number of similar symptoms are witnessed with the psalmist; such as general weakness or exhaustion and tears (Pss 31:10; 38:8; 39:10; 73:26). Terrence Collins, in his excellent study *The Physiology of Tears*, examines the connection between crying and tears with the internal organs, that is, between the eyes and the intestines.[23] Let us now investigate several Psalms that will exhibit not only the abdominal region, but also the relationships between the abdominal region and other parts of the human body (throat, eyes). We shall look more closely into Psalm 31; Psalm 38; Psalm 119 and Psalm 139.

---

21. Smith, "Heart and Innards," 434.
22. Smith, 434.
23. Collins, "The Physiology of Tears," 18–38.

15.2.3.1 Psalm 31

In medical terms, it is true that grief wears a person out physically. In Psalm 31, the psalmist's eyes are wasting away, worn out through crying, and his body is exhausted.

> Be gracious to me, O LORD, for I am in distress;
> my eye is wasted from grief,
> my soul and my body (*belly*) also (Ps 31:10 RSV).

Here "my body" is "my belly" (בטן), representing the most intimate experience. Collins provides interesting links between the eyes and tears and the internal organs, via the soul (throat). The soul (נפש, throat) is in the "service" of tear production. Collins then argues that this is a continuous process which includes "the eyes and stomach as extremities with the throat holding a crucial position as the link between the two."[24] It is also noted that the order of appearance in which the body parts are listed matter. Other particularly appealing instances are found in Jeremiah 13:17 and Psalm 119:28. In the former, Jeremiah warns the people of imminent punishment.

> If you will not listen, my soul (נפש) will weep in secret (סתר)
> for your pride; my eyes will weep bitterly and run down
> with tears,
> because the LORD's flock has been taken captive.
> (Jer 13:17 RSV)

Here, Collins translates "for your pride" as "even before the congregation" for מפני גוה,[25] that is, "my soul will weep in secret and even before the congregation." He also argues that here נפש should be understood in its physiological connotation of "throat." Collins explains from Psalm 119 that tears come from the throat, "My soul is dripping (דלף) through grief" (Ps 119:28).[26]

The symptoms of bodily weakening through grief are evident in such descriptions of private and even public manifestations and can hardly be dismissed as fossilized literary conventions. It is difficult to concur with those who view such texts as stereotyped language.[27]

---

24. Smith, "Physiology of Tears," 23.
25. Smith, 24.
26. Smith, 24. The verb דלף is exclusively used of water dripping.
27. For example, Anderson and Mays, in their comments on the similar context of Psalm 38, conclude it is "conventional word pictures of trouble" (Anderson) or "carefully composed prayer" (Mays, *Psalms*, 162).

15.2.3.2 Psalm 139

Here, the personal, intimate and private experience of the poet is set in a decidedly theological and doctrinal context. The Psalm is organized around two essential doctrines: affirming the divine *omnipresence* ("Where can I hide from your spirit?", 139:7–12), and God's *omniscience* ("you know when I sit and stand," 139:1–6). In content, meaning and even wording, it resembles Job's experience (Job 10:8, 18).[28] The psalmist's heart is probed, "Search (חקר) me and know me," (139:1). In the same way, Job says, "He knows the way that I take; when he has tried me" (כי־ידע דרך עמדי בחנני) (Job 23:10).

There are further parallels between the psalmist (Ps 139:23–24) and Job's trials (Job 23:10). Job, in his protestation of innocence, concludes, "I shall come forth as gold" (23:10), while the psalmist also infers his innocence, purity and piety, "Search me, O God, and know my heart, try me," (Ps 139:23 RSV). The psalm also refers to the secrecy of divine providence and the miracle of creation that the psalmist perceives as a very intimate experience. Alter suggests an associative link between the womb and the *chthonic depths*, that is, the subterranean underworld of the deities and spirits.[29] The womb (life) and netherworld (death) have archetypal religious associations with "mother earth."[30] This reinforces the *merimic* nature of the womb.[31]

> You formed my inmost being;
> you knit me in my mother's womb. (139:13)
> כי אתה קנית כליתי תסכני בבטן אמי[32]

And,

> My bones were not hidden from you,
> When I was being made in secret,

---

28. Acknowledging God's might and miraculous creative work, "Thy hands have framed me and fashioned me together round about" (Job 10:8–22.

29. the Greek adjective "chthonic" (*subterranean*) comes from the nominal form of one of the Greek words for the earth.

30. Alter, *Book of Psalms*, 481. Greek χθόνιος = under, or beneath the earth (from χθών = earth). The word *khthon* is one of the words for *earth*. The term specifically refers to the interior of the soil, rather than the surface of the land. In religious-historical terms, it also designates the abode of deities or spirits of the underworld.

31. Perry, *Honeymoon Is Over*, 31. "merism" (adj. "*merimic*") is a figure of speech, referring to two contrasting ideas of the same entity, thus the womb may be a seat of new life or a grave. Thus, the expression, "mother earth" as "mother" or earth as "grave."

32. "For Thou hast made my reins; Thou hast knit me together in my mother's womb" (JPS).

Anthropology

fashioned as in the depths of the earth. (139:15)

רקמתי בתחתיות ארץ

The ending of the Psalm (139:23–24) echoes its opening, "You search me and you know me," (139:1).

> Search me (חקר), O God, and know my heart,
> try me, and know my thoughts (בחן).
> And see if there be any way in me that is grievous,
> and lead me in the way everlasting. (139:23–24 JPS)

The pious man is being led in his public and private life. His experience is both doctrinal and personal, with similar overtones to Job's experience (Job 23).

15.2.3.3 Psalm 40

The psalm exemplifies the complementary nature of public worship with a deep personal piety. The psalmist emphasizes his participation in the tradition of public worship and witness:

> I have preached righteousness in the great congregation ...
> I have not hid Thy righteousness within my heart (לב);
> I have declared Thy faithfulness and Thy salvation. (40:10–11)

The psalmist decides not to keep the majesty and glory of God for himself, he concludes that as an individual he can also access God outside the "great congregation." He expresses this in words which seem to repudiate the sacrificial system:

> Sacrifice and offering you do not want;
> but ears open to obedience you gave me.
> Holocausts and sin-offerings you do not require. (Ps 40:7)

The psalmist resolves that it is better to delight in God's will and internalize the Torah, rather than have a public, yet merely formal cultic observance. Consequently, he declares that the Law is seated "in my inmost parts" (בתוך מעי) (Ps 40:9).[33] The Law of God should particularly become a close companion primarily to the the king (Deut 17:18–19).

---

33. Delitzsch defines the term מעה as "the soft parts of the body, which ... appear preeminently as the seat of sympathy, but also of fear and of pain." Keil and Delitzsch, *Commentary*, vol. 5, 40.

When he sits on the throne of his kingdom, he shall write for himself in a book a copy of this law, from that which is in the charge of the Levitical priests. and it shall be with him, and he shall read in it all the days of his life, that he may learn to fear the LORD his God, by keeping all the words of this law and these statutes, and doing them. (Deut 17:18–19 RSV)

Again, we have here another example where a translator for מעה (innards, innermost parts) has *heart*, which diminishes and betrays the gist of the author's original intent.

15.3 Limbs, Head and Soul

15.3.1 Lifting Up or Falling Down

The gestures of the body, that is, the limbs (hands, palms) ("I lift my hands" – Ps 28:2, etc.); head (face, eyes) ("I lift up my eyes" – Ps 121:1, etc.; "lift up His countenance upon thee" – Num 6:26; or "face fallen" – Gen 4:6) all involve motion, whether *upward* or *downward*. Even the soul itself can be lifted up or fall down (Ps 24:4, etc). In terms of grammar and syntax, *verbs of motion* (נשא נפל פרש) play a significant role in the psalmist's piety.

Motion is an event, *real* or *fictive*. It involves a physical *change* in the location or position of an object, relative to time. But equally, motion is conceptual and metaphorical. Throughout history, *orientational metaphors* have featured in language and culture, chiefly in relation to vertically vectorized experiences. In the history of religion, for example, God is *up* there (in heaven), while we are *down* here (on earth). In human communication, everyone knows what *thumbs up* or *thumbs down* refer to. In general, feeling happy and healthy is *up*, while being sad or sick is *down*. Conscious, positive actions are expressed by phrasal verbs with *up*, and involuntary, or unconscious actions by phrasal verbs with *down* (wake up, sit up, look up, go down with, slow down, die down, etc.). Lakoff groups them in the following clusters: * happy is up; sad is down/ * conscious is up; unconscious is down/ * health and life are up; sickness and death are down/ * having control is up; being subject is down/ * more is up; less is down/ * good is up; bad is down/ * high status is up; low status is down/ * foreseeable future events are up and ahead/ * rational is up; emotional is down.[34]

---

34. Lakoff, "*Contemporary Theory of Metaphor*," 202–251.

15.3.2 Hands Up

Lifting up the hands. The psalmist lifts up his *soul* (נשא) to YHWH (Ps 25:1), that is, he fervently addresses himself before God (see below).[35] But he also stretches, or spreads (פרש) out his *hands*: "I spread out my hands to you" (פרשתי ידי אליך) (Ps 143:6). The lifting or spreading of hands towards heaven is a liturgical gesture of prayer. For the psalmist, it would also have been in the direction of the temple (Ps 28:2).[36] But does he also lift his hands in his personal piety and private living quarters? Whichever, Psalm 143:6 clearly indicates a very personal yearning ("I thirst for you like a parched land"). His spirit faints within him when he feels devastated and deserted (143:4). Beyond any reasonable doubt, here we have a very personal experience, and most likely a very private demonstration of personal experience. Clearly, texts like this cannot be thought of as merely a formal liturgical exercise. Weiser speaks of it in the following words:

> how closely the individual and the cult community belong together in virtue of their faith. What happens to the faith of an individual member of the cult community is the concern of the cult community as a whole.[37]

We will assume, and argue on the basis of evidence so far, that the personal and private piety of the individual is a presupposition for the living cult community. In some way, this may be putting things upside down to previous postulates, but as it has been noted already, prayer-liturgy should not be seen merely as a verbal exercise. Besides, it is accompanied by actions which engage not only the mind or soul, but also the body. Outstretched or lifted hands are a gesture of anticipation of receiving something from God.

15.3.3 Eyes Lifted Up

Eyes are good indicators of the state of the body and soul, and tears are expressive of one's emotional disposition. Either of these is of personal and private make-up and very intimate in its emotive experience. Eyes are in many ways paralleled with the innards, the soul and heart (see: "Biblical Gastroentereology"). Jeremiah's experience over the fate of his people was a tearful one, coming right from his inner being:

---

35. Cf: Pss 28:2; 31:6; 143:6 (hands). Pss 63:5; 88:10; 119:48 (palms).
36. בנשאי ידי אל- דביר קדשך (28:2).
37. Weiser, *Psalms*, 816.

> Oh, that my head were a spring of water,
> my eyes a fountain of tears (מקור דמעה).
> That I might weep day and night
> over the slain of the daughter of my people! (Jer 8:23) (see also Jer 9:17)[38]

As noted above, Terence Collins in his "The Physiology of Tears in the Old Testament" connects the *tears*, the *soul* and the *throat* with "physical wearing out of the body parts."[39] It is worth noting here the incidence when the Israelites, led by Saul's son Jonathan, fought the Philistines. The victorious party, utterly exhausted after the battle (1 Sam 14:24) were forbidden to eat that day. But Jonathan dared to taste some honey from a honeycomb, it says then that "his eyes brightened" (14:27, 29).[40] There is another gesture that relates to eyes. The psalmist is "lifting up" his eyes (נשא עיני) towards the mountains, "I lift up my eyes to the hills. From whence does my help come?" (121:1 RSV). Although this is a rhetorical question, the psalmist is aware that only in God is his help. Or, he lifts up his eyes towards God, "To thee I lift up my eyes (אליך נשאתי את-עיני), O thou who art enthroned in the heavens!" (123:1 RSV).[41] But is God being far away in all this? The psalmist prays for his return (שובה יהוה) (Ps 6:5). Without God's help, the psalmist is in his traumatic experience. In his privacy he testifies to a similar ordeal as does Jeremiah (Jer 45:3):

> I am weary with my moaning;
> every night I flood my bed with tears;
> I drench my couch with my weeping.
> My eye wastes away because of grief. (Ps 6:6–7 RSV)

Psalm 121 and the lifting up his (psalmist) eyes to the mountains may refer to several things. One is the pilgrim's journey to the temple in Jerusalem and his return home, with all the dangers that such journey might entail in the

---

38. There are many examples of this emotional deluge with the "rivers of tears." In Jeremiah's lament it is: "my eyes flow with rivers of tears" (פלגי-מים תרד עיני) (Lam 3:48–49; cf. Lam 1:16). Ps 119:36, etc.

39. Collins, "Physiology of Tears," 23.

40. There is another episode in Gen 27 where taking of food physically enables a person to act. It is repeatedly pointed out that Isaac seemed to be needing food to be able to bless Esau (cf. Gen 27:4, 7, 10, 19, 25).

41. Ps 141:8 – "My eyes are upon you, O GOD" אליך יהוה אדני עיני.

mountains (vv. 3, 6, 8).⁴² It may be confirming and confessing the worshipper's trust in God, which may be another case of *synecdoche*, where the eyes represent the whole person. Dahood interprets the mountain as "YHWH's celestial abode and YHWH himself."⁴³ He also assumes that "mountain" in general in a religious context usually designates the divinity. It is true that in the Old Testament, the "high places" (במות) were the sites of pagan worship, the location of baals, fertility gods, etc. (e.g. 2 Kgs 23:5). But, the expression: "I raise my eyes toward the mountains," (121:1) may also refer to the worshipper's amazement at the grandeur and majesty of creation. Yet, there is a further context in which the psalmist indicates his need for help and protection: "My help comes from the LORD, the maker of heaven and earth. God will not allow your foot to slip (מוט); your guardian (שמרך) does not sleep" (Ps 121:2–3).

A rather different interpretation of the psalmist's reference to the mountains relates to their function as the sanctuaries of other gods.⁴⁴ In this context, the psalmist being protected from slipping may mean something else. Terrien reckons that the pilgrim

> will resist and reject the attraction of these half-pagan, half-Yahwistic places of worship. His foot might hesitate here and there, but the Lord will not permit stumbling confusion.⁴⁵

From this Psalm it is clear that the pilgrim speaks out of the devotion of his heart. His faith is confirmed and strengthened. His eyes, here a synecdoche, actually view the surrounding landscape, but he is a pilgrim rather than a recreational hiker.

---

42. Hans Joachim Kraus sets this in the context of the pilgrim's returning home from temple worship. He leaves the sanctuary and "enters the realm where he faces dangers in rugged mountains, under the burning sun, and from the threat of many perils." Kraus, *Theology of Psalms*, 100.

43. Dahood, *Psalms*, III, 200. See Ps 18:32 – "who is God, but the LORD? And who is a rock, except our God?" (RSV). Dahood translates, "Who is a mountain except our God?" Dahood, *Psalms*, III, 200.

44. Mowinckel, *Psalms in Israel's Worship*; Gunkel, *Introduction to Psalms*; Terrien, *Psalms*. Leslie Allen in this text extensively considers diferent views over the exegetical values of the "mountains." Allen, *Psalms*, 151.

45. Terrien, *Psalms*, 812.

15.3.4 Face Lifted Up

Many homonymous anatomical idioms in the Old Testament should be assumed to be synecdoche (literary devices by which a part denotes the whole). In the Psalter, as elsewhere in OT, a case in point is the soul (נפש), as synecdoche for the whole person. However, to render the soul and generalize it only for a whole person, uncritically, is mistaken. The anthropological dimension and anatomical idioms (postures, gestures or facial expressions) convey and describe psychosomatic conditions of an individual in his personality and privacy. This cannot be regarded as a synecdoche uncritically.[46]

The "face" is often reckoned to be a mirror of the soul (person), generally also displaying the intentions or mood(s) of a person. In the Psalter, the face abounds with a number of anatomical idioms. In anthropomorphic presentations of divine nature, it often exhibits affirmative dispositions towards his chosen people (for example, Ps 4:7; Ps 31:17, etc). An alternative to this is when a divine face is being hid from the psalmist or his chosen people (for example, Ps 13:1; Ps 27:9, etc).

The face can be *raised* (נשא) or *fallen* (נפל), it may *shine* (Num 6:25; Ps 31:17; Ps 61:7) or even be *hidden* (Exod 3:6; Deut 31:18). In entreating or begging, the face can be anxious, worried or even sick (חלה): "I was begging your favour" (חליתי פניך) (Ps 119:58).[47]

An example from Nehemiah's audience before the king is instructive. There, the face can be sad ("evil") (פנה רע) as noted in this episode of Nehemiah standing before the Persian king Artaxerxes. Nehemiah's mood and anxiety was clearly shown on his face (Neh 2:2).[48] He was also greatly troubled because his face did not "shine" in the royal presence. When he was asked by the monarch: "Why is your face sad (רע)?" Nehemiah reacted: "I was very much afraid" (ואירא הרבה מאד) (Neh 2:2).

Somewhat comparable is the episode of Cain and Abel, when in the presence of God Cain evidently had a grimace on his face and the Almighty asked him: "Why has your countenance (face) (פנה) fallen (נפל)?" (Gen 4:6). In both episodes (Cain, Nehemiah), face may be reckoned as synecdoche, but surely

---

46. Gruber, "Many Faces of Hebrew."
47. In the literal terms, it can be translated as: "my face was sick for you" (Ps 119:58).
48. The face can show a favourable disposition towards the sovereign subjects (cf. Ps 45:13).

not only as synecdoche. We can clearly find there elements of personal and bodily features. On the other hand, when the psalmist encourages himself to seek the "face" of the Lord:[49]

> Seek the LORD and his strength,
> seek his face continually! (Ps 105:4 NASB)
> (דרשו יהוה ועזו בקשו פניו תמיד)

He also gets worried sick if the divine face (favour) is turned away from him (119:58). In the Aaronic blessing the face being lifted up (נשא פנים) is equivalent to showing favour or mercy (Num 6:24–26). It is, as Mayer Gruber suggests, a "functional equivalent of 'smile.'"[50]

> The LORD bless you and keep you!
> The LORD make his face to shine upon you, and be gracious
>   to you!
> The LORD lift up his countenance upon you, and give you
>   peace. (Num 6:24–25 RSV)

Here, the NAB translates "The LORD let his face shine upon you" indicative of, "The LORD look upon you kindly," which really expresses YHWH's pleasure and affection.

15.3.5 Soul Lifted Up

The expression "I lift up my soul" (נפשי אשא) (Pss 24:4; 25:1; 86:4; 143:8) appears in several psalms. How do you do that, how does one "lift up the soul"? In the colloquial speech there is a close idiom when we speak of "lifting one's spirit," where the "lifting" ought to be seen as a conceptual metaphor.[51] This heavenward (conceptual) motion, for the psalmist, means coming personally closer to God ("in you I trust," Ps 25:2) in anticipation. Clearly, this is a very personal experience and yearning. This expression, "lifting up one's

---

49. Ps 27:8.
50. Gruber, "Many Faces of Hebrew," 253.
51. Conceptual metaphors, and those which relate to orientation in space and motion, particularly vertical motion, show us that that which is UP is better than that what is DOWN. Opposite from "I feel down" or depressed is "I am cheered up" or encouraged. Conceptually downward movements (sinking, falling, dropping, etc.) designate negative feelings or emotional conditions, while the upward motion or position (raise, lift, upright, etc.) designate more positive conditions. On this subject, see Berković, "Grammar of Death," particularly chapters "Motion as an Event and a Concept," and "Motion and Space."

soul" is synecdoche where the soul refers to the whole person. In the troubled, emotional turmoil of Psalm 86, one can easily replace "soul" with either "life" or "self."[52]

Psalm 86:1 "Hear me (נטה), LORD, and answer me, for I am poor and needy." The psalm begins with a masterly use of *assonance* (אני ענני כי עני ואביון) (86:1), which strongly punctuates the state the psalmist found himself in. At this point, we ought to give some attention to those poetic literary devices which are designed to accentuate the psalmist's personal emotional condition. *Repetitions* and *play on words* are ubiquitous in the Psalter and other poetic sections of biblical texts. In this particular example, assonance with the play on words, heighten the suspense and amplify the psalmist's grim emotional condition. This is particularly obvious in repeating the sounds of "ani"; as well as play on words with those sounds. With the assonance of repeating the vowel sound "i," and the profound play on words (me, poor, answer) – אני (me), then comes עני (poor), with the ענני (answer me). With all this, the author achieves a very dramatic description of the condition the psalmist is in.[53]

But, do we have here a pious individual privately crying out to God? Can this be only a spokesman (*performer, poet*) representing a whole group of worshippers in their personal adversities?[54] If so, are they socially and economically deprived? Does the *poor* (עני, pl.ענוים) *and needy* (אביון) perhaps refer to a specific group, like a community of the poor?[55]

> Preserve my life, for I am godly
> שמרה נפשי כי-חסיד אני (86:2 RSV)
>
> Gladden the soul of your servant;
> to you, Lord, I lift up my soul
> כי אליך אדני אשא נפשי (86:4 RSV)

---

52. Most translators here (Ps 86:2, 4a, 4b, 13) prefer "life" for "soul."

53. Much has been written on the psalmodic literary devices. A good insight into the poetic devices in the psalms is found in Gillingham's work, particularly on the assonance. Gillingham, *Poems and Psalms*, 192–94.

54. See here, in the "Interpretation of the Psalms" the threefold understanding of how the term the "psalms" can be conceived.

55. This problem has been tackled earlier. See previous chapters, "The Pious Man" and "The Anavim."

Alfred Rahlfs interpreted the *poor* and *needy* in the Psalter as a group or a "party of committed followers of Yahweh."[56] Others will go as far as saying that "the Psalter is the book of Israel's poor."[57] Over the issue one way or the other, one thing seems to be certain and that is, that the poor and the needy "out of the depth of their need come into the presence of Yahweh and plead him to intervene and save."[58] This only confirms our thesis, that beyond and besides the context of a collective access to the divine "throne," there must be an individual in his/her personal and private approach to the divine.

---

56. Cf. Kraus, *Theology of Psalms*, 150. Cf. Rahlfs, *Psalmi Cum Odis*.
57. Antonin Causse in Kraus, 150.
58. Antonin Causse in Kraus, 150.

CHAPTER 16

Location

Worship of a localized divinity (*numen locale*) is a primeval aspect of any religion. A theophanic, personal religious experience often leads to equating the location in which it took place with a deity. The god becomes localized, assigned a permanent worldly address and is expected to confirm his presence through occasional apparitions.

The psalmist's piety also relies on God's localization. YHWH dwells in Zion (Ps 9:11) where he has chosen to have his earthly abode (Ps 74:2; 76:2). From there, he releases his help and salvation (Ps 14:7; 20:3; 53:6).[1] The rhetorical question of who is worthy to come into the very presence of the Lord, or "Who shall go up on the mount of the Lord?" (Ps 24:3) is answered unequivocally in a "sister" Psalm 15 (Ps 15:1–2).[2]

Yet, private devotion is not exclusively dependent on a sacred location or the Torah liturgy[3] though there is a legitimate and logical suggestion that the right to approach God individually is also dependent on "ritual fitness," that is, the attendance at public worship.

Apropos of this, Weiser suggests that,

> Questions such as the one which is asked here, the question of the ritual fitness required for taking part in public worship, were customary in antiquity in various forms and have been

---

1. Most frequently, the root ישב designates YHWH's earthly dwelling. Less frequently, מעון also carries the meaning to dwell (Pss 26:8; 71:3; 90:1), usually with the meaning, to cover or conceal, protect, as in צור מעון ("rock of refuge") (Ps 71:3). Also, "LORD, I love the habitation (מעון) of thy house (בית)" יהוה אהבתי מעון ביתך (Ps 26:8).

2. Cf. Isa 33:14.

3. cf. Gunkel, *Introduction to Psalms*, 289, 292.

preserved right into the Christian cultus. Once, every sanctuary probably laid down its own rules in accordance with which admission was granted by the priest. Those rules above all included the requirement of ritual purity.[4]

It is also fascinating to note here how fervently Gunkel supports the odds that the individual and private piety is not locally attached to one "sacred" location.[5]

16.1 Private Places

There are occasions when there is no opportunity to participate in public worship, in such times personal piety must have been practised in private. Daniel, far away from Jerusalem in Babylon, was accustomed to exercise his personal piety, facing Jerusalem in the privacy of his Babylonian home.[6] Though far from the temple in Jerusalem, in his privacy, he experienced the presence of God.

> He continued his custom of going home to kneel in prayer and give thanks to his God in the upper chamber three times a day, with the windows open toward Jerusalem. (Dan 6:11)

In the same routine, the psalmist prays three times a day: "Evening and morning and at noon I utter my complaint and moan, and he will hear my voice" (Ps 55:18 RSV). Upon receiving the news of the death of his son Absalom, King David was deeply shaken and he "went up to the room over the city gate to weep" (ויעל על עלית השער) (2 Sam 19:1).[7] Jonah also "prayed to the Lord from the belly of the fish" (Jonah 2:2). The belly of the fish was the enclosed location in which Jonah expressed his piety. Along the same lines, Jesus, a Jewish rabbi, instructed his followers to approach God in their needs in privacy:

---

4. Weiser, *Psalms*, 167.

5. Gunkel, *Introduction to Psalms*, par.6:3, p.122.

6. Facing Jerusalem when praying is a custom which probably dates back to the time of the dedication of the temple by Solomon, that is, "praying towards this place" (cf.1 Kgs 8:33–35).

7. The עליה is the "roof chamber." King Eglon of Moab was sitting in a "cool roof chamber" (בעלית המקרה) when Ehud the judge visited him (cf. Judg 3:20). The wealthy woman from Shunem requested her husband to build a small "roof chamber" for Elisha (cf. 2 Kgs 4:8–10).

when you pray, go into your room and shut the door and pray to your Father who is in secret; and your Father who sees in secret will reward you. (Matt 6:6 RSV)

It is beyond any doubt that an individual in the Old Testament could legitimately encounter God in personal as well as private circumstances.

16.2 Bed

Their bed is the place where a weary person finds rest (Ps 132:3–5) and a sick person recuperates. It is also where the most intimate, private episodes take place.[8] Its dignity and privacy should not be breached. The bed is a sacred place whose desecration results in very serious consequences. The whole tribe of Reuben had to suffer grave reprisals for his defiling (חלל) the intimacy and privacy of his father's bed. It was also detrimental to his father Jacob, since Reuben was the first in rank among his sons and should have taken over the leadership of Israel. Instead, when Jacob came to bless his sons, for his firstborn Reuben he had to say,

> Reuben, you are my first-born, my might, and the first fruits of my strength, pre-eminent in pride and pre-eminent in power. Unstable as water, you shall not have pre-eminence because you went up to your father's bed (משכב); then you defiled it – you went up to my couch (יצוע)! (Gen 49:3–4 RSV)[9]

Throughout the night, in the privacy of his bed, the psalmist ruminates and declares the most intimate attachments to God: "I think of you on my bed, and meditate on you in the watches of the night" (Ps 63:6 NRSV).[10] In trials and deep distress, he has sleepless nights when he weeps before God and soaks his bed with tears (Ps 6:7), he is exhausted and physically ill; "I am weary with my crying; my throat is parched. My eyes grow dim with waiting for my God" (Ps 69:4 NRSV).[11]

---

8. Ps 63:7 יצוע Ps 6:7 ערש

9. Reuben's crime was sleeping with Bilhah, his father's concubine.

10. Terrien rightly notes that in Hebrew piety the *unio mystica*, a mystical union with divinity is actually "a refusal to bend the evocation of God into pantheism." Terrien, *Psalms*, 464.

11. Jer 45:3.

16.2.1 Psalm 63

This psalm is one of the finest testimonies to the piety of the Psalms, in the context of both private and public life.[12] It is usually understood to describe a Levite priest in exile, yearning for Jerusalem and the temple, and the opportunity of participating in temple worship.[13] Others think that the "poet is probably in the sanctuary, where he had been allowed to behold the revelation of the majesty of God."[14] This is supported by the illustration in 63:6, "My soul is satisfied as with marrow and fatness." Briggs comments that the poet probably makes an association with sacrifice, as "it is true that the fat pieces of animals always went to the altar."[15]

On the other hand, some commentators suggest that the nearness of God actually refers to the heavenly sanctuary. According to Dahood, such nearness can only be achieved in the celestial abode.[16] He also suggests that the situation described here is similar to that in the letter to the Philippians, in which the apostle prays to be delivered from this life, for his desire is "to depart and be with Christ, for that is far better" (Phil 1:23). This he compares with:

> When I think of thee upon my bed, and meditate on thee in the watches of the night; for thou hast been my help, and in the shadow of thy wings I sing for joy. My soul clings to thee; thy right hand upholds me. (63:6–8 RSV)

The suggestion is that this yearning to abide in the "shadow of thy wings" refers to the security of the afterlife.[17] However, it is also a description of private spiritual musing in the nocturnal privacy of the psalmist's bed.

> O God, thou art my God, I seek thee, my soul thirsts for thee; my flesh faints for thee, as in a dry and weary land where no water is. So I have looked upon thee in the sanctuary, beholding thy power and glory. Because thy steadfast love is better than

---

12. Weiser, *Psalms*, 454.
13. Briggs, *Critical and Exegetical*, 2: 72.
14. Weiser, *Psalms*, 454.
15. Briggs, *Critical and Exegetical*, 2: 73. Weiser's comment that the poet is probably in the sanctuary is somewhat obscure. Who is allowed into the sanctuary, apart from the priest? May the king be an observer there?
16. Dahood, *Psalms*, 2, 96–97.
17. Dahood, 2, 100.

life, my lips will praise thee. So I will bless thee as long as I live;
I will lift up my hands (כַּפָּי) and call on thy name. . . . I think of
thee upon my bed (יְצוּעָי), and meditate on thee in the watches
of the night. (Ps 63:1–6 RSV)

This is similar to Jeremiah's situation in his second lament (Lam 2:19). He clings to God with all his being (63:9) and proclaims that God's love and grace are better than life (63:4). Communion with God is continuous prayer, within or without the sanctuary. But is the psalmist conducting a deliberate vigil, or simply having a sleepless night, burdened by personal worries? Though he meditates (הגה) he is restless, even afraid (vv. 10–12). Since sleep does not come, he prays and this becomes an imposed vigil. Even if the worshipper yearns for the temple experience (63:3), he realizes that the house of God, or the place of cultic encounter, is only a part of daily life.[18]

16.2.2 Psalm 6

This Psalm is clearly an individual lament of a sick and weary person. He soaks his bed with tears: "every night I flood my bed with tears; I drench my couch with my weeping" (Ps 6:6). He is afflicted and exhausted, in body and soul (vv. 3–4).[19] Most commentators, such as Anderson and Briggs, consider these passages as metaphors, figures and exaggeration. Or, commentators such as Anderson and Brown envision them as metonymy, perhaps only as a "picturesque oriental style" with the "exaggerated figurative language of the tears."[20] These seem to be unqualified assumptions and not compelling. This is to say that the language of the texts quoted above are so explicit with personal "colour" that it is hardly conceivable to be only an "exaggerated" language and "oriental" style. Only few authors consider the physiological aspect of the psalmist's emotional turmoil. Craigie hints at the realism of the situation.

> The psalmist's sickness had created both exhaustion and insomnia . . . the insomnia was the result partly of the pain accompanying sickness, and partly of the spiritual anguish.[21]

---

18. Weiser, *Psalms*, 455.
19. Dahood translates אמל here as "I am spent." In many other places it refers to being *dry* and *withered away*. Cf. Isa 16:8; Joel 1:10. Here it is rendered as adjectival (אמלל אני).
20. Weiser, *Psalms*, 132.
21. Craigie, *Psalms 1–50*, 93.

In examining the anthropological dimension of the psalmist's private piety and the use of anatomy, particularly the abdominal region and internal organs, it has been shown that some descriptions are fairly accurate portrayals of psychosomatic conditions, and not only a "picturesque oriental style." It is hardly acceptable that all this is simply a poetic, picturesque hyperbole. In the privacy of his bed, the psalmist prays and cries to God in desperation. He shows confidence and is certain of being heard (6:10–11): "Have mercy on me, LORD, for I am exhausted (אמל); heal (רפא) me, LORD, for my bones are trembling (בהל)" (Ps 6:3).

Once again, the description is more than a literary figure. The psalmist is clearly suffering in his body, experiencing real physical manifestations as a result of his emotional and religious experience. Though the אמלל אני ("I am exhausted" or "I am spent") is adjectival, it more than likely describes a shivering motion.[22] Sometimes, it can be difficult to separate emotional disturbance from physical symptoms. So it is unwise to attribute certain phrases to poetic convention. There are several passages in which this approach is difficult to support. Psychosomatic reality and experiences are regularly imputed to body parts or internal organs, particularly the digestive system. Thus the pious man completely absorbs YHWH's Law, "I delight to do Thy will, O my God; yea, Thy law is in my inmost parts (מעה)" (Ps 40:9). Again, most translators inaccurately and needlessly put *heart* for בתוך מעי.[23] After claiming that the Law resides in his intestines, he then decides not to keep it to himself. It makes its way up to the heart, from where he speaks about it (vv. 10–11).[24]

---

22. On the *double ayin verbs* or the repetition of two consonants, the first or the last indicate repetition of an action. This is supported and well presented in Gesenius-Kautzsch (GK) as the form which "commonly expresses rapidly repeated movement," GK, 153: *Gesenius' Hebrew Grammar*, as edited and enlarged by the late; E. Kautzsch.

23. That is, "in my innermost parts."

24. Collins, "Physiology of Tears," 29.

CHAPTER 17

Conclusion

This research journey began with definitional clearance and clarification of key notions and ideas as used in this work, and also in general use. This is particulerly true for the (false) synonymies which seem to be a prevailing definitional problem. A demarcation line of how we comprehend and understand concepts and notions, which sometimes may be conceived as synonymous, actually may be an obstacle. Here, we examined only several examples relevant to this work, such as: *personal* and *private*; *psalmist* and *poet*; *subject* and *subjectivity*; *personal* and *personality*.

Let us first take a glance back at scholarship which set a foundation for psalmodic studies. For quite a while, reconstructionist zeal attempted to revise the literary history of the Psalter. Objectivism was the *sine qua non*, or in the words of Adele Berlin, "long-entrenched 'objectivism' that sought the one true meaning of a text."[1] While dissecting textual and literary forms in the attempt to reconstruct the history objectively, it often failed to recognize the actual content or message of the text, which became a collateral casualty of the process. Rebuilding the Psalter as religious poetry or cultic songs, and focusing on its place in the liturgical life of Israel, meant that the actual message and individual were nowhere to be found. Yet, *form-criticism* traditions not only greatly improved psalmodic studies, but also in many ways established it. Authors like Hermann Gunkel (*An Introduction to the Psalms*), Hans-Joachim Kraus (*Theology of the Psalms*), Sigmund Mowinckel (*The Psalms in Israel's Worship*), and others analyzed literary forms in the Psalter through historical and extra-literal research.

---

1. Berlin, "Role of Text," 143.

However, there are also important internal-historical elements, such as "original location," "original audience," "personal individuality" and "privacy," which were not equally explored. Most of all, there was little effort to identify the psalmist as an individual in his personal and private piety. And yet the language of the Psalter strongly suggests the presence of an individual and personal and private religious experience. And this is our second objective, which is also the overall focus of this work – to try to identify the psalmist as a personal individual, and to show that his piety is often recognizable in his privacy. Here, we need to reemphasize the demarcation between the *personal*, which can be manifest in public, and the *private*. The two are not synonymous.

The psalmist may be fully emotionally involved in identifying with the community, but this does not deny his existence as an individual with a personal and private life, including personal devotions. In this work, we have presented this as the "realms of privacy" in chapters 12 and 13. We unveiled the temporal aspects of the psalmist's personal piety (day and night, every day, always) in chapter 14. One crucial question is, where do all these manifestations of the psalmist's personal piety take place? It is clear that that they are not limited to public places (the temple) and public events (liturgy). His experiences also occur in very private places (his room, or bed, for example), as explained in chapter 15. Finally, the element of *personal anthropology* argues against collectivism. The psalmodic texts exhibit strong elements of psychology, anthropology, physiology and even biopsychology, all that would be difficult to assign to a corporate personality. For example, anatomical idioms extend throughout many psalmodic situations. We can hardly envisage the internal body parts (kidneys, liver and stomach) belonging to a corporate body, as argued in chapter 14 of this work.

Through this analysis of the psalmodic text(s), we can conclude that, (i) there is a psalmist, a pious man with a personal individuality, (ii) there are clear traces of the *tsadiq* (the righteous one), or individual in a very personal relationship with God, even in the Pentateuch, though some assume that this notion was a later development in Israelite history, and (iii) personal invocations are not only part of formal liturgical events, but often take place in privacy. Finally, (iv) one of the most deafening aspects of personal piety is silence, the times when the psalmist, totally exhausted in his distress, cannot speak, cry or even invoke his God (Ps 77:4).

Bibliography

Achtemeier, Elizabeth. "Overcoming the World: An Exposition of Psalm 6." *Interpretation* 28(1974): 75–88.
Addinall, Peter. "The Soul in Pedersen's Israel." *Expository Times* 92 (1981): 299–303.
Albertz, Reiner. *Persönliche Frömmigkeit und offizielle Religion*. Stuttgart: Calwer Verlag, 1978.
Allan, Keith, and Kate Burridge. *Euphemism and Dysphemism: Language Used as Shield and Weapon*. New York: Oxford University Press, 1991.
Allen, Leslie. *Ezekiel 1–19*. Dallas: Word Books, 1994.
———. *Psalms 101–150*. Waco: Word Books, 1983.
Allison, William. "The Poetry of the Psalms." *Biblical World* 22/1 (1903): 42–48.
Alter, Robert. *The Art of Biblical Narrative*. New York: Basic Books, 2011.
———. *The Art of Biblical Poetry*. New York: Basic Books, 1985.
———. *The Book of Psalms*: A Translation with Commentary. New York: W. W. Norton, 2007.
Alter, Robert, and Kermode, Frank. *The Literary Guide to the Bible*. Cambridge: HUP, 1987.
Anderson, Arnold. *The Book of Psalms*. Vol. 1. London: Oliphants, 1972.
———. *Psalms 1–72*. London: Marshall, Morgan & Scott, 1972.
Anderson, Ray S. *Theology, Death and Dying*. Oxford: Basil Blackwell, 1986.
Andresen, Jensine. *Religion in Mind*. Cambridge: Cambridge University Press, 2001.
Augustine, St. *Expositions of the Psalms, 73–98*. New York: New City Press, 2002.
Austin, John L. *How to Do Things with Words*. 2nd ed. Oxford: Oxford University Press, 1982.
Avis, Paul. *God and the Creative Imagination: Metaphor, Symbol and Myth in Religon and Theology*. London: Routledge & Kegan Paul, 1999.
Avishur, Yitzhak. *Stylistic Studies of Word-pairs in Biblical and Ancient Semitic Literatures*. Kevelaer: Butzon & Bercher, 1984.
Bach, Alice. *Women in the Hebrew Bible*. London: Routledge, 1998.

Bar-Efrat, Shimon. *Narrative Art in the Bible.* London: T&T Clark, 2004.
Barr, James. *Biblical Words for Time.* London: SCM Press, 1962.
———. *Comparative Philology and the Text of the Old Testament.* London: SCM Press, 1968.
Barre, Michael. "Psalm 116: Its Structure and Its Enigmas." *Journal of Biblical Literature* 109, no.1 (1990): 61–79.
———. "Wandering About as a Topos of Depression in Ancient Near Eastern Literature and in the Bible." *Journal of Near Eastern Studies* 60, no. 3 (2001): 177–87.
Barre, Michael, and John Kselman. "Psalm 55: Problems and Proposals." *Catholic Biblical Quarterly* 60, no. 3 (1998): 440–62.
Barrick, W. B. "The Meaning and the Usage of RKB in BH." *Journal of Biblical Literature* 101, no. 4 (1982): 504–52.
Basson, Albert. "Only Ruins Remain: Psalm 74 as a Case of Mundus Inversus." *Old Testament Essays* 20, no. 1 (2007): 128–37.
Bazak, J. "The Geometric-Figurative Structure of Ps 136." *Vetus Testamentum* 35, no. 2 (1985): 129–38.
Berkovic, Danijel. "Grammar of Death in the Psalms with Reference to Motion as Conceptual Metaphor." PhD Diss., OCMS, Middlesex University, 2016.
Berkowitz, L. *Causes and Consequences of Feelings.* Cambridge: Cambridge University Press, 2000.
Berlin, Adele. *The Dynamics of Biblical Parallelism.* Bloomington: Indiana University Press, 1985.
———. *Introduction to Hebrew Poetry.* Nashville: Abingdon Press, 1996.
———. "The Role of the Text in the Reading Process." *Semeia* 62 (1993): 143–47.
Bewer, J. A. *The Literature of the Old Testament.* New York: Columbia University Press, 1962.
Beyerlin, Walter (ed). *Near Easten Religious Texts relating to the Old Testament.* London: SCM Press, 1978.
Birkeland, H. *Die Feinde des Individuums in der israelitischen Psalmenliteratur.* Oslo: Gondhl and Sons, 1933.
Biti,V. Pojmovnik suvremene knjizevne teorije.Zagreb, MH 1997.
Black J., and A. Green. *Gods, Demons and Symbols of Ancient Mesopotamia.* 2nd ed. London: British Museum Press, 1998.
Bloustein, E. "Privacy as an Aspect of Human Dignity." *NYU Law Review*, 1964/38, 962–1007.
Booij, Th. "Psalm 127:2: A Return to Martin Luther." *Biblica* 81 (2000): 262–68.
———. "Psalm 133: Behold How Good and How Pleasant." *Biblica* 83 (2002): 258–67.
———. "Psalm 139: Text, Syntax, Meaning." *Vetus Testamentum* 55, no. 1 (2005): 1–19.

Booth, W. *A Rhetoric of Irony*. Chicago: University of Chicago, 1974.
Bosma, C. J. "Discerning the Voices in the Psalms." *Calvin Theological Journal* 43 (2008): 183–212.
Bostrom, L. *The God of the Sages*. Stockholm: Almqvist, 1990.
Botica, S. *Biblija i hrvatska tradicijska kultura*. Zagreb: Školska knjiga, 2011.
Botterweck, G. J., and H. Ringgren, eds. *Theological Dictionary of the Old Testament*. Grand Rapids: Eerdmans, 1990.
Boyle, M. "The Law of the Heart: The Death of a Fool." *Journal of Biblical Literature* 120, no. 3 (2001): 401–27.
Briggs, Charles A. *Critical and Exegetical Commentary on the Book of Psalms*, 2 volumes. Edinburgh: T&T Clark, 1907.
Briggs, C. A. & Briggs E.G. *Critical and Exegetical Commentary on the Book of Psalms*, Edinburgh: T&T Clark, 1907, vol. 1.
Broadribb, D. *An Attempt to Delineate the Characteristic Structure of Classical Hebrew Poetry*. Australia: Beverly Bookleaf Pub, 1995.
Brown, R. "The Messianism of Qumran." *Catholic Biblical Quarterly* 19 no. 1 (1957): 53–82.
Brown, R.E. *The Gospel according to John (I-XII)*. New York. Doubleday&Company, Inc. 1966.
Brown W. P. *Seeing the Psalms: A Theology of Metaphor*. London: John Knox Press, 2002.
Brown, F., S. R. Driver, and C. A. Briggs. *Hebrew and English Lexicon of the Old Testament*. Oxford: Clarendon Press, 1979.
Broyles, C. C. *The Conflict of Faith and Experience in the Psalms: A Form-Critical and Theological Study*. Sheffield: JSOT Press, 1989.
Broznick, N. M. "More on HLK 'L.'" *Vetus Testamentum* 35, no. 1 (1985): 98–99.
Brueggemann, Walter. *Genesis: A Bible Commentary for Teaching and Preaching*. Atlanta: John Knox Press, 1982.
———. *The Message of the Psalms: A Theological Commentary*. Minneapolis: Augsburg Fortress, 1984.
———. *Praying the Psalms*. Winona: St Mary's Press, 1993.
———. *Spirituality of the Psalms*. Minneapolis: Fortress Press, 2002.
———. *Texts That Linger, Words That Explode*. Minneapolis: Fortress Press, 2000.
———. *Theology of the Old Testament*. Minneapolis: Fortress Press, 1997.
———. *Vitality of Old Testament Traditions*. Atlanta: John Knox Press, 1982.
Burrows, Millar. *The Dead Sea Scrolls*. London. Secker and Warburg, 1956
Butler, Trent. "Piety in the Psalms." *Review & Expositor* 81, no. 3 (1984): 385–94.
Buttenwieser, Moses. "The Importance of the Tenses for the Interpretation of the Psalms." *Hebrew Union College Annual*, Jubilee – Special, 1925.
Christenson, Randall. "Parallels between Depression and Lament." *Journal of Pastoral Care and Counselling* 61, no. 4 (2007): 299–308.

Clines, David. "The Book of Psalms Where Men are Men . . . On the Gender of Hebrew Piety." Paper presented at the Society of Biblical Literature Annual Meeting, Philadelphia, November, 1995. http://www.academia.edu/2469780/ The_Book_of_Psalms_Where_Men_are_Men_On_the_Gender_of_Hebrew_

Clines, David. *Job 1-20*. Dallas. Word Books Publisher, 1989.

Collins, Terence. "The Physiology of Tears in the Old Testament: Part I." *Catholic Biblical Quarterly* 33, no. 1 (1971): 18-38.

———. "The Physiology of Tears in the Old Testament: Part II." *Catholic Biblical Quarterly* 33, no. 2 (1971): 185-97.

Cooper, Alan. "Ps 24:7-10: Mythology and Exegesis." *Journal of Biblical Literature* 102, no. 1 (1983): 37-60.

Cox, Dermot. *The Triumph of Impotence*. Roma: Universita Gregoriana Editrice, 1978.

Craigie, Peter. *Psalms 1-50*. Waco: Word, 1983.

Cranfield, C.E.B. *The Gospel according to St Mark*. Cambridge: CUP, 1959

Croft, S. J. L. *The Identity of the Individual in the Psalms*. Sheffield: JSOT Press, 1987.

Cross, Frank M., and David N. Freedman. *Studies in Ancient Yahwistic Poetry*. Missoula: Society for Biblical Literature, 1975.

Cruse, Alan. *Meaning in Language: An Introduction to Semantics and Pragmatics*. 2nd ed. Oxford: Oxford University Press, 2004.

Culler, Jonathan. *Literary Theory: A Very Short Introduction*. Oxford: Oxford University Press, 1997.

Culley, Robert. *Oral Formulaic Language in the Biblical Psalms*. Toronto: University of Toronto, 1967.

———. "Oral Tradition and Biblical Studies." *Oral Tradition* 1, no. 1 (1986): 30-65.

Dahood, Mitchell. *Psalms II, 51-100*. New York: Doubleday, 1968.

———. *Psalms I, 1-50*. New York: Doubleday, 1965.

———. *Psalms III, 101-50*. New York: Doubleday, 1970.

———. "The Divine Name Eli in the Psalms." *Theological Studies* 14, no. 3 (1953): 452-57.

Dalglish, E. R. "The Use of the Book of Psalms in the New Testament." *Southwestern Journal of Theology* 27 (1984): 25-39.

Daube, D. "Death as a Release in the Bible." *Novum Testamentum* 5, no. 2 (1962): 82-105.

Davidson, R. S. *Flame of Yahweh: Sexuality in the Old Testament*. Peabody: Hendrickson Publishers, 2007.

Davis, B. C. "Eccl 12,1-8 – Death, an Impetus for Life." *Bibliotheca Sacra* 148 (1991): 298-318.

Day, J. N. "The Imprecatory Psalms and Christian Ethics." *Bibliotheca Sacra* 159 (2002): 166–86.
De Claisse Walford, N. L. "Psalm 44: O God, Why Do You Hide Your Face?" *Review & Expositor* 104 (2007): 745-759.
De Moor, J. C., and M. C. A. Korpel. *The Structure of Classical Hebrew Poetry: Isaiah 40–55.* OTS, 41 ed. Leiden: Brill, 1998.
De Sion, M. Thaddea. "The Jewish Burial Service." In *The Bridge: A Yearbook of Judaeo-Christian Studies*, edited By J. M. Oesterreicher, 243–55. New York: Pantheon Books, 1955.
De Vaux, R. *Ancient Israel: Its Life and Institutions.* 3rd ed. London: Darton, Longman & Todd, 1973.
Deissler, A. *Die Psalmen.* Dusseldorf: Patmos Verlag, 1964.
Dell, K. J. "'I Will Solve My Riddle to the Music of the Lyre' (Psalm 49:4[5]): A Cultic Setting for Wisdom Psalms." *Vetus Testamentum* 54, no. 4 (2004): 445–58.
Dentan, R. C. "Kidneys." In *The Interpreter's Dictionary of the Bible* vol. 3, edited by George A. Buttrick, 9–10. Nashville: Abingdon Press, 1962.
Dodd, C.H. *The Interpretation of the Fourth Gospel.* Cambridge. CUP, 1953
Doyle, B. "Howling Like Dogs: Metaphorical Language in Ps 59." *Vetus Testamentum* 54, no. 1 (2004): 61–82.
Dommershausen, Werner. גורל. *Theological Dictionary of the Old Testament (TDOT)*, vol.2. Botterweck G.J. and Ringgren H. (eds.). Grand Rapids. Eerdmans Publishing. 1972
Driver, G. R. "Some Hebrew Medical Expressions." *Zeitschrift für die alttestamentliche Wissenschaft* 65 (1953): 252–62.
———. "Textual and Linguistic Problems of the Book of Psalms." *Harvard Theological Review* 29, no. 3 (1936): 171–95.
Driver, S. R. *A Critical and Exegetical Commentary on Deuteronomy.* Edinburgh: T&T Clark, 1896.
Du Bois, J. W. "Self-evidence and Ritual Speech." In *Evidentiality: The Linguistic Coding of Epistemology*, edited by W. Chafe and J. Nichols, 313–36. Norwood: Ablex Publishing, 1986.
———. *Theology of the Old Testament.* London: SCM, 1961.
Eich, Eric. Cognition and Emotion. Oxford: Oxford University Press, 2000.
Eichrodt, W. *Theology of the Old Testament, vol.1.* Philadelphia. The Westminster Press, 1975, p.103.
Eichrodt, W. *Ezekiel.* London. SCM Press, 1970.
Ekman, P. "All Emotions Are Basic." In *The Nature of Emotion*, edited by P. Ekman and R. Davidson, 15–19. New York: Oxford University Press, 1994.
Eliade, M. *The Music of Poetry.* 1942.
———. *On Poetry and Poets.* London: 1957.

———. *The Sacred and the Profane: The Nature of Religion*. New York: Harcourt, 1987.
Emerton, J. A. "Sheol and the Sons of Belial." *Vetus Testamentum* 37, no. 2 (1987): 214–17.
Encyclopaedia Judaica. S.v. "Prosody, Hebrew," by B. Harshav. Jerusalem, 1972.
Estes, D. J. "Poetic Artistry in the Expression of Fear in Psalm 49." *Bibliotheca Sacra* 161 (2004): 55–71.
Feinberg, C. L. "The Date of the Psalms." *Bibliotheca Sacra* 104, no. 416 (1947): 426–40.
Feininger, B. "A Decade of German Psalm-Criticism." *Journal for the Study of the Old Testament* 20, no. 1 (1981): 91–103.
Fishbane, M. "Accusation of Adultery: A Study of the Law and Scribal Practices in Numbers 5:11–31." *Hebrew Union College Annual* 45 (1974): 25–45.
Fokkelman, J. P. *Major Poems of the Hebrew Bible at the Interface of Hermeneutics and Structural Analysis* (Ex 15, Deut 32, Job 3). Assen: Van Gorcum, 1998.
Foucault, M. "Discourse and Truth: The Problematization of Parrhesia." Lectures at University of California, Berkeley, during October–November, 1983.
Fohrer, Georg. *Introduction to the Old Testament*. London: SPCK, 1970.
Fox, Michael V., Victor Avigdor Hurowitz, Avi M. Hurvitz, Michael L. Klein, Baruch J. Schwartz, and Nili Shupak, eds. *Texts, Temples, and Traditions. A Tribute to Menahem Haran*. Winona Lake: Eisenbrauns, 1996.
France, R.T. *The Gospel According to Matthew*. Leicester: IVP, 1985.
Freedman, D. N. *Pottery, Poetry and Prophecy*. Winona Lake: Indiana University Press, 1980.
Fritscher, L. "Thanatophobia." In *Diagnostic and Statistical Manual of Mental Disorders*. Arlington: American Psychiatric Association, 2003.
Frye, Northrop. *Anatomy of Criticism: Four Essays*. Princeton: Princeton University Press, 1957.
———. *The Great Code, the Bible and Literature*. 1st ed. Toronto: Academic Press Canada, 1982.
Futato, M. D. *Interpreting the Psalms: An Exegetical Handbook*. Grand Rapids: Kregel Publishing, 2007.
Geller, S. A., E. L. Greenstein, and A. Berlin. *A Sense of Text: The Art of Language in the Study of Biblical Literature*. Winona Lake: Indiana University Press, 1983.
Gervitz, S. *Patterns in the Early Poetry of Israel*. Chicago: University of Chicago Press, 1963.
Ghalioungui, Paul. *The Ebers papyrus: a New English Translation, Commentary and Glossary*. Cairo: Academy of Scientific Research and Technology, 1987.
Gillingham, Susan. *The Poems and Psalms of the Hebrew Bible*. Oxford: Oxford University Press, 1994.

Gillingham, Susan. "Personal Piety in the Study of the Psalms." PhD Diss., Keble College, Oxford University, 1987.

Giora, Rachel. *On the Cognitive Aspect of the Joke*. Tel Aviv: Tel Aviv University, 1997.

———. *On Irony and Negation*. Tel Aviv: Tel Aviv University, 1995.

———. *Understanding Figurative and Literal Language: The Graded Salience Hypothesis*. Tel Aviv: Tel Aviv University, 1997.

Glass, Benjamin, and Susanna Cahn. "Privacy Ethics in Biblical Literature." *Journal of Religion and Business Ethics*, 3 (2017): 1–23.

Gordis, Robert. *The Word and the Book: Studies in Biblical Language and Literature*. 1st ed. New York: Ktav Publishing House, 1976.

Goulder, Michael. "David and Yahweh in Psalms 23 and 24." *Journal for the Study of the Old Testament* 30, no. 4 (2006): 463–73.

Green, Barbara. *Like a Tree Planted: An Exploration of Psalms and Parables through Metaphor*. Collegeville: Liturgical Press, 1997.

Grohmann, Marianne. "Ambivalent Images of Birth in Ps 7." *Vetus Testamentum* 55, no. 4 (2005): 439–49.

———. "Metaphors of Miscarriage in the Psalms." *Vetus Testamentum* 69 (2019): 219–31.

Gruber, Mayer. *Aspects of Nonverbal Communication in the Ancient Near East*. Rome: Studia Pohl 12, 1980.

———. "Fear, Anxiety and Reverence in Akkadian, Biblical Hebrew and Other North-West Semitic Languages." *Vetus Testamentum* 40, no. 4 (1990): 411–22.

———. "Hebrew 'Daabon Nepeš,' Dryness of Throat: From Symptom to Literary Convention." *Vetus Testamentum* 37, no. 3 (1987): 365–69.

———. *Rashi's Commentary on Psalms*. Philadephia: Jewish Publication Society, 2007.

———. "The Many Faces of Hebrew 'Nasa Panim': Lift Up the Face." *Zeitschrift für die alttestamentliche Wissenschaft* 93 (1983): 252–260.

———. "The Tragedy of Cain and Abel: A Case of Depression." *The Jewish Quarterly Review* 69, no. 2 (1978): 89–97.

Gunkel, Hermann. *The Folktale in the OT*. Sheffield: Almond Press, 1987.

———. *Introduction to Psalms: The Genres of the Religious Lyric of Israel*. Macon: Mercer Univerity Press, 1998.

Haik-Vantoura, S. *The Music of the Bible Revealed*. San Francisco: California University Press, 1991.

Haran, Menahem. *Temples and Temple Service in Ancient Israel: An inquiry into the character of cult phenomena and the first setting of priestly school*. Oxford. OUP, 1979.

Haris, R. L., G.L. Archer, and B.K. Waltke. *Theological Workbook of the Old Testament*. Chicago: Moody Press, 1980.

Harrison, E. F. "A Study of Psalm 51." *Bibliotheca Sacra* 92, no. 365 (1935): 26–38.
Heiler, Friedrich. *Das Gebet: religionsgeschichtliche und religionspsychologische Untersuchung*. Munchen: Reinhardt, 1919.
Hill, David. *The Gospel of Matthew*. London. Marshall, Morgan and Scott, 1972.
Holladay, William. "Erets-Underworld: Two More Suggestions." *Vetus Testamentum* 19, no. 1 (1969): 123–24.
———. *The Root Shub in the OT: With Particular Reference to Its Usage in Covenantal Contexts*. Leiden: Brill, 1953.
Hornsby, Jennifer. "Free Speech and Illocution." *Legal Theory* 4 (1998): 21–37.
———. "Illocution and Its Significance." In *Foundations of Speech Act Theory: Philosophical and Linguistic Perspectives*, edited by S. L. Tsohatzidis, 187–207. London: Routledge, 1994.
Horowitz, M. J. "Some Psychodynamic Aspects of Respiration." In *Hyperventilation and Hysteria*, edited by T. P. Lowry, 128–32. Springfield: Charles C. Thomas Publishing, 1967.
Hunt, I. "Recent Psalm Study." *Worship* 47, no. 2 (1967).
Illman K.-J. *Old Testament Formulas about Death*. Turku: Abo Akademi, 1979.
James, W. *The Varieties of Religious Experience*. New York: The Modern Library, 1936.
———. *The Varieties of Religious Experience: A Study in Human Nature*. Longmans.Green and Co, New York, London, Bombay, 1902. Lect XX, 485–518.
Janowski, B. *Arguing with God: A Theological Anthropology of the Psalms*. New York: John Knox Press, 2003.
Janzen, J. G. "Another Look at Ps 12: 6." *Vetus Testamentum* 54, no. 2 (2004): 157–64.
Jenni, E. "Das wort 'Olam im Alten Testament." *Zeitschrift für die alttestamentliche Wissenschaft* 65 (1953): 1–35.
Johnson, Aubrey R. *The One and the Many in the Israelite Conception of God*. 2nd ed. Cardiff: University of Wales Press, 1961.
———. "The Psalms." In *The Old Testament and Modern Study*, edited by H. H. Rowley, 162–210. Oxford: Clarendon Press, 1961.
———. *The Vitality of the Individual in the Thought of Ancient Israel*. 2nd ed. Cardiff: University of Wales Press, 1964.
Johnston, Philip. *Shades of Sheol: Death and Afterlife in the Old Testament*. Downers Grove: InterVarsity Press, 2002.
Jonas, Hans. *The Phenomenon of Life, Toward a Philosophical Biology*. Evanston: Northwestern University Press, 1966
Jouon, Paul (Muraoka). *A Grammar of Biblical Hebrew*, vols I and II. Rome: Pontifical Institute of the Bible, 1993.
Kaufman, Yehezkel. *The Religion of Israel*. Chicago: Chicago University Press, 1960.

Kaiser, Walter. *Toward an Old Testament Theology*. Grand Rapids: Zondervan, 1978.
Kautzsch E. *Gesenius' Hebrew Grammar*. 2nd ed. Oxford: Clarendon Press, 1910.
Keane, Webb. "Religious Language." *Annual Review of Anthropology* 26 (1997): 47–71.
Keble, John. *Keble's Lectures on Poetry 1832–1841*. Oxford: Clarendon Press, 1912.
———. *The Psalter or Psalms of David in English Verse*. Oxford: John Henry Parker, 1839.
Keel, Othmar. *The Symbolism of the Biblical World*. New York: Seabury Press, 1978.
King, Philip. *Surrounded by Bitterness: Image Schemas and Metaphors for Conceptualizing Distress in Classical Hebrew*. Eugene: Pickwick Publications, 2012.
Keil, C. F., and F. Delitzsch. *Commentary on the Old Testament, Vol. 5, Psalms*. Grand Rapids: Eerdmans, 1983.
———. *Commentary on the Old Testament, Vol. 1*, The Pentateuch. Grand Rapids: Eerdmans, 1983.
———. *Commentary on the Old Testament, Vol. 7, Isaiah*. Grand Rapids: Eerdmans, 1983
———. *Commentary on the Old Testament, Vol. 9, Ezekiel, Daniel*. Grand Rapids: Eerdmans, 1983.
———. *Commentary on the Old Testament, Vol. 10*, Minor prophets. Grand Rapids: Eerdmans, 1983.
Kitchen, Kenneth. *Ancient Orient and Old Testament*. Chicago: InterVarsity Press, 1966.
Klein, E. *A Comprehensive Etymological Dictionary of the Hebrew Language for Readers of English*. New York: MacMillan Publishing, 1987.
Klingbeil, G. A. "Between 'I' and 'We': The Anthropology of the Hebrew Bible and Its Importance for a 21st Century Ecclesiology." *Bulletin for Biblical Research* 19, no. 3 (2009): 319–39.
Knierim, R. P. *The Task of the Old Testament Theology*. Grand Rapids: Eerdmans, 1995.
Knight, L. C. "'I Will Show Him My Salvation: The Experience of Anxiety in the Meaning of Psalm 91." *Restoration Quarterly* 43, no. 4 (2001): 280–92.
Knohl, I. "Between Voice and Silence: The Relationship between Prayer and Temple Cult." *Journal of Biblical Literature* 115, no. 1 (1996): 17–30.
———. *The Sanctuary of Silence: The Priestly Torah and the Holiness School*. Winona Lake: Eisenbrauns, 2007.
Koehler, L., and W. Baumgartner. *Lexicon in Veteris Testamenti Libros*. Leiden: E. J. Brill, 1958.
Kotze Z. "Metaphors and Metonymies for Anger in the OT: A Cognitive Linguistic Approach." *Scriptura* 88 (2005): 118–25.

Kraus, Hans Joachim. *Psalms 1–59: A Commentary*. Minneapolis: Augsburg Publishing House, 1988.

———. *Psalms 60–150: A Commentary*. Minneapolis: Augsburg Publishing House, 1988.

———. *Theology of the Psalms*. Minneapolis: Fortress Press, 1992.

Kruger, Paul. "A Cognitive Interpretation of the Emotion of Anger in the Hebrew Bible." *Journal of Northwest Semitic Languages* 26, no. 1 (2000): 181–93.

———. "A Cognitive Interpretation of the Emotion of Fear in the Hebrew Bible." *Journal of Northwest Semitic Languages* 27, no. 2 (2001): 77–89.

———. "Depression in the Hebrew Bible." *Journal of Near Eastern Studies* 64, no. 3 (2005): 187–92.

———. "The Face and Emotions in HB." *Old Testament Essays* 18, no. 3 (2005): 651–63.

———. "The Inverse World of Mourning in the HB." *Biblische Notizen* 124 (2005).

———. "Non-Verbal Communication and Symbolic Gestures in the Psalms." *The Bible Translator* 45, no. 2 (1994): 213–22.

———. "Non-Verbal Communication in the Hebrew Bible: A Few Comments." *Journal of Northwest Semitic Languages* 24, no. 1 (1998): 141–64.

———. "On Emotions and the Expression of Emotions in the OT." *Biblische Zeitschrift* 48, no. 2 (2004): 213–28.

———. "The Psychology of Shame." *Journal of Northwest Semitic Languages* 22, no. 2 (1996).

———. "Symbolic Inversion in Death: Some Examples from the Old Testament and the Ancient Near Eastern World." *Verbum et Ecclesia* 26, no. 2 (2005): 398–411.

———. "The World 'Topsy-Turvy' and the ANE Cultures: A Few Examples." *Anthropology Southern Africa* 29, no. 3 (2006): 115–21.

Kselman, J. S. "Psalm 3: A Structural and Literary Study." *Catholic Biblical Quarterly* 49, no. 4 (1987): 572–80.

Kugel, J. *The Idea of Biblical Poetry: Parallelism and Its History*. New Haven: Yale University Press, 1976.

LaBarre, W. "The Cultural Basis of Emotions and Gesture." *Journal of Personality* 16, no. 1 (1947): 49–68.

Labuschagne, C. *The Incomparability of Yahweh in the Old Testament*. Leiden: Brill, 1966.

Lacocque P-E. "Fear of Engulfment and the Problem of Identity." *Journal of Religion and Health* 23, no. 3 (1984): 218–28.

Lacocque, A. *The Book of Daniel*. London: SPCK, 1979.

Lakoff, G. "The Contemporary Theory of Metaphor." In *Metaphor and Thought*, edited by A. Ortony, 202–51. Cambridge: Cambridge University Press, 1993.

Landes, G. M. "The Kerygma of the Book of Jonah." *Interpretation (A Journal of Bible and Theology)* 21, no. 1 (1967): 3–31.

———. "The 'Three Days and Three Nights' Motif in Jonah 2:1." *Journal of Biblical Literature* 86, no. 4 (1967): 446–50.

Laney, J. C. "A Fresh Look at the Imprecatory Psalms." *Bibliotheca Sacra* 138 (1981): 35–45.

Langacker, R. W. "Viewing in Cognition and Grammar." In *Grammar and Conceptualization*, edited by R. W. Langacker, 203–5. Berlin. New York: Walter de Gruyter, 1999.

Langacker, R. W. Concept, Image and Symbol: The Cognitive Basis of Grammar. New York: Mouton de Gruyter, 2002.

Leick, G. *Mesopotamia: The Invention of the City*. London: Penguin, 2002.

Lemmens, M. "Motion and Location: Toward a Cognitive Typology." In Girard-Gillet, G. (ed.), *Parcours linguistiques: Domaine anglais* [CIEREC Travaux 122], 223–244. Saint-Etienne: Publications de l'Université St.-Etienne.

Lester D., and A. Abdel-Khalek. "Religiosity and Death Anxiety Using Non-Western Scales." *Psychological Reports* 103, no. 3 (2008): 652.

Leupold, H. C. *Exposition of Ecclesiastes*. Welwyn: Evangelical Press, 1952.

Levenson, J. D. "The Jerusalem Temple in Devotional and Visionary Experience." In *Jewish Spirituality: From the Bible through the Middle Ages*, edited by A. Green. New York: Crossroad, 1986.

Lewis, C. S. *Reflections on Psalms*. Glasgow, Collins Fount Paperbacks, 1977.

Limburg, J. *Psalms*. Louisville: John Knox Press, 2000.

———. "The Root ריב and the Prophetic Lawsuit Speeches." *Journal of Biblical Literature* 88, no. 3 (1969): 291–304.

Linfoot-Ham, K. "The Linguistics of Euphemism: A Diachronic Study of Euphemism Formation." *Journal of Language and Linguistics* 4, no. 2 (2005): 227–63.

Lipton, D. "Early Mourning? Petitionary versus Posthumous Ritual in Ezekiel 24." *Vetus Testamentum* 56, no. 2 (2006): 185–202.

Lowry, T. P. "The Development of the Concept of Hyperventilation." In *Hyperventilation and Hysteria: The Physiology and Psychology of Overbreathing and Its Relationship to the Mind-body Problem*, edited by T. P. Lowry. Springfield: Charles C. Thomas Publishing, 1967.

———, ed. *Hyperventilation and Hysteria: The Physiology and Psychology of Overbreathing and Its Relationship to the Mind-body Problem*. Springfield: Charles C. Thomas Publishing, 1967.

Lyon, M. L. "Emotion and Embodiment: The Respiratory Mediation of Somatic and Social Processes." In *Biocultural Approaches to the Emotions*, edited by A. L. Hinton, 182–212. Cambridge: Cambridge University Press, 1999.

Macky, P. *The Centrality of Metaphors to Biblical Thought: A Method for Interpreting the Bible*. New York: Edwin Mellen, 1990.
Mandolfo, C. "Psalm 88 and the Holocaust: Lament in Search of a Divine Response." *Biblical Interpretation* 15 (2007): 151–70.
Martin-Achard, R. *From Death to Life: A Study of the Development of the Doctrine of the Ressurection in the OT*. Edinburgh: Oliver & Boyd, 1960.
Martin, C. "The Imprecations in the Psalms." *Princeton Theological Review* 1, no. 4 (1903): 537–53.
Matitiahu, T. "Psalm 90." *Vetus Testamentum* 35, no. 1 (1985): 115–17.
Matlock, T. "The Conceptual Motivation of Fictive Motion." In *Studies in Linguistic Motivation*, edited by Günter Radden and Klaus-Uwe Panther, 221–48. Berlin: De Gruyter Mouton, 2004.
Mays L. James. *Psalms*. Louisville: Westminster John Knox Press, 2011.
McDonald, D. "Idea of Immortality." *Vox Evangelica* 7 (1971): 17–38.
McNamara, P. *The Neuroscience of Religious Experience*. Cambridge: Cambridge University Press, 2009.
McNeal K. E. "Affecting Experience: Toward a Biocultural Model of Human Emotion." In *Biocultural Approaches to the Emotions*, edited by A. L. Hinton, 215–55. Cambridge: Cambridge University Press, 1999.
Meek, Th. J. "Job 19,25–27." *Vetus Testamentum* 6 (1956): 100–103.
Messer, Neil. "Judging the Secret Thoughts of All: Functional Neuroimaging, Brain Reading and Theology Ethics of Privacy." *Studies in Christian Ethics* 34, no. 1 (2021): 17–35.
———. *Theological Neuroethics: Christian Ethics Meets the Science of the Human Brain*. London: Bloomsbury, 2017.
Michel, W. L. "Slmwt,'Deep Darkness' or 'Shadow of Death.'" *Biblical Research* 29 (1984): 5–13.
Mitchell, D. C. "'God Will Redeem My Soul from Sheol': The Psalms of the Sons of Korah." *Journal for the Study of the Old Testament* 30, no. 3 (2006): 365–84.
Monloubou, L. *L'Imaginaire des Psalmistes: Psaumes et Symboles*. Paris: Les Éditions du Cerf, 1980.
Moore, G. F. "The Covenanters of Damascus: A Hitherto Unknown Jewish Sect." *Harvard Theological Review* 4, no. 3 (1911): 330–77.
Morgenstern, J. "The Cultic Setting of the Enthronement Psalms." *Hebrew Union College Annual* 35 (1964): 1–42.
Mowinckel, S. "Drive and/or Ride in OT." *Journal of Biblical Literature* 12, no. 3 (1962): 278–99.
———. "Psalm Criticism between 1900 and 1935." *Vetus Testamentum* 5, no. 1 (1955): 13–33.
———. *The Psalms in Israel's Worship*. Oxford: Basil Blackwell, 1962.

———. "Traditionalism and Personality in the Psalms." *Hebrew Union College Annual* 23, no. 1 (1950): 205–31.

Mrozek, A., and S. Votto. "The Motif of the Sleeping Divinity." *Biblica* 80, no. 3 (1999): 415–19.

Muilenburg, James. *The Way of Israel*. London: Routledge & Kegan Paul, 1962.

Mulder M. J. "Rešeph." In *Theological Dictionary of the Old Testament*, vol. 14, edited by G. J. Botterweck, H. Ringgren, and H-J. Fabry, 10–16. Grand Rapids: Eerdmans, 2004.

Myhill, J. "What Is Universal and What Is Language Specific in Emotion Words?: Evidence from Biblical Hebrew." *Pragmatics and Cognition* 5, no. 1 (1997): 79–129.

Nicholson, E.W. *Deuteronomy and Tradition*. Oxford.Basil Blackwell, 1967.

Niditch, S. "Eroticism and Death in the Tale of Jael." In *Women in the Hebrew Bible*, edited by A. Bach, 305–16. London: Routledge, 1998.

Oesterley, W. O. E., and T. H. Robinson. *Hebrew Religion: Its Origin and Development*. London: SPCK, 1937.

Oesterreicher, J. M. *The Bridge: A Yearbook of Judaeo-Christian Studies*. Vol. 1. New York: Pantheon Books, 1955.

Ortony, A., and T. Turner. "What's Basic about Basic Emotions?" *Psychological Review* 97, no. 3 (1990): 315–31.

Otto, R. *Das heilige: Uber das Irrationale in der Idee des Gottlichen ind sein Verhaltnis zum Rationalen*. Munchen: Verlag C. H. Beck, 2004.

Otzen B. "Bhl." In *Theological Dictionary of the Old Testament*, vol. 2, edited by G. J. Botterweck, H. Ringgren, and H-J. Fabry, 3–5. Grand Rapids: Eerdmans, 1975.

Patterson, R. D. "Psalm 22: From Trial to Triumph." *Journal of the Evangelical Theological Society* 47, no. 2 (2007): 213–33.

Pedersen, J. *Israel: Its Life and Culture*. Vol.1. Atlanta: Scholars Press, 1991.

Peels, E. "Ps 139: I Hate Them with Perfect Hatred." *Tyndale Bulletin* 59, no. 1 (2008): 35–51.

Perry, T. A. *The Honeymoon Is Over: Jonah's Argument with God*. Peabody: Hendrickson Publishers, 2006.

Pinker, A. "Sheol." *Jewish Bible Quarterly* 22, no. 3 (1995): 168–79.

Pollio, H. R., J. M. Barlow, H. J. Fine, and M. R. Pollio. *Psychology and the Poetics of Growth: Figurative Language in Psychology, Psychotherapy and Education*. Hillsdale: Lawrence Erlbaum Assoc., 1977.

Pope, M. H. *El in the Ugaritic Texts*. Leiden: Brill, 1955.

———. "The Word שַׁחַת in Job 9: 31." *Journal of Biblical Literature* 83, no. 3 (1964): 269–79.

Power M. J., and T. Dalgleish. *Cognition and Emotion: From Order to Disorder*. London: Psychology Press, 1998.

Posser, William. "Privacy." *California Law Review*, 48, 3, 1960.
Prestige, G.L. *God in Patristic Thought*. London, SPCK, 1952.
Prinz, J. "Which Emotions Are Basic?" In *Emotion, Evolution and Rationality*, edited by D. Evans and P. Cruse, 1–19. Oxford: Oxford University Press, 2004.
Prothero, Rowland E. *"The Psalms in Human Life, Bound up with the Authorised Version of the Psalms."* London: John Murray, 1906.
Putz, M., and R. Dirven. *The Construal of Space in Language and Thought*. Berlin: Walter de Gruyter, 1996.
Quell, G. *Das kultische Problem der Psalmen. Versuch einer Deutung des religiösen Erlebens in der Psalmendichtung Israels* [The Cultic Problem of the Psalms. An Attempt at interpretation of the religious experience in the Psalms' Poetry of Israel]. Stuttgart: Kohlhammer, 1926.
Rahlfs, A. ed. *Psalmi cum Odis*. Septuaginta. Vetus Testamentum Graecum auctoritate Academiae Litterarum Gottingensis editum X. Göttingen: Vandenhoek and Ruprecht, 1979.
Ratzinger, J. *Einfuhrung in das Christentum*. Muchen: Kosel-Verlag, 1968.
Reimer, D. J. "Good Grief? A Psychological Reading of Lamentations." *Zeitschrift für die alttestamentliche Wissenschaft* 114, no. 4 (2002): 542–59.
Rice, G. "The Integrity of the Text of Psalm 139:20b." *Catholic Biblical Quarterly* 46, 1 (1984): 28–30.
Richards, I. A. *Coleridge on Imagination*. London: Routledge & Kegan Paul,1962.
———. *Verse vs Prose*. London: English Association, 1978.
Ricoeur P. "Biblical Hermeneutics." *Semeia* 4 (1975): 29–148.
Ringgren H. "Gava." In *Theological Dictionary of the Old Testament*, edited by G. J. Botterweck, H-J. Fabry, and H. Ringgren, 438–39. Grand Rapids: Eerdmans, 1975.
Robinson, B. P. "Psalm 131: Form and Meaning." *Biblica* 79, no. 2 (1998): 180–97.
Rom-Shiloni, D. "Psalm 44: The Power of Protest." *Catholic Biblical Quarterly* 70, no. 4 (2008): 683–98.
Roth, L. *Judaism: A Portrait*. London: Faber, 1960.
Rowley, H. H. *Worship in Ancient Israel: Its Forms and Meaning*. London: SPCK, 1967.
Rubinstein, E. "On the Mechanism of the Semantic Shift: Causation of Symmetric Locativity." *AfroAsiatic Linguistics* 3, no. 7 (1976): 1–10.
Russell, James A., José-Miguel Fernández-Dols, Antony S. R. Manstead and J. C. Wellenkamp eds. *Everyday Conceptions of Emotion: An Introduction to the Psychology, Anthropology and Linguistics*. Dordrecht: Springer, 1995.
Sadock, J. M. "Figurative Speech and Linguistics." In *Metaphor and Thought*, edited by A. Ortony, 42–57. Cambridge: Cambridge University Press, 1993.
Saebo, Magne (ed). *Hebrew Bible/Old testament: The History of its Interpretation*, vol.1. Goettingen: Vandenhoeck & Ruprecht, 2000 (1st ed).

Saggs, H. W. F. "'External Souls' in the Old Testament." *Journal of Semitic Studies* 19, no. 1 (1974): 1–12.

Salkinson-Ginsburg, *Hebrew New Testament*, Theology Library, School of Theology at Claremont, California, 1886.

Sarna, N. "The Psalm Superscriptions and the Guilds." In *Studies in Jewish Religion and Intellectual History Presented to Alexander Altmann*, edited by S. Stein and R. Loewe, 281–300. Tuscaloosa: University of Alabama Press, 1979.

Sawyer, J. F. A. "Hebrew Words for Resurrection of the Dead." *Vetus Testamentum* 23 (1973): 218–34.

———. *Semantics in Biblical Research: New Methods of Defining Hebrew Words for Salvation*. 1st ed. London: SCM Press, 1972.

Schachter, S., and J. Singer. "Cognitive, Social and Physiological Determinants of Emotional States." *Psychological Review* 69, no. 5 (1962): 379–99.

Scherer, K. R., and P. Ekman, eds. *Approaches to Emotion*. Hillsdale: Lawrence Erlbaum Associates, 1984.

Schilderman H. "Religion and Emotion." *Journal of Empirical Theology* 14, no. 2 (2001): 85–96.

Schlant, E. *The Language of Silence: West German Literature and the Holocaust*. London: Routledge, 1999.

Schmutz, P. "The Grammar of Resurrection in Isa 26:19." *Journal of Biblical Literature* 122, no. 1 (2003): 145–55.

Schokel, L. A. *A Manual of Hebrew Poetics*. Rome: Pontifical Institute of the Bible, 1988.

Seeligman, I. L. "A Psalm from Pre-Regal Times." *Vetus Testamentum* 14, no. 1 (1964): 75–92.

Seiling, J. R. "The 'Radical' Revisions of the Commentary on the Seven Penitential Psalms: Luther and His Enemies." *Reformation and Renaissance Review* 8, no. 1 (2006): 28–47.

Sells, M. *Mystical Language of Unsaying*. Chicago: Chicago University Press, 1994.

Semin, Guen. R., Carlen A. Görts, S. Nandram, and Astrid Semin-Goossens. "Cultural Perspectives on the Linguistic Representation of Emotion and Emotion Events." *Cognition and Emotion* 16, no. 1 (2002): 11–28.

Sheriffs, D. "The Human Need for Continuity." *Tyndale Bulletin*, no. 55 (2004): 1–15.

Silberman, L. H. "The Two Messiahs of the Manual of Discipline." *Vetus Testamentum* 5, no. 1 (1955): 77–82.

Smith, M. S. "The Heart and Innards in Israelite Emotional Expression." *Journal of Biblical Literature* 117, no. 3 (1998): 427–36.

Smith, Anthony. *"National Identity."* London. Penguin Books, 1991.

Soffer, A. "The Treatment of Anthropomorphisms and Anthropopathisms in the Septuagint of the Psalms." *Hebrew Union College Annual* 28 (1957): 85–107.

Solomon, Norman. "The Bible and the Preservation of the World." In *Concilium 1995/1: The Bible as Cultural Heritage*, edited by Wim Beuken and Sean Freyne, 97–107. London: SCM, 1995.

Soskice, J. M. *Metaphor and Religious Language*. Oxford: Clarendon Press, 1985.

Szoreny, Andreas. *Psalmen und Kult im Alten Testament*, Budapest: Sankt Stefan, 1961.

Stevens, M. E. "Between Text and Sermon (Ps 105)." *Interpretation* 57, no. 2 (2003), 187–89.

Stieglitz R. R. "Ebla and the Gods of Canaan." In *Eblaitica: Essays on the Ebla Archives and Eblaite Language*, vol. 2, edited by C. H. Gordon and G. A. Rendsburg, 79–89. Winona Lake: Eisenbrauns, 1990.

Svi, R. "The Mwt of Grandeur." *Vetus Testamentum* 9, no.1 (1959): 324–25.

Swenson, K. M. "Ps 22:17: Circling around the Problem Again." *Journal of Biblical Literature* 123, no. 4 (2004): 637–48.

Tate, M. E. *Psalms 51–100*. Dallas: Word Books, 2002.

———. "The Interpretation of Psalms." *Review & Expositor* 81, no. 3 (1984): 363–75.

———. "Psalm 88." *Review & Expositor* 87, no.1 (1990): 91–95.

Tawil, H. "The Semantic Range of the Biblical Hebrew חלל Lexicographical Note X." *Zeitschrift für die alttestamentliche Wissenschaft* 117, no.1 (2005): 91–94.

Terrien, S. *The Psalms: Strophic Structure and Theological Commentary*. Grand Rapids: Eerdmans, 2003.

Thiselton, A. "From Semiotics to Deconstruction and Post-Modernist Theories of Textuality." In *New Horizons in Hermenutics: The Theory and Practice of Transforming Biblical Reading*, edited by A. Thiselton, 80–141. Grand Rapids: Zondervan, 1992.

Thomas, A. *Anatomical Idiom and Emotional Expression in the Hebrew Bible and the Septuagint: A Comparative Study*. Sheffield: Sheffield Phoenix Press, 2014.

Thomas, D. W. "צלמות in the Old Testament." *Journal of Semitic Studies* 7, no. 2 (1962): 191–200.

Thorpe, J. B. "Psalm 23: A Remix." *Journal of Religious Thought* 59/60, 1/2/1 (2007): 165–79.

Tobin, Y. "The Hebrew Prepositions mi-/min- 'from, of.' Same or Different? A Sign Oriented Approach." In *Prepositions in Their Syntactic, Semantic and Pragmatic Context*, edited by S. Feigenbaum and D. Kurzon. Amsterdam: John Benjamins Publishing, 2002.

Tomasello, M. *The New Psychology of Language: Cognitive and Functional Approaches to Language Structure*. Mahwah: Lawrence Erlbaum Associates, 2003.

Tomberlin, J. *Language and Mind*. Oxford: Blackwell Publishing, 2002.

Torresan, P. "Silence in the Bible." *Jewish Bible Quarterly* 31, no. 3 (2003): 153–63.
Tsevat, M. "Chalaq." In *Theological Dictionary of the Old Testament* vol. 4, edited by G. H. Botterweck, H. Ringgren, and H-J Fabry, 4:470–72. Grand Rapids: Eerdmans, 1980.
Tucker, W. D. "A Polysemiotic Approach to the Poor in the Psalms." *Perspectives in Religious Studies* 31, no. 4 (2004): 425–39.
Turner, M. *Death Is the Mother of Beauty: Mind, Metaphor, Criticism*. Chicago: University of Chicago, 1987.
———. *Figurative Language and Thought*. New York: Oxford University Press, 1997.
Ullmann, S. *Language and Style*. Oxford: Basil Blackwell, 1964.
Von Rad, G. *Genesis*. London: SCM Press, 1972.
———. *Wisdom in Israel*. 1978 ed. London: SCM Press, 1972.
———. *Deuteronomy: A Commentary* (Old Testament Library). Philadelphia: Westminster John Knox. 1966.
———. Old Testament Theology: The Theology of Israel's Historical Traditions. Vol. 1. New York: Harper & Row, 1962.
Villanueva, Federico. "A Study of the Sudden Change of Mood in the Psalms of Lament." Leiden: Brill, 2008.
Vos, J. G. "The Ethical Problem of the Imprecatory Psalms." *Westminster Theological Journal* 4, no. 2 (1942): 123–38.
Wachter, L. *Der tod im Alten Testament*. Stuttgart: Calwer Verlag, 1967.
Waltke, B. K., and M. O'Connor. *An Introduction to Biblical Hebrew Syntax*. Winona Lake: Eisenbrauns, 1990.
Warnock, M. *Imagination*. Berkeley: University of California, 1976.
Warren, Samuel, and Louis Brandeis. "The Right to Privacy." *Harvard Law Review*, 4/5 (1890): 193–220.
Watson, W. G. E. *Classical Hebrew Poetry: A Guide to Its Techniques*. Sheffield: JSOT Press. Supplement 26, 1986.
Watts, J. W. "This Song: Conspicuous Poetry in Hebrew Prose." In *Verse in Ancient Near Eastern Prose*, edited by J. de Moor and W. G. E. Watson. Kevelaer: Verlag Butzon & Bercker, 1993.
Weiser, A. *The Psalms*. London: SCM Press, 1962.
Weitzman, M. P. "Verb Frequency and Source Criticism." *Vetus Testamentum* 31, no. 4 (1981): 451–71.
Wen, Y-H. "Religiosity and Death Anxiety. *Journal of Human Resource and Adult Learning* 6, no. 2 (2010): 31–37.
Wenham, G. J. *Genesis 1–15*. Waco: Word Books, 1987.
———. *Genesis 16–50*. Dallas: Word Books, 1994.
Westermann, C. *Genesis 12–36*. Minneapolis: Augsburg Publishing, 1985.

———. *Isaiah 40–66*. London: SCM Press, 1969.

———. "The Role of Lament in the Theology of the Old Testament." *Interpretation* 28 (1974): 20–39.

Wevers, J. W. M. "A Study in the Form Criticism of Individual Complaint Psalms." *Vetus Testamentum* 6, no.1 (1956): 80–96.

Whybray, N. *Reading the Psalms as a Book*. JSOT Supplement. Sheffield: JSOT Press, 1996.

Wierzbicka, A. "Everyday Conceptions of Emotion: A Semantic Perspective." In *Everyday Conceptions of Emotion: A Semantic Perspective*, edited by James A. Russell, Jose-Miguel Fernández-Dols, Anthony S. R. Manstead, and J. C. Wellenkamp, 17–48. Dordrecht: Springer, 1995.

Wijngaards, J. "Death and Resurection in Covenantal Context (Hos 6:2)." *Vetus Testamentum* 17, no. 2 (1967): 226–39.

Wilder, A. *Jesus Parables and the War of Myths: Essays on Imagination in the Scripture*. London: SPCK, 1982.

———. *Theopoetic: Theology and the Religious Imagination*. Philadelphia: Fortress Press, 1976.

Willesen, F. "The Cultic Situation of Psalm 74." *Vetus Testamentum* 2 (1952): 289–306.

Wolff, Hans W. *Anthropology of the Old Testament*. 2nd ed. London: SCM Press, 1974.

Wolverton, W. I. "Meaning of Zion in Psalms." *Anglican Theological Review* 47, no. 1 (1965): 16–32.

Worthman, C. M. "Emotions: You Can Feel the Difference." In *Biocultural Approaches to the Emotions*, edited by A. L. Hinton, 41–74. Cambridge: Cambridge University Press, 1999.

Wrenn, Rachel. "Is the Psalmist Angry at God? Psalm 88 and the Absent Nose." *Word & World* 40/3 (2020): 236–45.

Wright, Christopher J. H. *The Ethical Authority of the Old Testament: A Survey of Approaches*. Cambridge: Tyndale House, 1992.

Yaron, R. "The Meaning of Zanah." *Vetus Testamentum* 13 (1963): 237–39.

Young, Edward. *Daniel*. London. Eerdmans Publishing Company, 1949.

Yu, N. "Body and Emotions: Body Parts in Chinese Expression of Emotion." *Pragmatics and Cognition* 10, no. 1–2 (2002): 341–67.

Zajonc, R. B. "Feeling and Thinking: Preferences Need No Inferences." *American Psychologist* 32, no. 2 (1980): 151–75.

Ziegler, Y. "So Shall God Do . . . Variations of an Oath Formula and Its Literary Meaning." *Journal of Biblical Literature* 126, no. 1 (2007): 59–81.

Zobel, Hans-Jurgen. "בדד." In *Theological Dictionary of the Old Testament*, edited by G. J. Botterweck and Helmer Ringgren, 1: 473–79, translated by J. T. Willis. Grand Rapids: Eerdmans, 1974.

Langham Literature, with its publishing work, is a ministry of Langham Partnership.

Langham Partnership is a global fellowship working in pursuit of the vision God entrusted to its founder John Stott –

> *to facilitate the growth of the church in maturity and Christ-likeness through raising the standards of biblical preaching and teaching.*

Our vision is to see churches in the Majority World equipped for mission and growing to maturity in Christ through the ministry of pastors and leaders who believe, teach and live by the word of God.

Our mission is to strengthen the ministry of the word of God through:
- nurturing national movements for biblical preaching
- fostering the creation and distribution of evangelical literature
- enhancing evangelical theological education

especially in countries where churches are under-resourced.

Our ministry

Langham Preaching partners with national leaders to nurture indigenous biblical preaching movements for pastors and lay preachers all around the world. With the support of a team of trainers from many countries, a multi-level programme of seminars provides practical training, and is followed by a programme for training local facilitators. Local preachers' groups and national and regional networks ensure continuity and ongoing development, seeking to build vigorous movements committed to Bible exposition.

Langham Literature provides Majority World preachers, scholars and seminary libraries with evangelical books and electronic resources through publishing and distribution, grants and discounts. The programme also fosters the creation of indigenous evangelical books in many languages, through writer's grants, strengthening local evangelical publishing houses, and investment in major regional literature projects, such as one volume Bible commentaries like the *Africa Bible Commentary* and the *South Asia Bible Commentary*.

Langham Scholars provides financial support for evangelical doctoral students from the Majority World so that, when they return home, they may train pastors and other Christian leaders with sound, biblical and theological teaching. This programme equips those who equip others. Langham Scholars also works in partnership with Majority World seminaries in strengthening evangelical theological education. A growing number of Langham Scholars study in high quality doctoral programmes in the Majority World itself. As well as teaching the next generation of pastors, graduated Langham Scholars exercise significant influence through their writing and leadership.

To learn more about Langham Partnership and the work we do visit **langham.org**

www.ingramcontent.com/pod-product-compliance
Lightning Source LLC
Chambersburg PA
CBHW071820230426
43670CB00013B/2519